CENSORED MESSIAH

The Truth about Jesus Christ

PETER CRESSWELL

BOOKS

Winchester, UK
New York, USA

DEDICATION

To Jesus, who laid down his life for his friends

Copyright © 2004 O Books
46A West Street, Alresford, Hants SO24 9AU, U.K.
Tel: +44 (0) 1962 736880 Fax: +44 (0) 1962 736881
E-mail: office@johnhunt-publishing.com
www.0-books.net

U.S. office:
240 West 35th Street, Suite 500
New York, NY10001
E-mail: obooks@aol.com

Text: © 2004 Peter Cresswell

Design: Text set in Sabon by Nautilus Design, Basingstoke, UK
Cover design: Krave Ltd., London, UK

ISBN 1 903816 67 X

A CIP catalogue record for this book is available from the British Library.

Printed by Tien Wah Press Ltd., Singapore

Contents

———◦———

DEDICATION 2

ACKNOWLEDGMENTS 4

INTRODUCTION 6

CHAPTER 1   HIDDEN TRUTH 9

CHAPTER 2   PERFECT MAN 21

CHAPTER 3   MIRACLES 27

CHAPTER 4   PERFECT WOMAN 39

CHAPTER 5   FAMILY WEDDING 49

CHAPTER 6   PROMISED LAND 59

CHAPTER 7   FREEDOM 67

CHAPTER 8   ROMANS AND HERODIANS 75

CHAPTER 9   THE POOR 87

CHAPTER 10   KINGDOM ON EARTH 101

CHAPTER 11   THE RELIGION OF SAUL 111

CHAPTER 12   PASSION 127

CHAPTER 13   FULFILLMENT OF PROPHECY . . .141

CHAPTER 14   RAISING LAZARUS 165

CHAPTER 15   GLIMPSES 175

CHAPTER 16   SONS OF DAVID 193

CHAPTER 17   CENSORED REBELLION 215

CONCLUSION 239

FURTHER READING 248

———◦———

ACKNOWLEDGMENTS

Like everyone who has investigated Jesus and his followers, I owe a debt to those first gospel writers who put down in writing what they knew or believed to be true.

Some of what was written is lost and what remains has been much altered by later copyists. But without these sources it would not be possible to look at the movement which led to Christianity.

I also owe a debt to the scholarship of many modern writers. Professor Robert Eisenman has provided a seminal study based around James, the brother of Jesus, which illuminates developments in Jerusalem after the Crucifixion and also provides a crucial context by which to evaluate the character of Jesus himself.

Eisenman's work makes it possible to build on an understanding of the role of Jesus' family as it probably operated, in contrast with the way it has been represented.

I have developed the theme that the Nazoraean movement, centered on James, did not simply disappear but played an important part in the Jewish uprising. I owe my insights to the lead provided by Professor Eisenman, though any mistakes I may have made or misconceptions I may have arrived at are entirely mine.

Professor John Crossan is another biblical scholar whose work is of fundamental importance in understanding the nature of Jesus and the times in which he lived. I have followed many of Crossan's ideas, including his suggestions for the sequences in which the gospels arose and the ways in which they relate to each other. I have also followed his analysis of the sayings of Jesus, as they are presented in different sources, to arrive at a core which, as far as can be judged, constitutes the message that Jesus preached. This perspective is augmented by the position taken by Hyam Maccoby, which I follow, that Jesus was not at odds with the Pharisees nor indeed most of his fellow Jews.

Many writers have suggested that Jesus might also have been influenced by the Essenes. Some references in the gospels and other texts lead me to the conclusion that Jesus may have been involved with an assembly of the "poor", most probably in Jerusalem.

In looking at the influence of Saul, who became the Apostle Paul, I have generally followed Maccoby though with modifications suggested by the analysis provided by Professor Eisenman.

A number of writers have pointed to ways in which the gospels were edited to provide interpretations which are pro-Roman and spuriously anti-Jewish. I have developed the idea of censorship carried out to disguise Jesus' Jewish roots and to protect sources. As well as looking at the gospels, I have also applied this to the Jewish historian Josephus, resolving I believe some important discrepancies.

The interpretation given of the miracles is mine alone, though it is possible that I may unconsciously absorbed ideas first circulated by others. I have also brought together several strands of evidence to suggest a much greater role for Lazarus, one of the followers who was close to Jesus.

Donovan Joyce, Hugh Schonfield and many others have pointed to some odd aspects of the passion narrative, which are only amplified on reading and rereading the gospel texts. The analysis which I have developed is therefore not entirely original, though I believe that I have taken more aspects of the story into account. I am grateful here to Professor Crossan for providing an alternative theory of the passion story, against which I have been able to test my own ideas.

INTRODUCTION

Ajourney has to begin somewhere. For anyone investigating the life of Jesus and the movement of which he was a part, that journey will start with the four gospels of the New Testament which are, in order of origin, Mark, Matthew, Luke and John. That is where the bulk of the surviving evidence, though not all of it, lies.

It is a difficult beginning point because of the way the gospel stories have inculcated not just the Christian religion, but the whole of Western society and culture. It is even harder for someone like myself who has been a part of it all, a church attender, baptized and confirmed, absorbing beliefs as part of the natural order of things–even before an age when I could develop and exercise critical judgment.

On the other hand, there are those who would discount it all as just a set of myths and storytales, often from a standpoint of never having been involved. The trouble with this approach is that it involves dismissing, without proper consideration, something which has very great significance. This is whether one believes the Christian message, as it has evolved, or not.

Though it has been a difficult journey, it has also been enlightening, astonishing, and liberating. Looking at long last at the evidence, after years of simply taking many doctrines for granted, I have finally been freed from my ingrained preconceptions. I began also to understand the original context in which Christianity evolved.

As I read and researched more, so I revised, adjusted, changed and fine-tuned my ideas. As an inevitable consequence, I have had to rewrite some sections of the book as I went along. Doubtless if I had kept on with this, I would have continued to make changes and the book would never have been completed!

Eventually, I reached a point where I was satisfied with the generality of my conclusions. I can envisage further adaptations but not any fundamental rethinking, based on the information now available.

Though I have made changes, I have still sought to retain a flavor of my journey of discovery. Readers may well at points detect my frustration at the way evidence about Jesus and his followers was disguised by those who wrote or later edited the gospels. They will hopefully also share my subsequent satisfaction and often excitement at what can be discovered and deduced. It is a journey in which I believe I have done something to retrieve Jesus from the land of religious dogma, into which he has been kidnapped, and restore him to his historical context.

While I have looked at a range of sources, some like the canonical gospels and works by Josephus are central to the investigation. Not everyone will want to look up all the references for themselves, since this would make for very slow progress. On the other hand, certain passages are crucial for understanding the argument. I have provided some of these, along with other quotes, as reference points at the beginning of each chapter.

I have tried to maintain an analytical approach, while crossing where necessary the boundaries of academic disciplines. Historians have on the whole sought to keep out of religious debate, while there is much discussion among theologians based on no real analysis or evidence. Popular writers in some cases generate sensational theories without substance, while others sensationalize what is actually quite reasonable and sensible. This is an area where views are deeply held. What contradicts orthodox belief is likely to be taken as inflammatory, and it can be the material that makes for tabloid headlines.

This is not in my view a reason for avoiding the issues. Much of the evidence has either been produced or processed by Christian writers and editors and this needs to be examined, along with assertions about the nature of Jesus based upon it.

So I do not avoid looking at the Christian view of Jesus as represented in orthodox interpretation of the gospels. However, I treat the subject matter analytically and, if anything sensational arises out of this, it is because that is the nature of the subject matter. What could be more sensational than the gospel or "good news" that Jesus died, divine sacrifice for the sins of the world, and was then miraculously brought back to life again? The answer is unfortunately, given the emotion invested in these beliefs, almost any other explanation, no matter how rational, well thought out or soundly based.

My approach is to take the Christian view of Jesus, analyze it and then work outwards from it.

The first chapter provides an overview and looks at some of the difficulties and challenges in considering the evidence. The next four chapters consider, in relation to the gospel evidence, certain propositions about Jesus himself: that he was a perfect man, that he could perform miracles, that he was born from a virgin impregnated by God and that he remained unmarried and celibate.

I then give a whistle-stop tour of the history of the Jewish people, assuredly limited and imperfect but useful in providing some sort of context.

The next chapters deal with the Nazoraean movement of which Jesus was a part, its relation with other contemporary groups, particularly "the poor" or Essenes, Jesus' message and how this was altered.

I go on to investigate the passion story, looking at two possibilities. One is that it was invented from Old Testament text and prophecies. The other is that it offers a coherent account of something that really happened, though not what is superficially presented in the gospels as they have been altered and edited.

In one version, Jesus died and his body was discarded and forgotten. The passion story came into being as Jesus' followers tried to make sense, with little information available to them, of an otherwise tragic occurrence. In the alternative account, Jesus survived through a sequence of events which are, astonishingly, still there to read in the pages of the gospels.

In making my analysis, I put Jesus back into context in the stormy times under Pilate's rule as procurator, when taxes were extortionate, Roman justice was swift and brutal and memories were fresh of mass executions in which many people had personally lost friends or relatives. In terms of what actually may have happened, I suggest that the gospels provide a narrative and a basis for explanation that make sense.

Finally, I look forward in time to see what happened to the followers of the Nazoraean movement, associated with Jesus, and the descendants of Jesus and his brothers.

Again, there appears to have been an effort at censorship, this time by the turncoat Jewish historian Josephus and this time even more effectively.

But there are surprisingly some strong clues in the way that Josephus presented his characters, some traces which indicate the fate of followers of the "Sons of David".

I find in the Jewish uprising a final resolution of the tension between the active and passive elements, present in the Nazoraean movement and also existing all along in messianism throughout Jewish history. I find that the Nazoraeans were there in the battle for Jerusalem because they were Jewish and because there were so many of them.

They died or were scattered and their movement, though the death throes took a while, died with them.

What replaced it was the religion of the Roman Empire, Christianity.

CHAPTER I

HIDDEN TRUTH

What I say three times is true...
  The Hunting of the Snark, Lewis Carroll

How often have I said to you that when you have eliminated the impossible, whatever remains, however improbable, must be the truth.
  The Sign of Four, Sir Arthur Conan Doyle

———◦———

Whereas once even scholars took the bible as simply given, there has now been more than a century of serious academic study. The ways in which the canonical gospels and other books of the New Testament came to be written, their contradictions and their limitations are much better understood. Yet there still persists an irrational view that the bible, no matter how it came to be composed by flesh-and-blood men, is beyond criticism, absolutely true because it is absolutely the word of God.

The persistence of this viewpoint is not helped by the fact that ministers of the Church, having been well trained at theological college, then fail to pass any sense of critical analysis and judgment on to their flocks! The same absolute certainties are preached from the pulpit and the same errors in interpretation are absorbed in bible reading classes, just as if nothing had happened.

Many previous believers have found, when they began to read the sources for themselves, that they have been treated dishonestly. If they have then turned away, it is not so much because the Church lacks relevance to contemporary society but because it lacks integrity.

What I will show first, many will find unsettling and disturbing. The traditional gospel story of the sacrifice of a God, incarnate in man, to save the world from its sins is not what the gospels actually describe.

Read critically and carefully, the gospel accounts tell something radically different. It is still a tale of passion and belief, of charismatic leadership and showmanship, of confrontation and great daring. Above all, it is the story of how a Jewish man tried to change the direction of the religious leadership of his people. It describes a breathtaking piece of brinkmanship carried out against the Roman occupiers of Israel, leading to a journey into the mouth of death which appeared to succeed.

I suggest that Jesus, according to the evidence in the gospels, planned if possible to survive his execution. The same body of evidence indicates that he could have and indeed did survive the ordeal of crucifixion. His appearances afterwards, described in the gospels, at the beginning of the Acts of the Apostles and in an early letter written by Paul, provide further confirmation.

The idea that Jesus did not die on the cross is not a new one. Where it comes from is the mass of direct and circumstantial detail in the gospels themselves. This evidence, and not the preconceptions of myself or others, is what really makes the case.

For those who are new to the idea that Jesus survived, and was not dead and resurrected, this may be a shocking revelation. It certainly threatens the fundamental premise on which present Christianity is based. I can only say, read the analysis which follows and look again at the original texts.

Ironically, this is probably not an issue that would have bothered the early followers of Jesus. They would have seen survival of the ordeal as a form of individual resurrection. They were also not dealing with a world-redeeming savior but a Jewish messianic figure who, they hoped, would return to lead them.

This to me is the most revealing and challenging aspect. Jesus was not acting alone, but was the lead part of a movement that continued through time, up to and beyond the Jewish revolt thirty years after the Crucifixion.

The pivotal family which emerges from analysis of the gospel story is not then the traditional one we are used to: mother and infant, with a father somewhat sketchily in the background. The family which changed the course of history were a group of brothers, largely acting with a common purpose but differing over the means to achieve their aims.

Within the lines and between the lines, the gospels tell all this, despite what so many authors and editors have done to them over the years for a variety of purposes.

Put back into their context, the stories begin to reveal even more. There is a lot of other evidence from past history, other contemporary writings and the fate of Jesus' followers, relatives and friends.

On the face of it, Jesus by his teaching did not accomplish his objective. He addressed large crowds and attracted scores, perhaps even hundreds, of followers. But in his own lifetime there was no mass movement, no fundamental change in the worldview of the Jewish people. The Jewish kingdom on earth that he preached simply failed to come about. It may have been, in the way that Jesus saw it, a spiritual dominion existing in parallel with the political reality of Roman occupation. But the anticipated revival, whether spiritual or political, did not happen.

When there was a rebellion against the Roman authorities thirty years later, it was bound to fail, with disastrous consequences for the Jews. Would it have made any difference if there had been a risen Messiah fighting alongside the rebels? Or would Jesus have simply been cut down and forgotten, like Menahem–who also offered himself up as a Messiah and then died fighting Rome?

Analysis of the gospel material and the context of the times in which Jesus lived suggests that he may have had a good reason for giving himself up and putting his life on the line. Not saving the world, but saving his friends–and in this latter enterprise he may well have succeeded.

Jesus' early followers expected him to return fairly swiftly, following his resurrection and temporary departure after the Crucifixion. This idea was carried forward, as a diminishing theme, progressively losing credibility with the passage of time. It is there, however, as a strong message in the gospels.

Jesus, if he had simply died, could not come back in an attempt to liberate his people. Jesus, if he was still living after the Crucifixion, for whatever reason did not do so.

The defeat and dispersal of Jesus' followers, the Nazoraeans, provided the opportunity for, and contributed towards, the creation of a new worldwide religion. That was something that Jesus did not plan and had not envisaged.

This new religion made Jesus into a godlike figure, savior of the world rather than the savior for the Jews that he claimed to be. It manufactured rituals and beliefs, some of which have little to do with the original movement.

For those who believe there is more merit in the values that Jesus preached than in the religion which has been created out of him, there is a saving consolation. It lies in the fact that dozens of other messianic figures have arisen in Jewish history, but without providing a legacy of teaching. In all cases, we know something about what they did and what happened to them, but nothing or next to nothing about what they said. Who knows what great ideas were preached and then lost to posterity? In Jesus' case, thanks to the gospels, we do still have and can identify the essentials of his message. Whatever the fate of Jesus, that message remains powerful and appealing.

Once Jesus was absent from the scene, however, influence over the course of events and thereby the making of history was in the hands of others. One person who had a determining influence was Saul, or Paul as he came to be known, once a persecutor of the followers of Jesus. A man very much with his own agenda, he almost single-handedly generated a religion designed for a wider, Gentile audience, based on his followers at Antioch, the first to be described as Christians.

Though Paul came on side by his self-proclaimed vision of Jesus on the way to Damascus, he continued to be in conflict with the original followers of Jesus, led by James at Jerusalem. He conspired against them and he may even have contributed to their destruction.

As will be seen, the Christianity which Paul so successfully sold to the Gentiles and especially to the Romans, was not the still-Jewish religion of Jesus' immediate followers.

Paul and his followers modified the beliefs of the people who had known Jesus to suit their market. This was a pagan world in which many of the elements of Paul's reconstructed "Christian" religion were already circulating. There were well-established tales of mortal men and women consorting with the gods to produce semi-divine offspring. The idea of the divine, mystical blood sacrifice was a part of popular consciousness. Jesus was slotted into this framework to become something other than the man he had been.

The message was further altered, for a variety of reasons, and these changes were incorporated into the text as the gospels were subsequently edited. The Christian Church convened councils to vote on and adopt doctrines, such as the Trinity and the divinity of Jesus, which have little basis in scripture. Like other religions, Christianity evolved as people's ideas changed over time.

In mainstream Jewish society, there was a strong emphasis on males growing up to become full adults within society by marrying and having children. The expression of an alternative ideal of celibacy could only be found in certain minority sects, such as the upper echelons of the Essenes. But early Christian writers, beginning with Paul, advocated that marriage was a less perfect state, acceptable for those who could not manage the ideal of celibacy.

From the position of marriage as an inferior state, there developed the idea that sex itself was impure. By the middle of the second century, there were Christian groups following the teachings of Marcion, forbidding the union of the sexes entirely.

The Catholic Church rejected much of Marcion's philosophy as heretical, but the idea that sex was somehow sinful stuck. So celibacy became the rule for priests while, for the mass of followers, sex was allowed within marriage as a necessary means of procreation.

The gospel stories were also edited to remove from Jesus any hint of human sexuality. That's even though there was a strong cultural obligation to marry and Jesus as a normal Jewish man, around 30 to 40 years old, would certainly have been married.

Because sex had come to be regarded as essentially sinful, to be carried out only as a duty for the purposes of procreation, it was even eliminated from the account of the Jewish Messiah's birth. The Nativity stories in the Gospels of Matthew and Luke tell us that Mary was a "virgin" when Jesus was conceived. But these stories were founded on the mistranslation of the Hebrew word for a young woman (almah) into the word for a virgin (parthenos) in the Greek Old Testament. This allowed for something quite ordinary to be portrayed as quite miraculous.

With the human male ruled out, either Joseph or someone else, it could then be God who mystically impregnated the mother of Jesus. With God then as his biological father, Jesus was well on the way to being accepted as himself divine.

There is no evidence that the early followers of Jesus adopted a sacramental meal or did anything other than follow the normal Jewish practice of blessing and breaking bread before eating. But Paul and his Gentile community introduced a ritual, incorporated into the gospels, in which bread and wine were communally consumed. The act commemorated the last Passover meal shared by the disciples and Jesus, with the bread and wine representing his body and blood.

The metaphor of the wine and bread soon came to be taken literally, culminating in the extraordinary and still widely believed doctrine of transubstantiation. This is the belief that the bread and wine are not just symbolically but actually, by some miraculous process, real flesh and blood. It is not hard to see where this came from. Paul took the elements of a Jewish custom and combined it with pagan ideas of eating the body and drinking the blood of the sacrificed god.

While there was some fluidity and change in the early years, after a very short time doctrines became embodied in a conceptual straitjacket, about which no debate was allowed and from which there was no escape.

The subsequent development of Christianity has been characterized by intolerance towards alternative views. Dissenters of all kinds have been hounded, persecuted, tortured and killed.

The irony is that the beliefs so tyrannically imposed have fluctuated over time with changing political and social conditions. So what was, at one point, the orthodox view was at another moment the heresy for which one could be put to death.

Following Paul, Christian apologists maintain that, to believe, all that is needed is to have faith. But, for Paul and the Church down the centuries, what this seems to have meant is trusting in what one is told rather than one's own judgment or the evidence.

When it comes to the life of Jesus, however, it is not just a matter of faith or conjecture. There is a body of evidence in the gospels, some included in the bible and some also with historical value which is not. There are other contemporary writings. There is, moreover, a well-understood social and historical context.

Jesus wasn't a "Christian", as many present-day Christians would understand this. He was a fully practicing Jew, living at a time of great tension with his country, Israel, under Roman occupation. He was one of a number of messianic figures who came forward over a relatively short period of time, apparently in fulfillment of the Jewish (Old Testament) scriptures.

The Christian religion which the world now has was not invented by Jesus, nor indeed by his immediate followers, the Nazoraeans or Nazarenes, who were based in Jerusalem as a sect fully within Judaism. They differed from their fellow Jews in one essential only, their belief that the Messiah who would liberate the Jewish people had already come.

Christianity was the product of a split away from the Jerusalem Church. It came about as Paul, one-time persecutor of the followers of Jesus, began to promote a novel religion which would both appeal to the Gentiles and also appease the Romans. This religion differed in fundamental respects from the Nazoraean view, resulting in a clash recorded in early documents, including letters from Paul to some of the newly-formed "Christian" groups.

Christians have preached the gospels, as proof of their beliefs. But these gospels can be examined as historical evidence, however distorted by the perspective of the authors, the time lag before events were actually recorded in writing and alterations made in copying and recopying.

The gospels are the evidence of the victors, or rather the survivors, in a struggle. After the fall of Jerusalem, Jewish national revivalism was crushed and the Nazoraeans were relegated to the sidelines. The religion with wider appeal was pro-Roman and anti-Jewish, adapting existing ideas of human incarnate deities from the Greek and pagan worlds. What was then recorded reflected this, or was edited subsequently to conform to the political status quo.

This is hardly surprising. Roman rulers were touchy in dealing with troublesome subject peoples and would often react sharply to early signs of discontent, or even find convenient scapegoats. The Emperor Nero subjected early Christians to horrendous persecution for the fire that nearly destroyed Rome, something they were probably not involved in at all. After the first Jewish Revolt of AD 66–70, the Romans did not ban Judaism as such but only the Nazoraean followers of Jesus, correctly perceiving that messianic cults were the real threat to Rome.

The Nazoraeans had, as their leader, someone who had claimed to be the Jewish king and who had been killed by the Romans for that very reason. So it seems unlikely that the Nazoraean view could ever, in the context of the times, have formed the basis for a wider religion. That is even if the Nazoraeans had not been crushed and dispersed as a result of the Jewish rebellion.

Paul by contrast advocated, in his letters to Gentile congregations, a religion obedient to Rome, and one therefore well placed eventually to become the Roman Empire's official religion.

He was involved in a power struggle with the early followers of Jesus which, because they were eliminated from the scene, he or rather his successors eventually won. His version of events, recorded in his letters to the early Christian Church and reflected to an extent in the gospels, came to be accepted as the truth.

Any dispassionate reading of the gospels will nonetheless tend to shake many preconceptions. It is a sobering experience to realize that otherwise rational and intelligent people have for centuries suspended their critical judgment and ignored evidence of a very different sequence of events, told in the gospel stories, from the ones we have become accustomed to believe.

When Mark, for example, describes Jesus and the disciples celebrating the Feast of the Passover at a house in Jerusalem two days earlier than most other Jews, what does this mean? Why did Jesus switch abruptly from trying to escape from his enemies, including one or two attempts by his fellow Jews at stoning him to death, to giving himself up? Why were there so many glaring irregularities in the Crucifixion, including the fact that it was not completed as an act of execution?

One might add, perhaps, how did James, the brother of a supposed carpenter's son, get to acquire the standing of the Jew's High Priest in Jerusalem?

Any attempt at explanation is going to be full of imperfections. But I feel compelled to tell the story and I will do my best.

In looking at the source material, a number of guiding principles will be followed.

The first is that all of the text has to be taken into account. It may not always be possible to provide one explanation that fits all of the sometimes contradictory evidence. But it will, on the other hand, often be possible to provide a best fit, and occasionally something which seems to make all the pieces fit into place.

Another consideration to take into account is the background of the writers. This includes their culture, the context in which the events took place, their own involvement and access to sources.

A third guiding rule is to take what is written at face value, unless there is good reason for doing otherwise. Such reason might, for example, include evident mistranslation or a writer's known bias.

Use can be made in analysis of the fact that text may have been edited to generate a particular slant. Passages which lack the introduced bias, such as the anti-Jewish tone present in all four canonical gospels, are likely to be earlier and more authentic, having missed the attentions of later censors.

Where a version of events appears in more than one text, then in principle more reliance can be placed on it than, say, a single unsupported reference in one of the gospels. But it has to be borne in mind that the accepted, canonical gospels appear to have relied on one or more common sources, including an earlier collection of the sayings of Jesus (*Sayings Gospel Q*). These can be found imbedded in the gospels of Luke and Matthew, though not in Mark.

Luke and Matthew used Mark for stories about the life of Jesus and quite possibly the account of his Crucifixion, although it may be that all three were reliant on a single passion source. In view of the way that early writers borrowed from each other, it is not surprising that there are similarities across many of the accounts.

Difficulties in interpreting the evidence are compounded by the way that it has been molded and altered over the years. There is a considerable lag between the points in time when the gospels were first written down and the creation of the copies that are now available. Texts were copied, edited in the course of copying and then the earlier versions destroyed. Mark, the earliest of the four canonical gospels, can for example be dated to around AD 70. Used by Luke and Matthew and so earlier, it is described by the second century Church authority Irenaeus as having been written by Mark, the follower and interpreter of the Apostle Peter, following Peter's martyrdom in Rome around AD 64 or 65. There is some debate over whether the apocalyptic language used in Mark chapter 13 indicates that the gospel was written just before or just after the fall of Jerusalem.

Either way, the gospel is established as having been written very early in the first century. But the stark fact is that there are now no full copies of the gospels existing which date before the fourth century AD.

This latter point is worth a small digression. The Roman Emperor Constantine ended the persecution of Christians and then made Christianity the religion of empire. But at that time there were many different interpretations of belief, including one great divide. On the one hand, there were those who believed that Jesus was subordinate to God, although divine by virtue of being chosen as God's intermediary or adopted Son. On the other hand, there were the supporters of a more radical view that God and Jesus were really one and the same. The Emperor favored the latter position, embodying as it did the idea of a coherent and unified God who would act as the central focus for a strong and united empire.

In AD 325, Constantine convened the Council of Nicaea for the bishops to decide a common position on the true nature of Jesus. The Emperor got his way. An overwhelming majority of the assembled bishops voted for his position and a creed was adopted, which included the statement that Jesus was "of one substance" with the Father. Two bishops and a number of priests, who refused to sign up to the new creed, were sent off into exile. This is how, essentially, Christians gained one of their creeds, the Nicaean or Nicene creed, recited as an article of faith to this day.

Six years later, in AD 331, 50 new copies of the gospels were prepared under the Church historian Eusebius "for use in the Churches of Byzantium."

It appears that this was an attempt to impose uniformity to reflect the new orthodoxy. Local bishops had previously a great deal of autonomy in deciding what doctrine to promote and which texts to use from the large variety of gospels then circulating, including the four now used in the New Testament. It seems reasonable to assume that the gospels were edited in these replacement copies to reflect the new view of Jesus' divinity. Although there were undoubtedly many copies of the gospels in existence, requiring 50 replacements, none of the earlier texts survive. Discordant accounts could not have been allowed to exist alongside the newly-created official versions, and they would simply have been destroyed. It does appear that there was a concerted effort about this time to generate a standardized text to reflect prevailing religious correctness.

There may possibly have been even earlier revisions of the material, of which there is now no record.

A further possibility is that the eyewitness accounts and tales passed on from one person to another may well have been first written down many months or years after the actual events. Traditionally, it was thought that Mark or an earlier version of Mark was the first of the now-surviving gospels to be written down. However, comparative analysis of scroll fragments with dated material is beginning to suggest that other gospels, such as Matthew, may also have been first recorded when there were some eyewitnesses still alive. Modern scholarship is tending to push the dates of first writing back in time.

If the original gospels should prove in the main to have been very early written records, then the main sources of distortion will come from the mistakes, falsifications and prejudices on the part of the gospel writers themselves and also later copying and reediting. The earliest surviving texts date from the fourth century AD, so there had been a long period in which there could have been considerable creative rewriting. There is little or nothing left from earlier times to check the documents against. That presents a considerable problem.

It might be thought that nothing can be reconstructed of earlier versions of the gospels, now lost or destroyed. Certainly, nothing can be proved beyond doubt until perhaps a forgotten copy, saved from the censors, turns up on the dusty shelves of a monastery somewhere.

But it's rather like investigating a crime: though the perpetrator may have gone, he will inevitably have left a forensic impression, a trace of events. In trying to reconstruct, we are helped enormously by the fact that the gospel material is limited and precious. If the early editors also saw it that way, then they would have striven to keep as much of the original as possible, eliminating only the minimum of offending passages or references. There is a good chance this will have left a lot of indirect or circumstantial evidence in the rest of the text, suggesting what may have been cut out.

As will be seen, this is precisely what is often found when the gospels are subjected to close scrutiny.

There is also the fact that it is easier to remove or reposition small bits than attempt to rewrite passages entirely, while keeping within the ambit of the text as a whole. When bits were removed, it was common practice to put text back in to fill the gap, so avoiding the necessity to alter the pagination and rewrite whole sections. These insertions sometimes strike a very discordant note.

Help in deciding what is added or original may sometimes be provided by other texts, not subsequently edited, which refer to or even quote gospel passages which predate the fourth century, Constantine copies.

Passages in the letters attributed to Paul can be checked against the description of the same events in the Acts of the Apostles. The accounts in both of these, which do not appear to have been so severely edited, can also be related to what is said in the gospels. There are separate and very early historical references to James, the brother of Jesus, which also provide valuable context for the gospel-related events.

One further source of error needs to be considered and that is accidental or unconscious misrepresentation. The gospel story has become so imbedded in our culture and our consciousness that it now forms a script, which relates only imperfectly to the evidential text. This can be clearly seen in the description of the Nativity in Matthew and Luke.

How many wise men sought out the infant Jesus, future king of the Jews? Three, of course! But there is no mention of three wise men anywhere, only "wise men" in Matthew's Gospel. The story has subsequently been embellished and the invention of three wise men is now assumed as a matter of fact.

It is similarly assumed that Jesus came from a humble background. But there is no real direct evidence of this and the indirect evidence (see chapter five) is rather to the contrary. His father is furthermore described as a carpenter, though in fact the Greek word used suggests that he could equally well have been a builder.

Jesus was not born in a "stable" because there was no room at the "inn". There were in fact no wayside inns 2,000 years ago providing travelers with a pint, a bite to eat and a room for the night. But there were ordinary houses divided so that the upper floor provided living accommodation while livestock were kept on the lower floor. When there was no room left in the family area, visitors might well have had to lodge below where the animals were kept. More mistranslations here have generated perceptions which are widely held, repeated and reinforced every year in thousands of Nativity plays. But they are still nonetheless erroneous.

Another mistranslation, this time of the original Hebrew Old Testament into Greek, resulted in the misconstrued idea that Jesus' mother Mary was a "virgin" (see chapter four).

Other mistaken beliefs resulting from mistranslation will be encountered, for example that Jesus was able to walk on water (chapter three) and that he was betrayed by Judas (chapter twelve). Care is certainly needed when using translations of the original sources.

There are as outlined a number of ways of evaluating the often conflicting evidence in the gospel stories. My first port of call will be these accounts to see what they reveal of their subject, the Jewish Messiah who became a world-redeeming Christ.

The text provided by the gospels needs to be looked at dispassionately. This is a hard exercise even for those who are agnostic, not concerned with religion at all or simply lapsed Church attenders. The script is embodied in the whole of our culture, the images of the Nativity and other gospel scenes are now a part of our collective consciousness. Critical awareness will be tougher still for those who feel they must believe what their minister or priest tells them to believe. And it will be hard to reach those who believe, no matter how it came to be collated or what are the internal contradictions, that every word of the bible is the unimpeachable word of God.

For Christians, Jesus is beyond reproach: he has to be, as they perceive him to be the Son of God. But was the man portrayed in the gospels really that perfect?

CHAPTER 2

PERFECT MAN

*And Jesus went away from there and withdrew to the district of
Tyre and Sidon.*
*And behold, a Canaanite woman from that region came out and
cried, "Have mercy on me, O Lord, Son of David; my daughter
is severely possessed by a demon." But he did not answer her a
word. And his disciples came and begged him, saying, "Send her
away, for she is crying after us." He answered, "I was sent only
to the lost sheep of the House of Israel." But she came and knelt
before him, saying, "Lord, help me." And he answered, "It is not
fair to take the children's bread and throw it to the dogs." She
said, "Yes, Lord, yet even the dogs eat the crumbs that fall from
their masters' table." Then Jesus answered her, "O woman, great
is your faith. Be it done for you as you desire." And her daughter
was healed instantly.*

    Matthew 15:21–28

*On the following day, when they came from Bethany, he was
hungry. And seeing in the distance a fig tree in leaf, he went to
see if he could find anything on it. When he came to it, he found
nothing but leaves, for it was not the season for figs. And he said
to it, "May no one ever eat fruit from you again." And his
disciples heard it …*
*As they passed by in the morning [of the next day], they saw the
fig tree withered away to its roots. And Peter remembered and
said to him, "Master, look! The fig tree which you cursed has
withered." And Jesus answered them, "Have faith in God. Truly,
I say to you, whoever says to this mountain, 'Be taken up and
cast into the sea,' and does not doubt in his heart, but believes
that what he says will come to pass, it will be done for him. …"*

    Mark 11:12–14, 20–23

The material in the gospels was put there to serve a purpose, or rather a number of purposes, and what wasn't considered relevant was not included. There is very little, for example, about Jesus' early life.

A lot of dramatic events are certainly described. But there are fewer descriptions included of everyday life, except incidentally. It was not the prime purpose of the gospel writers to say much about Jesus' character. Yet there is evidence on which it is possible to make a judgment.

The question posed for this chapter and the following three chapters, is what kind of a man was Jesus? The point is to see whether the gospel evidence supports some of the cherished tenets established by the Christian Church.

If Jesus was the Son of God and identifiable with God, as the assembled bishops decided at their meeting at Nicaea in AD 325, then he had to be a perfect man, nothing less. But do the stories of his life and works show this?

They certainly indicate that he was a charismatic leader, a healer, a man capable of immense self-denial, a performer of good works. He is shown overall as a very good man. But there are also passages which show him in a less pleasing light: capable of rage, petulance and lack of compassion. These remain because they are an integral part of the plot or because they tell excellent stories which the gospel writers, and later editors, must have felt they just couldn't leave out.

Jesus was, as he is described, not entirely non-violent. He turned over the tables of the Temple money-changers, a physical and symbolic act against a system that reaped profit from an excessive rate of exchange. It can be argued that this was justified and carried out as an act of "righteous" anger. But who is to say that all those involved were guilty or equally guilty? And what about the possibility of injury to innocent bystanders caught up in the fracas? One man's righteous vengeance can be another man's perceived act of unprovoked aggression.

Jesus appears in this episode almost in an Old Testament mode, smiting the wicked. Decisive, courageous, righteous or even self-righteous, certainly. But was it the act of someone who was absolutely perfect?

Jesus is also presented at times as being inconsiderate or gratuitously rude. There is, for example, the comment to his mother at the wedding at Cana, "O woman, what have you to do with me?", when she was merely pointing out that they had run out of wine. It may be, as I will suggest later, that this phrase is inserted and out of context. But it suggests, along with occasions when Jesus refused to meet or rebuffed members of his family, that he could be harsh and somewhat insensitive. As Mark reports, Jesus' mother, brothers and, in some versions, sisters came seeking him but could not get through the crowd. Told of their presence, Jesus made clear his present priorities: he regarded his followers as his family now.

If a little unease surrounds such incidents, it is nothing compared to the questions arising from two other stories. These fall into the category of incidents included in the text because they have a moral and provide some drama.

The first is about a Canaanite or Greek woman as told in Matthew (15:21–28), in the passage quoted at the beginning of this chapter, and Mark (7:25).

This woman asked Jesus to heal her daughter who was "possessed" or mentally disturbed. But Jesus ignored her.

His disciples asked him to send the woman away, perhaps by implication after having dealt with her, because she was pestering them. Jesus replied in effect that he wouldn't help her because his mission only applied to the Jews, and she didn't qualify.

The woman persisted and Jesus relented and healed her daughter.

The moral to the story, which the gospel writer gives, is the power of the woman's humility and faith which produced results. Faith overcomes all barriers.

But what of Jesus' attitude? His effort to ignore the woman's pleas shows, by the standards of our conventional image, a distinctly uncharitable and even "unchristian" approach. As the story is related, he had no intention of acting and was only persuaded to do so by the disciples. Had the woman gone away, what then? The daughter would not have been healed. The story would not have been worth telling.

So what about the possibility that there were others in a similar position who did not make the text, who were excluded and even personally rejected by Jesus' narrow, though in the historical context completely comprehensible, definition of his mission?

It is likely that there were others, since Jesus had only so much time and a closely defined goal. Christian apologists, who hold to their concept of a perfect and divine man, may contend that he was just testing the Canaanite woman. But the story, as told, shows him turning away.

The wider issue, of what Jesus saw himself as doing, as opposed to what others might like to believe he was doing, will be returned to later.

For an even more graphic description of a less endearing side to Jesus, there's the famous tale of the withered fig tree, as recounted in Mark (11:12–14 and 20–23) and Matthew (21:18–21). The story in Mark's probably earlier version is that Jesus, returning from Bethany to Jerusalem, felt hungry and went up to a fig tree to look for fruit. Finding nothing but leaves, he cursed the tree. The next day, as Jesus took the same route back into the city, his disciples marveled at finding that the cursed tree had withered. Jesus' response, the same in both texts, is that anything can be done with faith, even moving mountains.

Here again is an excellent tale, with the bonus at the end of a moral message. It just had to go in from among the stories collected about Jesus' life. It was dramatic and had an effective message, and for these reasons later editors did not cut it out.

But what of the display of angry petulance which the story reveals? The fig tree was entirely inoffending, barren because of some malady which would shortly lead to its demise.

Jesus cursed it in the same way as a motorist today might kick his car for failing to start in the morning. He may have failed to realize that the figs were not in season, as Mark suggests. But it was just as likely that fruit could not be expected from the tree because it turned out to be diseased.

Jesus in the story displayed an all-too-human loss of control. "Well, curse you," he said to the tree. And it was.

In very short order, the fig tree withered and died.

The story is turned round, with a homily at the end about faith moving mountains. So, are we really to believe this is why Jesus cursed the tree, to get across this particular message? Just as we are supposed to believe he rejected the Canaanite woman to test her faith or demonstrate another moral lesson? Even for the believers in a nice-as-pie, monodimensional Jesus, this is stretching credulity a little. Isn't it far, far more likely that he cursed the tree in a fit of pique and avoided the Canaanite woman because she wasn't Jewish?

The outcomes in each case made great copy for the storytellers, but we are left with a picture of a human being with flaws as well as many great qualities.

Jesus was undoubtedly an outstanding individual, with enormous personality and will, someone who lived as a practicing Jew by a strict moral code. But he wasn't perfect, he wasn't a demigod.

Some might argue that these stories were not characteristic of Jesus and that other events described, such as the rescue of the woman about to be stoned for adultery, represent the "real" Jesus. What this boils down to is taking some of the evidence as valid and regarding other evidence as more likely to have been invented. But this, of course, is to fall into the traps in interpretation described in the previous chapter, that is not taking evidence at face value without good reason and not taking the whole of the text into account. It is only possible, in my view, to see Jesus as having an entirely blameless character by starting from the position that he had and then only accepting those parts of the text that tend to show that he had. That is not a logical or valid method of interpretation.

The doctrine that Jesus was the Messiah, biologically progeny of God and therefore divine and therefore perfect, gets theologians into all sorts of impossible quandaries.

The fate of Judas Iscariot provides a classic example of the hopeless difficulty in arguing from a set position and then trying to bend the evidence to fit it. The four gospels largely agree in their accounts of what Judas did. So, on the principles outlined, he will be taken as a real rather than a fictional participant in the drama. Some writers have argued that the character of Judas was invented and that consequently Jesus was not "betrayed" in the way described.

Because Jesus is seen as divine, he is accredited with the gift of prescience. He is depicted at several points in the narrative as being able to foresee his fate, down to the detail of who would betray him to his persecutors and when it would happen. That person of course was going to be Judas, one of the twelve disciples whom Jesus himself selected.

So, did he select an evil man just for this purpose? Or, worse still from a moral point of view, did he just select a weak man who could be molded to act according to the divine purpose? But, wait a bit, Judas was going to be eternally damned for this seminal act of betrayal. Surely, that shows a certain lack of "Christian" compassion? Jesus, being divine, could surely have found another way of fulfilling his destiny without sacrificing Judas. Judas certainly suffered in this life for his part in the drama. He was blamed for Jesus' fate, hanged by his own hand or by that of someone else, and disemboweled.

Are we to believe that destiny required this, and it was just tough on Judas?

This dilemma over how to deal with this story demonstrates the problem of the fixed script approach. In reality, the evidence is cloudy, perhaps collected years after the events and difficult to interpret. The underlying historical reality to which the imperfect evidence relates may be hard to grasp.

As it happens, I have no difficulty in dealing with the apparent fact that Jesus callously allowed Judas to damn himself. That's because the imposed script, as opposed to the underlying text, that we have adhered to is wrong in this part as it is wrong in many other parts of the narrative.

Judas Iscariot almost certainly didn't betray Jesus. He was as loyal as the other disciples, if not more so. As will be seen later, he simply did his job. And he has to go down as the most unfairly maligned person in the history of mankind.

So, here I can be more generous than many conventional theologians, without getting into a twist over the concepts of predestination versus freewill. Jesus may at times have been bad-tempered, blinkered, hard and insensitive. But he also appears as a man of moral stature, too compassionate knowingly to let his disciple Judas go to a grisly fate.

I have argued in this chapter, that Jesus was a man and undoubtedly a great man, but by no means perfect. Since God is presumed perfect, he was therefore not God.

But, if not divine on this score, what about the accounts of the miracles? If Jesus could do something impossible everyday, then he must surely be divine and questions about his character would be mere quibbles. Furthermore, if the miracles all worked as stated, then the miracle of the resurrection (the core of Christian faith) is no longer any great problem.

Jesus, as the Son of God, drove out evil spirits and conjured food out of thin air. So, as the Son of God, he could have resurrected himself, or called on God to do it.

It's what a part of all of us wants to believe, that death can be so conquered.

But, to be true to ourselves, we have to stand and look at the reality and not follow our own wish fulfillment.

So, before going on to the other issues of Jesus' life and his mission, I shall look at the prophets and their miracles, Old Testament and New.

Does the apparent ability to move mountains make for divinity? There would, on this criterion, be a lot of claimants.

CHAPTER 3

MIRACLES

Then Elijah said to the prophets of Baal, "Choose for yourselves one bull and prepare it first, for you are many; and call on the name of your god, but put no fire to it." And they took the bull which was given them, and they prepared it, and called on the name of Baal from morning until noon, saying, "O Baal, answer us!" But there was no voice, and no one answered. ...

Then Elijah said to all the people, "Come near to me"; and all the people came near to him. And he repaired the altar of the Lord that had been thrown down; Elijah took twelve stones, according to the number of the tribes of the sons of Jacob, to whom the word of the Lord came, saying, "Israel shall be your name"; and with the stones he built an altar in the name of the Lord. And he made a trench about the altar, as great as would contain two measures of seed. And he put the wood in order, and cut the bull in pieces and laid it on the wood. And he said, "Fill four jars with water, and pour it on the burnt offering, and on the wood." And he said, "Do it a second time"; and they did it a second time. And he said, "Do it a third time"; and they did it a third time. And the water ran around the altar, and filled the trench also with water.

And at the time of the offering of the oblation, Elijah the prophet came near and said... "O Lord, answer me, that this people may know that thou, O Lord, art God, and that thou hast turned their hearts back." Then the fire of the Lord fell, and consumed the burnt offering, and the wood, and the stones, and the dust, and licked up the water that was in the trench. And when the people saw it, they fell on their faces; and they said, "The Lord, he is God; the Lord, he is God." And Elijah said to them, "Seize the prophets of Baal; let not one of them escape." And they seized them; and Elijah brought them down to the brook Kishon, and killed them there.

Kings 1:18, 25–26, 30–40

Some of the events described in the Old Testament occurred, or were believed to have occurred, three thousand or more years ago–at the beginning of time, going back to the Genesis creation myth. The New Testament gospels relate to happenings around two thousand years ago, with the first written records made probably a few years later and the earliest surviving copies dating from seventeen hundred years ago.

This was a period before the generation of modern science, when people did not know how the weather happened or how the human body worked. The industrial revolution was still centuries away and, while cities did exist, most people lived in smaller rural communities.

Lives were shorter, misfortunes plentiful and many diseases incurable. There were no vaccines. Conditions which can now be simply remedied by antibiotics could and did lead to disfigurement and death. When crops failed, people routinely starved; there was no hope of rescue through international welfare. Fierce national and religious rivalries led to brutal wars and acts of repression.

In an uncertain social and economic climate, beliefs in magic and superstition flourished. People accepted then that the world of the spirit was all around them. Bad happenings were punishment for spiritual wrongdoing; victories over enemies were taken as reward for rectitude. Natural events were explained by reference to the supernatural.

A great many miracles described in the Old and New Testaments derive from this lack of knowledge, in combination with a particular mindset and frame of reference. The occasions when the Israelites were defeated and enslaved are explained as the consequence of deviations from "true" religion. But when they returned to the true path, they were shown to be rewarded.

For example, under Moses, the fleeing Israelites were able to walk over the bed of an inland sea when the waters were blown back. Scholars believe that it was not the Red Sea, but probably a marshy area north of Suez known as the Lake of Reeds. Exodus refers poetically to a wall of water being held back on either side. But the clue to a possible natural explanation lies in the description in Exodus of the clogged up chariot wheels of the Egyptian pursuers. As the water table rose, Pharaoh's forces were first immobilized and then trapped and engulfed.

It is necessary to look analytically at the gospel miracles since the character of Jesus is partly defined through the acts he is described as having performed. I do not deny that the universe is awe-inspiring and miraculous, a miracle in itself. But all the evidence suggests, at each stage of our understanding of it, that it is essentially coherent. The laws which govern the universe, however imperfectly understood by us, would appear to apply equally to all its regions, however far distant. The laws do not change randomly or capriciously from day to day. Constants, like the speed of light, do not vary from moment to moment; gravity does not operate in different ways on Tuesdays and Saturdays.

If this appears to be a painful and tedious statement of the obvious, consider the belief of many that there is a Creator-God intervening personally in day to day events, rectifying wrongs, punishing the wicked and creating miracles as signs to boost the morale of the faithful.

It might be said, if only that were the case! The idea of a Superman-type intervention to stop earthquakes or roll back the waters of the Red Sea and then release them on transgressors is patently not just absurd, but a human projection. The ideas of a divine jester, the old man in the sky with a beard and the wrathful deity, who must be appeased, are all products of human consciousness. We project what we want to believe.

But centuries ago, before modern science, before there was any real understanding of the way the human body worked or natural phenomena, when lives were short and disaster was always one bad harvest away, people did believe that magic and the world of spirits was all around them and that the gods did personally intervene in their lives.

Their leaders were part of the same culture and subscribed to the same belief system.

But leaders, spiritual and political, and prophets were supposed to perform great works and signs. They needed to get the natural order of things on their side, either rewarding people for listening to their true advice or (if things went wrong) punishing them for failing to stick to righteous ways. Either way, prophets would be looked up to and proved right.

They were not above performing acts of showmanship, using their understanding to exploit popular credulity.

So, here in the pages of Kings as quoted above, we have a tale, appearing fresh as it may have been first recounted more than 2,000 years ago. The story is a record of Elijah vanquishing the followers of Baal to restore the Israelites to their true faith.

What Elijah did was create a very public challenge, under his own specific conditions. The people were summoned to a mountain, Mount Carmel. The followers of Baal were given first chance of getting their god Baal to intervene directly and light a pyre for a burnt offering.

Elijah let the priests of Baal chant, imprecate and cut themselves, to draw the attention of Baal, though all to no avail. He chose his time, as the day wore on and conditions changed, to build a pyre. He built a stone altar, cut a trench around it, placed wood and the offering on top, doused the lot so that it was sopping wet and then filled the trench with water.

This all seems rather strange until it is appreciated that these actions, far from being random, were directed towards a specific end.

What Elijah had in actual fact done was build a perfect lightning conductor. The detail shows that it was not something that came together by accident. It was clearly done intentionally.

Elijah had engaged in a masterly piece of showmanship. The dousing of the pyre with water would have appeared to make Yahweh's task of igniting it more difficult, while in reality it greatly increased the chances of a successful outcome. Wet stones and wood, with water all around, provided in such a prominent place the likely route through which static electricity would discharge.

When the evening storm finally came, it all worked immaculately. A lightning bolt struck the pyre and consumed everything, the false prophets were confounded, the Israelites returned to belief in the Lord and the losers were slain.

The contest took place during a severe drought in Samaria. So, the point of the offering was to induce God or the gods to stir up a storm which would bring rain. After the lightning, as the text goes on to describe, the rain did come. Elijah thus scored a double victory: he prevailed on his God to light the pyre and also to bring an end to the famine and drought.

Lightning, of course, was the fire of the gods. Elijah had no detailed knowledge of the physics of static electricity. He did, however, know from a practical point of view what tended to attract lightning and when electrical storms took place. He had a parallel, commonsense understanding of the world. And he wasn't above exploiting his knowledge in order to further a political and religious goal.

The story was undoubtedly written down long after the events happened, and so is dependent on folk memory and subject to embellishment. What adds to its credibility as a record are the circumstantial details.

The writer of Kings is motivated to describe a miracle wrought by God and portray Elijah in a favorable light as his prophet, doing God's will against the heathen enemies of Israel and against enormous odds. He is not trying to show Elijah carrying out a confidence trick. But what the details of the story show is Elijah doing just that, engaging in a brilliant act of trickery, even if for what the prophet believed was a good purpose.

The probability that the story relates reasonably well to an historical event is increased by the fact that the details hang together to provide a somewhat different, and more plausible, account from the one the writer intended.

In a work of pure fiction this wouldn't happen. An invented account of Yahweh miraculously lighting a sacrificial pyre wouldn't have needed the trench of water round it and other such significant, circumstantial detail.

The same sort of consideration applies, as will be seen, to the core gospel narrative and also other parts of the gospel stories.

Jesus, several hundred years later, was also a religious figure, preaching for a return to what he believed were the central values of Judaism. His message may have run counter to the ruling religious elite's prevailing practice: not so much what they taught but what they did, how they lived their lives, how they treated people and the example they set. So he was also a prophet of a kind, and it appears he was also not above either creating signs or letting certain perceptive acts be interpreted as miraculous signs.

There are in fact surprisingly very few miracles described in the gospels, around 30 or so in all over a ministry which lasted more than three years. There appear to be more, because the same story is retold in more than one gospel and sometimes, like the feeding of the 5,000, in all four.

Try the experiment of saying "Jesus" and "miracle" to someone; ask what comes to mind and you will probably get one of the real headline miracles: walking on water, turning water into wine or indeed feeding the 5,000. The statistical or textual reality is actually quite different from common perception. The majority, about two thirds, of the miracle stories relate instead to acts of healing.

Jesus as a miracle worker was a faith healer and what he is reported as having done, and probably did do, was of a similar nature to the acts of healing undertaken subsequently by his disciples and followers. Such healing was also practiced by other Jews among the Pharisees and Sadducees. He used his charismatic strength to calm and restore people with mental illnesses and behavioral problems, "possessed by demons" according to the cultural perception of the time. He combined something of himself with the natural self-healing power of individuals to release and unblock themselves. He is described as healing the lame, the dumb, the blind, the deaf and the sick.

What he is not reported as doing in the instances of healing, with maybe the exceptions of the man with a withered hand and the slave's severed ear, is anything obviously contrary to physical limits. Missing limbs were not made to sprout again, the old were not suddenly rejuvenated, flesh was not put on dry bones.

Not fully understood certainly, but the powers involved are not necessarily contrary to the order of the created universe. Jesus can be accepted as a successful faith healer without having to invoke the idea of a jester god overturning natural laws to intervene selectively in human affairs. There have been many other such healers. This doesn't detract from the value or the wonder of it, but it does not make Jesus divine.

There are, however, nine reported miracles of a quite different order. These are the real "miracles", impossible acts which only a god could perform. With one exception, the immediate textual evidence or more general considerations explain what really happened or did not happen. Except in one case, the explanations for these fall into one of three categories: mistaken association, mistranslation or alternatively misunderstanding on the part of the writer or storyteller.

The eight miracles which can be explained within this framework are the feeding of the 5,000 (or 4,000), wine into water, the barren fig tree, calming the winds, the widow of Nain, walking on water, the woman of Samaria and the fish and the shekel.

The one instance depending on mistranslation is possibly the easiest to explain. The Greek and Hebrew words for "by" and "on" are the same. So, when Jesus was described in Mark, with the story repeated in Matthew, as walking on the lake or Sea of Galilee, he was actually walking by the lake.

Jesus had earlier gone up into the mountain to pray, leaving his disciples in their boat. But they were sailing into the wind and could make little progress, in fact so little that Jesus was able to walk along the shore and overtake them. He intended to go on, but the disciples saw him and cried out, thinking the lonely figure in the dark was a ghost. So Jesus got on board and joined them on the boat, driven by this time towards and against the shore. Out on the lake it was breezy but now, in the shelter of the land, there was no wind.

Here is the text of Mark with "by" substituted for "on", an equally valid and more probable translation:

> *Immediately he made the disciples get into the boat and go before him to the other side, to Bethsaida, while he dismissed the crowd. And after he had taken leave of them, he went up on the mountain to pray. And when evening came, the boat was out on the sea and he was alone on the land. And he saw that they were making headway painfully, for the wind was against them. And about the fourth watch of the night he came to them, walking by the sea. He meant to pass by them, but when they saw him walking by the sea they thought it was a ghost, and cried out; for they all saw him and were terrified. But immediately he spoke to them and said, "Take heart, it is I; have no fear." And he got into the boat with them and the wind ceased.*
>
> Mark 6:45–51

This was, I suggest, what the text as originally written intended.

Matthew, by most accounts a later compiler, embellished the tale. With the mistranslation from an earlier text possibly already there, he could not resist adding a touch of drama – Peter walking out to Jesus and sinking when his doubt overcame his faith.

As was noted earlier, mistranslation has contributed to the misinterpretation of much gospel evidence; this story provides one example.

The next category of presumed miracle depends on misunderstanding.

There are four stories where the writer described accurately what had happened, according to the evidence he had available, but in his interpretation misunderstood what was really going on.

The tale of the fish and the half-shekel Temple tax is only told in Matthew. It appears that the payment of this tax at Capernaum was resented, and there is a suggestion that Jesus had reason to be exempted. "From whom do kings of the earth take toll or tribute–from their sons or from others?" Jesus asked Peter. As we shall see later, Jesus did eventually stake a claim to kingship either by descent from David, which many could also claim, or less likely and not explicitly by descent from the more recent Maccabean kings.

According to what he claimed to be, he should by rights not have to pay their toll.

But the solution, "not to give offense to them", was typically ingenious, like Jesus' way of dealing with the question of tax by the Roman occupiers. Render to Caesar the things that are Caesar's.

They did not pay the tax from their funds, but they went and caught a fish specifically for the purpose, and sold it for a shekel. The money was therefore metaphorically, though not actually, in the fish's mouth.

But, through retelling, the metaphor became literal–and the shekel was described as really being found in the mouth of the fish.

The miracle in the story of the woman of Samaria, told only in John, depends on another sort of misunderstanding. It is full of metaphors and double meanings, about springs of water and eternal life. The miracle is supposed to be that Jesus, meeting the woman at a well where they had both gone to get water, could read the woman's mind and knew all about her. It does seem, on this and other evidence in the gospels, that Jesus was commonly presumed to have the gift of prescience. He could clearly perform miracles of healing, so it was thought he must also be able to read people's minds and predict the future.

So, what did Jesus tell the woman? He told her that she had had five "husbands", and that the man who she was currently with was not her husband. Among the Jews, at least, adultery was punishable by stoning. So the way to avoid public opprobrium and possible punishment was to divorce one's current partner and find a new one. For a man to embark on a long course of serial monogamy by divorce was nevertheless unusual. For a woman to do this was highly exceptional.

In a relatively small community, with no newspapers and television and not a lot to talk about, the actions of the Samaritan woman would have been a major talking point. Jesus traveled a lot with his disciples among the different communities. He heard the gossip. He was therefore only telling the woman what he already knew. But she went away, as the gospel story relates, and told her friends that she had met a man who was the Messiah and who had told her "all that I ever did." In this way, a relatively unexceptional event came in John's gospel to be reported as miraculous.

Two more mistaken miracles arise from events likewise reported accurately, but misunderstood in being retold or written down. These also reveal something of Jesus' acute perception of human nature. Here, we may be closer to the showman prophet, Elijah. Jesus did not apparently, like Elijah with the lightning and burnt offerings, set these situations up. But in each case he made a point and his reputation as a miracle maker was certainly enhanced.

The first incident, the turning of wine into water, is told in John's Gospel only. It was, according to John, Jesus' first miracle performed shortly after he had begun to recruit his disciples. It was, judging from the quantities of liquid involved, rather a large wedding feast at Cana. Jesus, invited with his mother and disciples, took charge when his mother pointed out that the guests had no more wine. He got the servants present to fill six stone jars, each holding 20 to 30 gallons, with water and serve from these.

It was the practice at such events to serve the best wine first and save the poor wine until last, when people were so drunk that they would not notice. The wedding feast must presumably have reached this stage because the master of ceremonies then commented to the bridegroom that, notwithstanding the usual practice, "you have kept the good wine until now". People already very merry would not, of course, have needed more alcoholic stimulus. What they got, cool and pure, was a refreshing change from the usual rough stuff served at this late stage in the proceedings. It may be that some believed they were drinking wine, or it may be that the master of ceremonies was simply complimenting the bridegroom on his brilliance in substituting water for something far less palatable. The miracle arises from misunderstanding an ironic or complimentary comment, or possibly from an exaggerated later retelling by a drunken guest, who really had thought he was drinking water turned into wine.

If you feel there are some very odd aspects to this miracle, having maybe not looked at it critically before, then you are right. Why for example did Jesus, merely one of the guests, take charge to deal with a major crisis? Was this simply a dramatic device in a story that was in any case simply fiction, or something else?

Like the stories of the barren fig tree and the good Samaritan, this is a good, dramatic tale which just had to be left in—even though it reveals, as will be seen, something about Jesus that the writer or a later editor would not have us know. The trouble with editing, as discussed in the previous chapter, is that it tends to leave traces of the original version, clues to what really may have happened.

This story will be returned to later, because it is a vital part of the mosaic in understanding the life of Jesus. The story does not appear in the other gospels. It may be that the anonymous original source, the "disciple whom Jesus loved" as he is referred to in the gospel, had personal knowledge and access to other material that the other gospel writers did not have. He is described as being present at the Last Supper, the Crucifixion and the discovery with Peter of the empty tomb. It is believed that this disciple, as is stated in the gospel, survived to a great old age and was interviewed by the person who actually compiled the gospel, a prominent figure known as John the Elder, around AD 90.

The fourth and final example of miracles based on misunderstanding provides another demonstration of superb people psychology. This, of course, is the story of the feeding of the five thousand which appears in all four gospels. Matthew, indeed, also has a second such story, the feeding of the four thousand, which is so similar in detail that it must have been a different version of the same event, collected by the gospel writer.

The essence of the story is that Jesus, by now pursued by people because of his reputation as a healer and teacher, wanted some space for himself and the disciples. So they took the boat across the Sea of Galilee to "a lonely place" which may have been near Bethsaida. But they were seen setting off and the crowds went on, some literally running around the lake, to intercept them.

Accepting the situation, Jesus preached and laid hands on the sick. But it began to get late and they were nowhere near shops to buy food. The disciples asked Jesus to tell the people to go back to the towns and villages, where they could get something to eat.

Instead, Jesus asked what they had: just five loaves and two fishes. He asked the disciples to sit people down in groups and divide up the food.

The rest, as they say, is history—well, biblical history. The multitude was fed and afterwards twelve baskets of crumbs were gathered up. So, where did all the food come from? A miracle?

Well, it was a miracle of a sort. The people who wanted to see Jesus knew he was in the vicinity. But they would have to go and find him. There would be crowds, it could be difficult simply locating Jesus and it might well prove to be a long day. Imagine being in the position of a family setting out for the equivalent of a modern, impromptu, open-air pop festival. With no guarantee of any facilities when they got there, the family would certainly take some provisions with them. Others, seeing or hearing about the boat leaving the lakeside would have quickly bought something, maybe in Magdala or Capernaum. But, when it was time to eat, those who had shown foresight could not take their food out. It would have been rude to eat in front of others who had nothing and sharing would have been a pointless sacrifice among so many. Everyone believed they were the only ones who had been wise enough to bring food in their bags or pockets, and so everyone held back.

Jesus demonstrated an extraordinary degree of perception and imagination in resolving the situation. He assumed the likely state of affairs and then did something calculated to unblock the problem.

As soon as food began to be passed round, people nearby took out and offered their own provisions as contributions. The unpacking and handing round of food passed like a great ripple through the crowd, and everyone had at least something to eat.

Jesus took a creative risk because it was possible that the food was not there in sufficient quantity, or that people would not share. In just the same way, he took a risk that the wedding guests, having recognized the water for what it was, would pour scorn on him. As will be seen, in this latter case, Jesus would have been able to withstand criticism because of his role in the ceremony.

The aspects of Jesus' character, revealed in these episodes, are important for understanding what happened when it came to his final confrontation with the Jewish authorities. Jesus could only control so much of the situation. For the rest, he had to rely on his intelligence and then take only those risks, minimized as far as possible, that he had to. He appears to have been an astute, perceptive and calculating risk-taker.

The third and final category of miracle, examples of mistaken association, are rather like the miracles which depended on misunderstanding, except that in these instances there was actually nothing at all going on.

In the case of the barren fig tree, Jesus wanted some fruit to eat on the way into Jerusalem from Bethany. He cursed the tree because there was no fruit on it. But the reason for the lack of fruit was the fact that the tree was already damaged or diseased. By the next day, when Jesus and the disciples passed the same way, it had begun to wither. The curse and demise of the tree were coincidental.

In the same way, in the story told identically in Mark and Matthew, when Jesus awoke during a storm on the Sea of Galilee, the wind dropped–a further coincidence. Either that, or you must believe the storyteller's embellishment that Jesus rebuked the wind and the waves and that they then subsided to order.

Given Jesus' demonstrable healing powers, and popular belief that magic and spirits influenced matters like the weather, it was understandable that anything unusual happening would be attributed to him. So here is my last case in this category, the story of the widow of Nain, told only in Luke's gospel.

Like the example of quelling the wind, this can be taken at face value. Jesus came upon a funeral party, outside the city of Nain. He took pity on the mourning widow whose only son was being taken for burial. So he resurrected the corpse, which then sat up and began to speak.

It's necessary here to look at the context, 2,000 ago. There was no modern medicine, no clear understanding of the distinctions between unconsciousness, coma and death, or brain death as opposed to body death. Mistakes would have been made and people revive, after having apparently died.

If this all seems rather condescending, consider the occasional stories which make the popular press today of individuals coming to on a mortuary slab. In Victorian times, just 100 years or so ago, many people had a real fear of being buried while still alive and so made provision in their wills to have their wrists cut before burial.

Even executions, which were intended to bring about death, sometimes failed. Before the drop was introduced to break the victim's neck, hanging as a method of execution often involved protracted strangulation. It was a messy and inefficient process. There are instances recorded of individuals being cut down and then coming to life, when they were about to be dissected.

So there may well have been an incident of someone being mistakenly laid out and then reviving later on a funeral bier at Nain. With Jesus' miraculous powers widely known and talked about, it was easy to attribute this event to him, if he had been anywhere in the vicinity or even if he had not. Luke collected the story and used his imaginative powers to provide the details.

While on the subject of resurrecting the dead, the story of Jairus' daughter properly belongs as a healing miracle, where I've included it (but see also chapter 16). It is told in all the gospels, except John, in various guises.

The story is that Jairus, "a ruler of the synagogue" in Galilee and thus an important man, had a daughter who was ill. He asked Jesus to lay his hands on her and make her well. Jesus went and a large crowd followed. In the versions in all three gospels, a woman touches Jesus' clothing on the way and is healed. When they arrived at the house, there was a great commotion, because the girl was apparently now dead. Jesus got most of the people out of the house, took the girl by the hand and got her to come to life.

Jesus knew about healing and it seems, by the standards of the time, that he knew something about medicine. But it would appear that he revived someone who was possibly deeply unconscious or near the point of death, though not actually dead. These are fine distinctions that we might make–though perhaps not the gospel writers or the people present at the time. They anticipated that Jesus would perform miracles and they saw, in an everyday world inhabited by magic, what they expected.

Jesus, incidentally, was here literally following in the footsteps of Elijah, who revived a widow's son by what would appear to have been an early form of artificial respiration (I Kings 17:17–24).

So this accounts for the eight "impossible" miracles. What about the ninth, another resurrection story, the raising of Lazarus? It can hardly, as in the case of Jairus' daughter, have really been an act of help or healing; Lazarus had reportedly been laid in his tomb for three days. Which of the three categories does it fall into: mistranslation, misunderstanding or misplaced association?

The answer is that it does not really fit well into any of them. There are just too many curious facts and too many links with other parts of the story. It wasn't a miracle but it was nevertheless something of vital importance–as will be seen.

CHAPTER 4

PERFECT WOMAN

Now the birth of Jesus Christ took place in this way. When his
mother Mary had been betrothed to Joseph, before they came
together she was found to be with child of the Holy Spirit; and
her husband Joseph, being a just man and unwilling to put her
to shame, resolved to divorce her quietly. But as he considered
this, behold, an angel of the Lord appeared to him in a dream,
saying, "Joseph, Son of David, do not fear to take Mary your
wife, for that which is conceived in her is of the Holy Spirit; she
will bear a son, and you shall call his name Jesus, for he will
save his people from their sins." All this took place to fulfill
what the Lord had spoken by the prophet:
"Behold, a virgin shall conceive and bear a son, and his name
shall be called Emmanuel (which means, 'God with us')."
When Joseph woke from sleep, he did as the angel of the Lord
commanded him; he took his wife, but knew her not until she
had borne a son; and he called his name Jesus.

Matthew 1:18–25

———◦———

If the bible text shows Jesus as less than perfect, if his miracles were acts
of faith healing, with a minority of improbable acts resulting from myth
or misunderstanding, what remains of the claim in Christian theology
that he was not only human, but also divine?

There remains his miraculous birth, his–for the time–abnormal unmarried
celibate life and his miraculous resurrection after death. These are all, in one
way or another, superimposed by the canonical gospel writers and editors,
that is those whom the Church has chosen to accept.

The gospel that most scholars agree is the earliest, Mark, says nothing
about Jesus' birth and there is likewise nothing in the Gospel of John. Both
these authors report, either at first or second hand, eyewitness accounts.
Mark accompanied Peter as his interpreter for Greek-speaking Gentile
audiences as he preached to the Early Church and "John-the-Priest", the

disciple whom Jesus loved, is thought to have given his recollections whilst in his old age to the author of the Gospel of John.

In the years after the Crucifixion, there was material available both from eyewitness and passed-on or passed-down accounts about Jesus' life. But Jesus in his preaching would almost certainly have said little, if anything, about his own early life. That sort of detail would only have been available directly from his own family: his mother Mary and his brothers and sisters.

If it were not collected at the time, that is within a few decades of Jesus' Crucifixion, then this part of the record would simply have been a blank. The gospel writers would have had to fill it in, as best they could.

It may also be that the immediate family of Jesus was not all that forthcoming, for good reason. It seems that Mary, the mother of Jesus, was not married when she conceived her firstborn. Joseph, as it would appear from the gospel story, came to the rescue.

There are several possibilities. Joseph may have taken on an already pregnant Mary and married her, saving her from shame and possibly punishment. He may have impregnated Mary himself and then regularized the situation by marrying her. He may have been betrothed to Mary, as both Luke and Matthew suggest, but then been cuckolded by someone else, before either marrying or rejecting her.

Joseph then disappears entirely from the story, apart from some references only in Luke which could refer to Joseph–or to someone else. Luke reports that "his parents", that is Jesus' parents, went to Jerusalem every year for the Passover Feast and he follows with a description of the twelve-year-old Jesus staying behind to talk to priests. When "they" discover him missing and return to track him down, Mary is quoted as saying to Jesus that she and "your father" had been looking anxiously for him. In not one of these references is Joseph specified by name as the father of Jesus.

Luke's version of Jesus' birth is similar to Matthew's given above, except that the angel in the dream with the good news appears to Mary rather than Joseph. Both assert that Mary was a virgin when Jesus was conceived.

Suggesting that God was the father was one way of evading scandal, and not without precedent. Alexander the Great was presumed to have been conceived in somewhat similar circumstances by the god Jupiter. Stories abound in ancient legends of gods consorting with mortals to produce half-human, half-divine offspring.

So the tale, told in Matthew and Luke, not only dealt with the potentially awkward circumstances of Jesus' birth, but it also laid the foundation for the doctrine of the divinity of Christ.

Casting about for evidence to fill in the gaps and justify elements of their narrative, the gospel writers turned to the Jewish testament writings.

Here Matthew found what he wanted. Isaiah wrote, "Behold a virgin shall conceive and bear a son and shall call his name Emmanuel." (Isaiah 7:14).

That would seem clear enough, but for one important fact. The version of the Old Testament which both the non-Jewish, Greek-speaking writers Matthew and Luke had access to was the Septuagint. This had been translated into Greek from the original Hebrew in the third century BC, reputably by seventy scholars in seventy days, for the benefit of Jews in Alexandria who could neither read nor speak Hebrew.

Hebrew had two words, almah and bethulah, that could be used to described Mary's state while in the Greek language there was only one word, parthenos. The Hebrew text crucially used the word almah which meant a young unmarried woman, or possibly any woman who had not yet had a child. It did not use the word bethulah which would have denoted a virgin in the strict physical sense.

The Septuagint writers had no exact Greek equivalent for the Hebrew word almah, so they translated it by parthenos. This word denoted a virgin in the physical sense, that is a woman who was intact and had not had sex.

So Isaiah's prediction became something else by mistranslation, that a "virgin", not a young woman as originally written, would conceive and bear a child.

It should, perhaps, be added that nowhere in any later part of the gospel texts is there any resonance of Jesus' supposed miraculous birth. People said, "Is not this the carpenter's/builder's son?" They were marveling at someone of such apparently ordinary origins being able to heal and preach. They might have said, "It's not surprising that someone can do and say such things who was himself the product of a miraculous intervention by God." That is, they might have said that if the story of the "virgin" birth had been current at the time and not a later invention by Matthew, followed by Luke.

Paul, who wrote letters to the early Christian communities following his conversion, stated firmly that Jesus was born "according to the flesh". Several of his letters which appear in the New Testament, and can safely be attributed to him, appear to have survived without too much alteration and in general predate the gospels. This suggests that Paul may in this respect be a more reliable source than Matthew or Luke.

The Hebrew-speaking gospel writers John and Mark did not repeat the mistakes of Matthew and Luke because there were able to read the prophecies of Isaiah in their original form. So their accounts contain no details of a supposed "virgin" birth.

The miraculous account of Jesus' birth was, however, useful in dealing with the possibly awkward circumstances surrounding Joseph and Mary's betrothal. It gave the Early Church, increasingly hostile to human sexuality of any sort, what it wanted: a sex-free conception plus the involvement of God. The extension of the doctrine made Mary, now the "mother of God", a perpetual virgin.

Given that women at that time married very young and, with no contraception, would ordinarily go on to have several children, this is more than a little odd. In the face of the evidence provided by the gospels themselves, it is in fact extraordinarily perverse. Jesus is described as Mary's "firstborn", which strongly implies that she went on to have other children. Moreover, Jesus' brothers and sisters are mentioned and named.

For example, Mark 6:3, has people wondering, "Is not this the carpenter (builder), the son of Mary and brother of James and Joses and Judas and Simon, and are not his sisters here with us?"

There's a similar passage in Matthew 13:55–56, "Is not this the carpenter's son? Is not his mother called Mary? And are not his brothers James and Joseph and Simon and Judas? And are not all his sisters with us?"

Joseph, incidentally, is nowhere specifically described in the gospels as a carpenter/builder. Jesus' father was. But by this point there has ceased to be any reference to Joseph by name. It is possible, as will be seen, that someone else had taken over the role of social father and head of the household.

Catholics have argued, in an implausible effort to shore up the doctrine of Mary's "perpetual" virginity, that the brothers and sisters of Jesus referred to in the gospels were really his cousins. However, the gospel writers are known to have reported other such relationships accurately. Luke, for example, describes Philip as the brother and not the cousin of Herod the Tetrarch (Herod Antipas). They were, indeed, half brothers, offspring of two of Herod the Great's wives.

It has been suggested that confusion could have arisen from the Hebrew word "akim", which might either refer to cousins or siblings. But the gospels are believed to have been originally compiled in Greek which has separate words for brother, sister and cousin. Distinctions were certainly made between brothers or sisters and more loosely related kin. Elizabeth, for example, was described as Mary's kinswoman, rather than her sister, while the disciples John and James were described as brothers, rather than cousins.

Furthermore, the gospel writers were not, as in the case of the problem with the Hebrew words almah and bethulah, dealing with an ancient, translated source. They wrote what they knew and what other writers, such as Paul, knew: Jesus had brothers and sisters. Paul wrote in Greek, in his letter to the Galatians (1:18–19), as follows. "Then after three years, I went up to Jerusalem to visit Cephas (who was possibly Peter), and remained with him fifteen days. But I saw none of the other Apostles except James the Lord's brother."

James, one of the four brothers listed by Mark and Matthew, is also quoted by other sources as the brother of Jesus, such as the Early Church historian, Eusebius. His comments, quoting Hegesippus, suggest that James may have been both religious leader of the Nazoraean sect, that is the original Jesus movement, and someone with a very significant basis of support within the Jewish community as a whole.

There is no real need or strong evidence for believing that there was a scandal surrounding Jesus' conception and birth. The only evidence is indirect and lies in the Nativity stories in Matthew and Luke. These stories are there to add substance to the argument that Jesus was divine, since procreated by God. But they derive, as I have argued, from a mistranslation of the original Isaiah prophecy from Hebrew into Greek in the Septuagint.

Betrothal was a solemn agreement, which was expected to lead to marriage, so it was socially acceptable for betrothed couples to have sex. So it may simply be that Jesus was conceived when Mary and Joseph were betrothed. This would not have been an entirely uncommon occurrence.

There are later stories that Mary was raped by a Roman soldier, Panthera, though it seems these originated from sources hostile to the emerging Christian Church.

Whoever the biological father was, the real point is that the mother of Jesus was not a virgin. This idea arose from a mistranslation which was then reinforced and compounded by the desire to portray Jesus as semi-divine.

But the consequence was to create an impossible virginal status for Mary as "the mother of God". This was in the teeth of the evidence that Jesus had brothers and sisters and the probability in any case that Mary, having married young, would have gone on to have a fairly large family.

Later editors of the original versions of the gospels would certainly have realized this difficulty. Their response is shown in the circumspection with which Jesus' family is described. In descriptions of the family later in the gospel stories, the name of the father is absent, presumably edited out.

Taking all the references together, it can be seen that Joseph is only mentioned by name as Mary's betrothed at the time of the Nativity.

Then, later in the gospel story, Jesus is mentioned in the same breath as his mother Mary and four named brothers and his sisters. He is also described in John 2:12, as coming from the wedding feast in Cana to Capernaum with his disciples, his mother and his brothers. In these references, the name of the father has been deliberately left out or edited out, unless Mary was by then a single mother.

The passage in John, which equates to the carpenter quotes in Matthew and Mark, suggests another possibility. In John 6:42, some people are upset by Jesus' reference to himself as "come down from heaven" and "the bread of life" and so query, "Is not this Jesus, the son of Joseph, whose father and mother we know?"

Why the rather repetition, with both "the son of Joseph" and "whose father" we know? It's either clumsy writing or intriguingly indicative of the fact that Jesus' biological and social father were not at this point one and the same. As in the other references, the names of Jesus' mother and social father have been edited out.

There are some later references, around three years on at the time of the Crucifixion, which provide a further clue. Matthew, Mark and Luke describe a group of women who stood by the cross, and who would have been significant people and very likely close family members. Luke doesn't name any of the women. But Mark describes three among those present: Mary Magdalene, Mary the mother of James the younger and Joses and Salome. Matthew lists the following three as being present, Mary Magdalene, Mary the mother of James and Joseph and the mother of the sons of Zebedee. Assuming these are the same three women, then Salome is the wife of Zebedee and mother of his sons, James and John.

Since Mark earlier describes James and Joses as among Jesus' brothers, and Matthew does likewise for James and Joseph, it is clear that the Mary present near to the cross (the mother of James the younger and Joses) was also Mary, the mother of Jesus.

But this could not be stated directly because it would have linked Mary's other children directly with her and so contradicted the myth of her "perpetual" virginity. Hence the circumlocution: Mary, the mother of James and Joses, or James and Joseph, rather than straightforwardly Mary, the mother of several children and also Jesus.

Whenever Mary and her children are mentioned in one breath, the text has been edited so that either Jesus is named or some of the other children but not both together. By this device, the fictional "virgin" Mary could be made separate from the real-life Mary who had other children beside Jesus. It is possible that the names Joses and Joseph, appearing alternately in Matthew and Mark, both refer to same brother of Jesus. It is also possible, as I will argue later, that there are only four brothers in all and that the names Jesus, Joseph and Joses all relate to one character.

Mary Magdalene, one of the three women present, was clearly an important character in the life of Jesus, as will be seen, as she appears frequently at key points in the narrative.

The sons of Zebedee—James and John—were among the twelve disciples. Comparison of the passages in Mark and Matthew describing the women present near the cross suggested that their mother may have been Salome.

In John's Gospel, 20:25, the description of the women at the Crucifixion is more specific, but confused: "But standing by the cross of Jesus were his mother, and his mother's sister, Mary the wife of Clophas, and Mary Magdalene."

Now there would appear to be four women present. Or, alternatively, there are still three including one Mary, the mother of Jesus, and another Mary, her sister– mentioned in the gospels for the first and only time! The confusion involved in calling two children in a family by the same name is usually avoided at all costs, and it is highly improbable that this would have happened.

Another curious point is that Salome, the mother of the sons of Zebedee, appears in this scene in John to have disappeared from the plot.

The answer would again appear to the later editing that took place to separate the fictional virgin Mary from the real-life persona, this time achieved by a simple transposition.

The passage makes sense, *and only really makes sense*, if it reads, "But standing by the cross of Jesus were his mother, Mary the wife of Clophas, and his mother's sister (Salome, the wife of Zebedee) and Mary Magdalene." It needs just one transplaced phrase "Mary the wife of Clophas" to be put back into position for the description to become coherent and fall into place with the other gospel records.

Now, John agrees fully with the descriptions in Mark and Matthew. There are the same three women present. There are no sisters, improbably and confusingly both called Mary and mentioned nowhere else. Salome is back on the scene.

The mystery of the lack of any direct reference to Joseph, Jesus' biological father, after the Nativity scenes is also resolved. He may have divorced Mary or more likely died, leaving Mary to marry a person named Clophas, who then fathered some or all of Jesus' brothers and sisters.

This explanation allows for a more comprehensible reading of the earlier reference in John. This, before editing, would now read: "Is not this Jesus, the son of Joseph, whose father Clophas and mother Mary we know?"

Jesus was the son of Joseph but his social father, probably since his very early years, may well have been Clophas.

There is interesting confirmation in the fact that the Greek historian Eusebius records a tradition that Joseph, Jesus' first named father, had a brother named Clophas. This brother might well have formally taken on the family responsibilities when Joseph died. As in other societies, there was a custom called the levirate which provided for a man in some circumstances to marry his deceased brother's widow.

Clophas or Cleophas most scholars agree was a name which became corrupted in use and translation into another name, "Alphaeus".

This interpretation is supported by a fragment from a medieval manuscript attributed to the Early Church father Papias which states that "Mary the wife of Cleophas or Alphaeus ... was the mother of James the Bishop and Apostle, and of Simon, Thaddeus, and one Joseph."

Eusebius states that James was succeeded after his death, as leader of the community of followers of Jesus in Jerusalem, by "Simeon the son of

Clophas mentioned in the gospel narratives, a cousin of the savior". The Early Church father Jerome takes this as a basis to conclude that the brothers of Jesus were in fact all his cousins. His motivation would have been to defend the virginal status attributed to Mary and the position of Jesus, disconnected from an immediate family.

But the evidence already outlined strongly indicates that Jesus had at least three brothers: James, who was frankly described as such by Paul and Josephus, plus Simon and Judas. If the indications that Clophas took on responsibility for his dead brother's wife are correct, then Simon or Simeon might well have been a half-brother of Jesus– though easy to portray as a cousin. That's because he was at the same time the son of Jesus' uncle and stepfather, Clophas. If Clophas had children from a previous marriage, then Simon could alternatively have been both a step-brother and cousin of Jesus.

The aim of the gospel writers or editors to cut Jesus' family out of the story as far as possible was, I have argued, linked with the objective of making the birth of Jesus appear miraculous and Jesus himself semi-divine. This was to fit with a Hellenistic version of events, competing with and supplanting a Nazoraean/Jewish theology supported by Jesus' immediate followers who had known him, and who were in some cases related to him. In this way, Mary had to be perfect and so, absurdly, a perpetual "virgin", despite having given birth to Jesus and despite the sound evidence in the gospels and elsewhere that Jesus had brothers and sisters.

Jesus as a character in the gospels had also to be cut from his family, as part of the process of divorcing him from his Jewish origins in order to make him the acceptable savior of a Gentile and Roman world.

But the evidence could not be obliterated entirely and, at the same time, leave a story to tell. Just as crucially, it could not be removed from other, independent sources.

Just acknowledging the bits that have been left in, and carrying out some simple detective work, reinstates Jesus' family with some astonishing results. Not only did Jesus have a fairly large family from what we know, and it may have been even larger taking into account what might have been excluded because it was not even deemed relevant, but his family played a very important role in Jesus' ministry.

Jesus is described as having four brothers–James, Simon or Simeon, Judas and Joseph or Joses, as well as two or more unnamed sisters.

References in Mark are to a degree ambiguous, allowing for the possibility that Salome was one of his two sisters. However, comparisons with similar passages in Matthew and John strongly indicate that Salome was the sister of Jesus' mother Mary and therefore his aunt.

That makes James and John, the sons of Zebedee, Jesus' cousins.

Even more striking is the fact that one of Jesus' brothers clearly appears in all the lists of the twelve Apostles whom Jesus appointed from his disciples. James, the son of Alphaeus, that is the son of Mary's husband and therefore the brother or stepbrother of Jesus, appears in the same position in the lists of Apostles given in Mark, Matthew, Luke and in the Acts of the Apostles.

In Luke's list, and in the Acts of the Apostles believed to have been written by the author of Luke, another brother appears, "Judas the brother of James".

Judas was, it will be recalled, one of the four brothers of Jesus–James, Judas, Simon and Joseph or Joses–named in the Gospels of Matthew and Mark.

This might be considered a bit of an oddity, a later addition by Luke, were it not for the fact that the corresponding Apostle in the lists provided in Mark and Matthew was Thaddeus (in Matthew, Lebbaeus surnamed Thaddeus). In the fragment attributed to Papias, who lived between AD 60 and 135, there are four sons of Mary listed: James, Simon, Joseph and, in place of Judas, Thaddeus.

So Judas is there also, not only in Luke's list but as Thaddeus in Mark and Matthew. He also appears as Judas Zelotes (Judas the zealous or zealot) in a list of Apostles provided in the apocryphal Gospel Epistula Apostolorum.

As further confirmation, in the *Apostolic Constitutions*, a second or third century Syriac document, there is a reference to "Thaddeus also called Lebbaeus and surnamed Judas the Zealot".

Two of Jesus' brothers, James and Simon, were leaders in the Jewish Nazoraean community in Jerusalem which thrived in the years following the Crucifixion. So it is not surprising that some or all of them would have been among Jesus' immediate followers in his lifetime.

James and Judas were among the twelve and so too may have been the third brother, Simon, in the guise of "Simon the Cananite" or "Simon the zealot", as given in the gospel lists.

The fourth brother "Joses" in Mark, corresponding to "Joseph" in Matthew, disappears after his early appearance in the gospels and also lacks references in other texts, unlike the others. It may be that the sources for the gospel writers were not absolutely clear and Joses or Joseph was, as the Papias fragment suggests, possibly Jesus himself. This, it will be recalled, stated that "Mary the wife of Cleophas or Alphaeus ... was the mother of James the Bishop and Apostle, and of Simon, Thaddeus, and one Joseph."

The picture which the gospels, as edited or reconstructed, seek to give is of the family of Jesus failing to understand his mission, trying to drag him away from his audience, while Jesus himself disowns them. Thus in Mark 3:20, his family are described as trying to seize Jesus at the start of his preaching ministry because people were suggesting that he had become deranged. They went to call for him (Mark 3:31–35) while he was talking to a crowd. On being informed that his mother and brothers were waiting for him, Jesus is quoted as suggesting that those who were around him were now his mother and his brothers.

Some family disagreement might well have been likely at the outset. There may have been misunderstandings as to what Jesus was about. But at least two, and possibly three, brothers are numbered among his close disciples. Two brothers went on in turn to lead the Nazoraean community in Jerusalem which grew up, continuing Jesus' ministry after the Crucifixion.

So it appears that, whatever initial disagreements there may have been, Jesus and his brothers worked together cooperatively in a movement with a broad, religious aim.

The gospels, as they have evolved, emphasize discord and either omit or disguise the cooperation. That it would seem was part of the effort to distance Jesus from his Jewish roots in the manufacture of a religion with appeal to the wider Gentile world.

The reality was that Jesus' brothers and cousins were inextricably involved from the outset as followers in his teaching and mission, as is shown by their place in the lists of the Apostles.

It was certainly a family affair. Why not? If Jesus had some sort of messianic claim by descent, as a "Son of David" or as part of a priestly lineage, then so too would his immediate blood relatives.

As will be seen, they did pursue their claim. James was stoned to death by his fellow Jews for his presumption, and other members of the family were sought out and killed by the Romans as actual or potential messianic claimants.

Another vital corollary is this. The Nazarene or Nazoraean community, first of all under James, had orthodox Jewish beliefs including strict observance of the Law of Moses, which made them little different from the Pharisees. Since they began as followers of Jesus, this makes it likely that Jesus was also like them in his way of life and beliefs.

The picture which has been built up of Jesus, and which to some extent is portrayed in the gospels, is quite different.

Did he really have scant respect for Jewish Law, for example in respect of Sabbath observance? Was he really, as we have been led to believe, seeking to bring about an entirely new religious order?

The answer is that Jesus wasn't, but the "Apostle" Paul and those who subsequently promoted the gospels were.

CHAPTER 5

FAMILY WEDDING

On the third day there was a marriage at Cana in Galilee, and the mother of Jesus was there; Jesus also was invited [called] to the marriage, with his disciples. When the wine gave out, the mother of Jesus said to him, "They have no wine." And Jesus said to her, "O woman, what have you to do with me? My hour is not yet come."

His mother said to the servants, "Do whatever he tells you." Now six stone jars were standing there, for the Jewish rites of purification, each holding twenty or thirty gallons. Jesus said to them, "Fill the jars with water." And they filled them up to the brim.

He said to them, "Now draw some out, and take it to the steward of the feast." So they took it. When the steward of the feast tasted the water now become wine, and did not know where it came from (though the servants who had drawn the water knew), the steward of the feast called the bridegroom and said to him, "Every man serves the good wine first; and when men have drunk freely, then the poor wine; but you have kept the good wine until now." This, the first of his signs, Jesus did at Cana in Galilee, and manifested his glory; and his disciples believed in him.

After this he went down to Capernaum, with his mother and his brothers and his disciples; and there they stayed for a few days.

John 2:1–12

The analysis of the previous chapters, relying chiefly on gospel sources, has shown that Jesus was neither entirely perfect, nor the product of an unusual liaison between an immortal god and a mortal woman, nor able to perform bizarre and fantastic miracles. This is no way detracts from the historical Jesus who claimed none of these things. He certainly appears to have been a successful faith healer and a strong and charismatic leader.

Having shaken away preconceptions, put in place by a Church obsessed by a false equation between sex and sinfulness, we can see Jesus more as the human being he would have been. He was part of a normal Jewish family with siblings who were either his full brothers and sisters or his half/step brothers and sisters.

He was not only born via the normal process of reproduction but he would, in Jewish society at that time, almost certainly have been married.

Marriage was a strong cultural obligation and those who did not marry, without good reason, were regarded as cursed and were pitied. Most boys married in their late teens to early twenties, while girls were married as young as thirteen.

It is worth considering where Jesus might have fitted in Jewish society either as a celibate or married individual.

The Essenes, or "the poor", are described by Josephus as a minority ascetic cult in the Jewish community. They practiced celibacy, though some among their number were permitted to marry for the purposes of reproduction and the sect also adopted children. Young men would have been taken on as initiates for training to keep the sect going.

There is evidence that Jesus was influenced by and sympathetic towards the ideas of this group. He reserves his condemnation, as it is recorded in the gospels, for the Pharisees and Sadducees and their scribes. Some references, as will be seen, suggest that members of the Essenes or a similar sympathetic group may have provided him with essential help.

Membership of these various sects within Judaism was not incidentally so very rigidly defined. The Jewish historian Josephus, for example, claimed to have belonged at one time or another to all of them, including the "fourth way" characterized by active opponents to Roman rule, the zealots! So, in a sense, these terms were simply labels which might or might not in every case refer to a distinct, organized group.

The Essenes at Qumran were apparently an offshoot of the Sadducees, distancing themselves from the secular excesses of Maccabean rule. They did not refer to themselves by, and might well not even have recognized, the term "Essenes" as it was applied to them. The word which they used for themselves was "the poor".

The situation is complicated by the fact that the gospel writers adopted, or were edited to adopt, an anti-Jewish stance though Jesus was himself a Jew.

Some writers have suggested, because of similarities in some of the terms used and some of the teachings, that Jesus was simply a prominent member of the Essenes who described themselves as "the poor". However, the gospel description of Jesus as a wandering prophet, who had family, disciples and friends, do not fit with him being a member of the group who set themselves deliberately apart, living at Qumran by the shores of the Dead Sea.

It seems that at Qumran celibacy was the ideal or expectation for at least the upper hierarchy of members of the covenant. But in other settlements in towns, where there was closer contact with other Jews, the rules were more relaxed and there was specific provision (as given in the Messianic Rule) for men to marry at twenty. Another important difference was that at Qumran members, once initiated, had to surrender their property to the community. Elsewhere, those in the towns were not required to do this but instead contributed from their wages to help those in need.

Jesus was one of probably four brothers. Judas or Thaddeus was certainly married because he had descendants who were later tracked down, persecuted and eventually killed by the Romans on the grounds that they were "Sons of David" with a claim to the Jewish throne. James, the leader of the Nazoraean community is described as a lifelong celibate. As for the third brother Simon or Simeon, who succeeded James, there is simply insufficient evidence.

This mixed picture suggests that, rather than being members of an upper echelon of the monastic community at Qumran, the brothers are more likely to have been in contact with one or more of the assemblies of the towns. Here marriage was permitted and celibacy was only an ideal for some, and not enforced.

There is a lot of surviving written material about Jesus, as there is also quite a bit about his brother James. But, while there are direct references to James' celibate state, there are no references which give similar information about Jesus. Had Jesus been a lifelong celibate like his brother, it can be expected that this would have come across directly or indirectly in the gospels.

As a normal man within Jewish society as a whole, Jesus would have been married. There was clearly an exception to this for religious groups, such as the mother church of the Essenes at Qumran, that practiced celibacy. But marriage was otherwise such a strong cultural expectation that those who reached adulthood and remained single often became objects of pity or derision.

At the time Jesus was preaching, the gospels indicate that Jesus was bound by conventional Jewish custom and practice, though not by any other rule.

As it happens, one of the gospels provides strong evidence which seems to resolve the issue.

The marriage in Cana was just too good an episode for the author of John to leave out because it contained the excellent tale of the miracle in which water was turned into wine. It should be noted, however, how essential information on the wedding is only sparingly included. There are very few details given, except those necessary to relate the water into wine miracle. There is no mention at all of the bride and the bridegroom, although featuring in the story, is not given a name.

What information there is, however, points overwhelmingly to the fact that this was Jesus' own wedding! Not just any old guest, he went to the wedding in a formidable wedding party with his disciples, his mother and his brothers. This rather implies that he and they were not just onlookers but part of the proceedings.

When the wine ran out, the master of ceremonies turned to Mary, the mother of Jesus. She was thus clearly acting as the hostess. So it would in that case have been a wedding for one of her own children.

Mary passed the problem on to Jesus who took charge and, in his own way, solved it.

The master of ceremonies then calls and compliments "the bridegroom". This is a character not so far mentioned in the story and apparently not involved in dealing with the difficulty over wine. But why would the MOC have congratulated someone else, when he had gone to Mary in her capacity as hostess and her son Jesus had solved the problem? This only makes sense if Jesus, son of the hostess, was also the bridegroom.

Jesus dealt with the wine shortfall; the master of ceremonies then complimented him–as the bridegroom–on his solution.

When the couples were from different villages, or when the prospective husband lived or worked away, it was the practice at that time to send a messenger to summon the bridegroom. Events were reckoned by days before and after important religious feasts and there were no names for days of the week. So the call was important to coordinate and avoid mistakes in a less calendar and clock-obsessed society.

Jesus and his family and disciples were indeed invited or called to the wedding. The text in John which immediately precedes the quote given above is somewhat disguised or garbled. But it indicates that the summons was delivered to Jesus by a Galilean named Nathanael.

The quantity of extra wine required, 120 to 180 gallons, merely as a supplement when the main provision had run out, indicates that this was a wedding on a substantial scale.

But there is no problem here either. It is only the Nativity myth which gives the impression that Jesus came from a humble background. He lived an itinerant life, accepting food and hospitality and alms and, with his disciples, assistance from a significant group of women. But he might also have come from a family of some standing–certainly, as will be seen, one with a priestly background and connections.

There is, however, one highly discordant phrase in the story of the wedding in Cana, and that is Jesus' reply to his mother Mary. In response to her comment, "they have no wine" with its implication "can you please do something about it?", Jesus according to the text retorts with a scorching, out-of-character and off-key put down, "O woman, what have you to do with me? My hour has not yet come."

Pretty fierce stuff in response to a simple observation that the guests had already managed to mop up all the drink provided for the wedding.

It is also a remark that is clearly out of context. The phrase "my hour has not yet come" is reserved in the gospels for those occasions when Jesus, in advance of his planned final confrontation, avoids any action which would put him at risk. For example, this is precisely what he says to his brothers, later in John's Gospel, when they exhorted him to go to the Feast of Tabernacles when he would have been at risk of capture: "My time has not yet come, but your time is always here."

So the phrase would appear to have been copied and put in to fill a gap. But what kind of gap?

I suggest that Mary's remark to Jesus, even though it provided a clue as to what was happening, was left in the text because it was necessary to give the dramatic context: the supply of wine for the guests had run out. But Jesus' original reported reply had to be deleted because it really gave the game away, making quite clear his status at the wedding. When deletions were made, material of the same extent was often inserted to avoid the need to copy out more than one page in a document.

The original text would have run something like:

"When the wine gave out, the mother of Jesus said to him, "They have no wine."

And Jesus said to her, "Be not troubled, the bridegroom provides for the guests; I will get them more to drink."

His mother said to the servants, "Do whatever he tells you."

This now makes more sense. The blistering "O woman, what have you to do with me?" is clearly a misplaced comment. If it was made by Jesus in some other context, it indicates an all too human degree of exasperation on his part.

It is interesting and in a way encouraging that in the wedding story, as in the stories of Jesus' birth, family and upbringing, editing and censorship seems for the most part to have been carried out by the simple expedient of deleting names. This suggests that some reliance can be placed on the framework that has been retained.

There was a practical reason why editing proceeded by this process of pruning rather than wholesale transplanting. Even with primitive methods of production and publishing through laborious copying, there were by the third and fourth centuries AD many copies of the gospels in circulation. Parts had also been copied and included in other texts as references. The religious authorities did not therefore have complete control over the situation. If they made drastic changes in copying the gospels, people would remember the old versions and complain–and there would be the possibility of a few texts surviving to back up their points. If, however, they made some selective and judicious excisions of names, they could still achieve their objective without offending anyone.

For example, those who knew the old texts would read in their minds when encountering "they" and "Jesus' mother and father" what had originally been in the texts–which, I have argued, were in this case the names "Mary" and "Clophas". But these mental associations in general would die with these readers and new readers would read the new texts as they stood. In time, the dislocated text, purged of awkward associations, would become the orthodoxy.

That's how Jesus came to be left out of the story as the bridegroom just as his mother, social father and brothers and sisters were pushed textually to one side.

But if Jesus was, as I have argued, the bridegroom, who then was the bride?

Whoever it was, would surely appear in one way or another later in the gospel texts.

There are indeed two candidates, Mary Magdalene and Mary of Bethany, sister of Martha, who provided somewhere for Jesus to stay while he was preaching in Jerusalem.

Both women in the text act in ways that a wife would do and they never appear together in the same scene. For these reasons, and the fact that Jewish society would not have tolerated Jesus having two wives or a wife and a mistress–especially as he was himself the advocate of a strict moral stance on adultery–there are grounds for regarding the two Marys as one and the same.

Mary Magdalene appeared to have met Jesus when she was cured of some form of "possession". She was one of a group of women, described in Luke, who provided for Jesus and the Apostles "out of their means", that is gave financial support. She was also one of the three women, besides Mary the mother of Jesus and his brothers and sisters and Salome, who were present at the scene of the Crucifixion and the empty tomb. In most of the instances, Mary Magdalene is mentioned first, an order of precedence which at least points to her being his wife; no one else would have ranked above his mother. If Jesus were married, then his wife like his mother would have sought to be near him in his final agony, at the Crucifixion scene. And she surely would not have been upstaged by someone who would otherwise have been no more than a family friend.

As with the wedding and family stories, editing was largely carried out by process of elimination. Mary Magdalene is left in the places where she would naturally be as Jesus' wife, but she is deprived of her true title and not described as such. However, in other early gospels which did not find a place in the New Testament and were therefore not so edited–the Gospel of Mary and the Gospel of Philip–she is frankly described as Jesus' partner. According to the Gospel of Philip, "the Savior loved Mary Magdalene more than all the disciples and kissed her on the mouth often". This suggests that, if not his wife, then she was his partner or betrothed at this time.

As for Mary of Bethany, she is described as having a special place in Jesus' affections and Jesus did indeed frequently stay at her house. This would have been socially unacceptable except in one particular circumstance whatever Jesus' status, even if he were single. It would certainly have been quite out of the question had Jesus been married, as I have argued he must have been, by that time. But, if he were married to Mary, and not someone else, then there's no longer any problem. In the story of Lazarus, Mary of Bethany does indeed behave as Jesus' wife.

When Jesus arrives, apparently rather late to save Lazarus, he is roundly upbraided by Martha, while Mary remained inside.

Then, Martha went and called Mary, "saying quietly: the teacher/master is here and is calling for you. And when she heard it, she rose quickly and went to him."

The difference in behavior of the two women, both sisters of Lazarus, can be accounted for by their different positions in relation to Jesus. Mary behaved as a wife would, despite her equal anger and despair over the fate of her brother, by meekly waiting to be summoned by her husband.

Luke also recounts an incident which provides separate corroboration for the different status of Mary, as compared with Martha. Jesus returns to Bethany and Mary sits at his feet while Martha is left to do the cooking and serving. Martha then complains of the lack of assistance. But, instead of talking directly to her sister, she addresses her complaint to Jesus, which indicates that Mary was under his control or authority. This would have been the case if, as the other evidence also suggests, Mary were his wife.

Jesus could not have had two wives: so it is far more probable that his wife was described in different terms in different parts of the gospel narrative.

Since Mary's sister Martha lived with her, and also her brother Lazarus, it seems that the place where Jesus stayed in Bethany was Mary's original family home. Only a mile or so from Jerusalem, this would have made a convenient stopping-off place for Jesus and the disciples' preaching missions in Jerusalem, as described in the Gospel of John. It was also a relatively safe place to return to spend the night. Jesus was aware that his teaching in the Temple precinct was antagonizing the High Priest and his followers among the Sadducees, and that they were plotting against him. So he was careful until the final confrontation came to go back and forth to Bethany in daylight hours.

Jesus was also entertained at the house of Simon the Leper, as the Gospels of Mark and Matthew relate, where he is anointed by an unnamed woman with some very costly ointment. The possible significance of this action will be discussed later on. What is interesting at this point is that the story appears in all four gospels with common key elements and some variations. It is really the same story. In which case, are the variations all that they seem?

Mark and Matthew both have the woman pouring the ointment over Jesus' head. Both Luke and John have the woman using the expensive ointment, spikenard, to anoint Jesus' feet and she also uses her hair to dry Jesus' feet, from her tears in the case of Luke and from the ointment in John's Gospel.

In Luke, the incident takes place in the house of an unnamed Pharisee. John skirts over the point: it is in Bethany, with Lazarus at the table, Martha serving and Mary applying the pound weight of costly ointment. The reader is left to presume that this is in Mary and Martha's home.

It could well be that some or even many of the facts are wrong in one or more version. But in Jesus' time, men by and large owned property. Mary and Martha's family home would have been that of their father. The evidence of Mark and John combined provides some slight indication that this person might have been Simon the Leper.

In Luke's version, the woman who wets Jesus' feet with her tears is described as "a woman of the city, who was a sinner". This accords with a Church tradition that Mary Magdalene had been a prostitute. But the only evidence for this appears to be the possibility that the name Magdalene might derive from the Hebrew word for harlot, *magdalah*.

According to Mark, Jesus did cure her of possession by casting out "seven demons", which is not the same as implying that she had led an immoral life. But if Luke was here referring even elliptically to Mary Magdalene, then this is the point in the text where the two Marys fuse in one historical character.

Jesus stayed at Mary's house in order to carry out his preaching in Jerusalem and, after his anointing, to fulfill his final mission.

It may be that Jesus and Mary lived for the rest of the time, when he was not traveling, in his home town of Capernaum.

There is one final point which needs to be resolved. Just why did the gospels avoid direct reference to Jesus' wife who the evidence suggests was called Mary?

Well, the references may very well have been there initially. But this fact was edited out in the same way and for the same reason that references to Jesus' father and to his brothers and sisters were obscured or eliminated.

Three hundred years on, Christian theology demanded that Jesus was not just symbolically but actually the "Son of God". So he could not have a biological father, his mother had forever to be pure and virginal (hence no other brothers and sisters) and he himself had to be pure and free from sex, which in the eyes of the Early Church came to be seen as simply sin, the corruption of the flesh. Christians ever since have suffered from a distinct lack of joyous procreation.

There may be similar reasons behind the omission of the name of the father of Mary/Mary Magdalene at points, such as the wedding at Cana and the anointing of Jesus, where he should have appeared in the text. This person, whether Simon the Leper or someone else, would have been Jesus' father-in-law.

One objective of the early gospel editors was to strip Jesus of real human relatives in order to retain a vision of him as austere, aloof, apart from the world and godlike. He was denied a wife and, by extension, denied relatives through marriage.

There is also a further possibility. When the gospels were first written, not many years later on, those who had helped Jesus or were linked to him in any way were still at risk, and men more than women, from the Romans or the Sadducee priestly hierarchy. This may also be why the writer of the Gospel of John refers elliptically to the provider of the information for the gospel, as "the disciple whom Jesus loved". This disciple was a close supporter and had possibly helped Jesus by providing a safe house in Jerusalem. A statement by a second century bishop of Ephesus, Polycrates, indicates that he was a priest, and this is supported by indirect evidence in the gospel. The beloved disciple, for example, outran Peter to reach the tomb, but did not go in until Peter had entered and found it empty. A priest entering the tomb with a corpse present would have become ritually unclean.

As a helper and as a priest, the disciple whom Jesus loved would have been in a precarious position in the years following the Crucifixion, had his support been identified. He could well have become a wanted man. The same applies to Jesus' male relatives by marriage and, as will be seen, especially to Lazarus.

As well as later editing, which removed or displaced some names, it seems highly probable that the early gospel writers, setting down their records maybe only a few years after the events took place, exercised a degree of self-censorship. They left clues, especially for those "in the know", but left out details which might have incriminated some of the people who had helped

Jesus. They were still in danger from the Roman and the Jewish authorities.

It is high time, having tried to sort out some of the consistencies and inconsistencies of the gospels themselves in evaluating current Christian beliefs, to look now at the historical context.

Jesus certainly lived at a time of great turbulence. He was also like other Jews, heir to a thousand years of struggle, triumph and subjection–a glorious past which was used as a means of understanding and even determining the present.

CHAPTER 6

PROMISED LAND

When the Philistines heard that David had been anointed king over Israel, all the Philistines went up in search of David; but David heard of it and went down to the stronghold [Jerusalem]. Now the Philistines had come and spread out in the valley of Rephaim. And David inquired of the Lord, "Shall I go up against the Philistines? Wilt thou give them into my hand?"

And the Lord said to David, "Go up; for I will certainly give the Philistines into your hand." And David came to Baalperazim, and David defeated them there; and he said, "The Lord has broken through my enemies before me, like a bursting flood." Therefore the name of that place is called Baalperazim [Lord of breaking through]. And the Philistines left their idols there, and David and his men carried them away.

    II Samuel 5:17–21

Then the king of Assyria invaded all the land and came to Samaria, and for three years he besieged it. In the ninth year of Hoshea, the king of Assyria captured Samaria, and he carried the Israelites away to Assyria, and placed them in Halah, and on the Habor, the river of Gozan, and in the cities of the Medes.

And this was so, because the people of Israel had sinned against the Lord their God, who had brought them up out of the land of Egypt from under the hand of Pharaoh king of Egypt, and had feared other gods and walked in the customs of the nations whom the Lord drove out before the people of Israel, and in the customs which the kings of Israel had introduced.

    II Kings 17: 5–8

At the time of Jesus, Jewish people living in Palestine could look back on some twelve hundred years of history. What they had, of course, were religious books in which over the years were assembled myths, stories, oral traditions and written accounts. The past, to which people looked back, was very much alive in their minds. Many Jews aspired to the independence which they had had under their old kings, beginning with Saul and David, and which had ended, apart form one relatively brief flourish under the Maccabees, with conquest by the Assyrians.

To the extent that it influences the present, a view of the past gains reality regardless of how it accords with what really may have taken place.

Twelve hundred years is, in a historical sense, a long time. It would be a mistake to assume that people at the beginning of such a great timespan saw things the same way, or lived in a similar context, as those at the end.

Documentary sources are much better than they would be for, say, looking at the history of the people of the British Isles over the same period. Even so, the sources are limited and were created often for purposes of providing something other than an objective account. Summarizing a thousand years in a few pages is bound to be fraught with difficulty and give rise to generalizations which simply cannot tell the whole story.

On the other hand it is possible, and desirable, to convey a flavor of the traditions that influenced the thinking of people at the time of Jesus of Nazareth.

Even this will provide a better framework than for most Christians who read their Old and New Testaments with no historical background at all. It is hardly surprising that some Western Christians have identified with the Israel of the Old Testament. It was even once argued that the British people and Queen Victoria were descendants of the "lost" tribes!

Technological change may have proceeding faster more recently, but social and cultural changes offer as great a gulf as say between now, at the time of writing, and Europe in the year 800. The deeds of the old kings of Israel were many centuries old at the time of Jesus. Although alive in people's minds, and relevant for pressing political and religious reasons, they were as much mythological as historical and part of the long-ago past.

Israel developed in an area east of the Mediterranean Sea, within what is generally known as Palestine. The area has a dry sub-tropical climate and varied topography, from rugged hills and deserts to plains and fertile river valleys. It was intersected by major trade routes, from Egypt to the Near East and from South Arabia to the Mediterranean. Not surprisingly, the great powers that arose successively in the region sought both to occupy and control the land. The Israelites were fated, because of the facts of geography, to be a subject people for most of their history. Philistines, Assyrians,

Babylonians, Persians, Macedonians, Egyptians, Syrians and Romans swapped control over a period of a thousand years.

From about 1,600 to 1,200 BC, Egyptian Pharaohs of the New Kingdom exerted control over the land of Syria/Palestine. It was more a question of domination rather than occupation, with power exerted by repeated military campaigns. When at last this power declined, the rule of the Pharaohs ended, leaving in Palestine a series of city-states inhabited by indigenous Bronze Age Canaanite peoples. Between these fortified towns and their immediate cultivated surroundings were large areas of sparsely populated land.

The Israelite tribes came in as semi-nomadic migrants, occupying land, creating their own towns and at times clashing with the original inhabitants. One group may have come from Egypt, where they had originally been driven perhaps by famine, in order to escape a system of forced labor. Out of this was elaborated the story of Moses and the divine bestowal of all the land of Palestine to the people collectively described in the Old Testament as Israel.

The tribes, nominally twelve, were only loosely associated, with each having at its head a tribal patriarch; hence references to the house of Joseph, the tribe of Judah and other similar groups. Somewhat confusingly, there are references in the Old Testament to Israel as the whole area occupied by the twelve tribes and also to the Kingdom of Israel, meaning the area to the north occupied by a majority of the tribes but excluding the smaller Kingdom of Judah. This Kingdom, later named Judaea, was occupied by the most powerful of the twelve tribes of Israel, tracing its descent from Judah, the fourth son of Jacob.

The Israelites had developed a monotheistic religion, with Yahweh as their god and deliverer of the people of Israel. They set up shrines to Yahweh at different places and took with them a sacred Ark, an empty throne for an invisible god. Their social organization was then fairly egalitarian. The Canaanites by contrast had a more feudal organization with language and religion, including fertility rites and the cult of Baal, derived from their former, Egyptian rulers. This is the religion the prophet Elijah is described as countering when the Israelites came to occupy "Canaan", their Promised Land.

The Israelites were involved in territorial conflicts with neighboring peoples and with the people whose land they were occupying. But the biggest threat came from a seafaring people, the Philistines, who first occupied part of the coastal plain and then moved inland, sweeping all before them with their fearsome iron chariots.

The need to counter the threat generated a need for overall leadership. Saul arose as the first acclaimed king around 1,000 BC, initially to rally the tribes against other enemies and then take on the Philistines. But after some initial successes, he was defeated and killed.

Saul's former armor-bearer, David, had fallen into disfavor with Saul and gone over to serve as a mercenary for the Philistines. He was allowed by the Philistines to become vassal king of a small part of Palestine around Bethlehem, territory of the house of Judah. David defeated Saul's son Eshbaal, ruler of the Kingdom of Israel, to take the rest of the tribal areas and thus assert control over the adjacent Kingdoms of Judah and Israel.

The Philistines woke up to the threat of an emerging, independent state but were then decisively defeated by David, and pushed right back to their original borders. David took Jerusalem from the Jebusites and moved the sacred Ark in to the city to make this the political and religious capital of the combined state of Israel. Further successes extended the influence of Israel over a number of neighboring states.

The story is told in the second Book of Samuel (5:6–8) of how the Jebusites blocked an entrance to Jerusalem by using their disabled, the blind and the lame, as a form of human shield. This stratagem failed because David ordered his troops to force their way through regardless.

The real point of this tale, however, is to justify the Jewish prohibition against people with any form of physical impairment from entering the Temple:

Therefore it is said, "The blind and the lame shall not come into the house." (II Samuel 5:8).

The Temple prohibition can be seen to have its origins in more general ideas of ritual purity and impurity, prevalent in many other religions as well as in early Judaism.

The empire established by David in Syria/Palestine was the high point of political power for the tribes of Israel. For the next two hundred years or so, there was intense rivalry between the Kingdoms of Judah and Israel. David resolved a potential conflict over his succession by appointing his son Solomon as king and after that, in Judah, the succession passed down the male line, with precedence given to the first-born son. The manner in which the kingship was passed on varied among the other tribes over the border in the Kingdom of Israel. The principle of succession passing to the firstborn son sometimes operated, but at other times the throne was simply seized and the old incumbent killed. On other occasions, a prophet proclaimed a successor king in the name of Yahweh. So, there was no continuous line of descent in the larger of the two kingdoms.

After David, Israel was no longer a regional power. There were no more gains and power over adjoining states was lost at an early stage. Friction and conflict continued between Israel and Judah.

Finally, over the period 733 to 721 BC, Assyrian expansion brought an end to the independence of the twin kingdoms. A large segment of the population in the greater part of Israel, chiefly the ruling classes, were deported to other parts of the empire and replaced by Assyrian officials. A smaller part remained in a politically dependent vassal state in Judah. Both areas were forced to accept the official Assyrian religion alongside the worship of Yahweh.

For a people who believed they had been given the land as a gift from God, this must have been difficult to accept. Religious belief was reconciled with hard political reality by the device of attributing events as part of the divine purpose. Conquest by a foreign power was thereby seen as a divine judgment and a punishment for wrongdoing, as in the quotation from the Second Book of Kings given above. So, even in a state of humiliation and submission, the tribes of Israel and their prophets could console themselves. It was all part of God's purpose–and it would all come right in the end.

The Assyrian Empire was ultimately destroyed by the Babylonians around 612 BC, a new power which would plunge the tribes into even deeper submission.

While the northern Kingdom of Israel had been turned into four provinces under the Assyrians, Judah had in the meantime remained as a separate vassal state. Under King Josiah, Judah expanded into the territory of Israel as Assyrian power declined. Josiah also centralized worship in Jerusalem. But these glimmerings of independence could not be sustained; Judah had to recognize the sovereignty of the Babylonian King Nebuchadnezzar who then proceeded to crush rebellions and finally inflict an awesome defeat on Judah's King Zedekiah.

After being besieged for a year and a half, Jerusalem was taken, the city wall was pulled down, the Temple destroyed and craftsmen and the ruling class removed to Babylonia where they and Zedekiah were forced to live in captivity.

The year was 587 BC. This turning point marked the end of any vestiges of political independence and the monarchy in the Kingdoms of Judah and Israel for the next 400 years.

Rather than becoming assimilated by the states to which they were deported, many of the Israelite exiles in Egypt and Babylonia adhered to their old traditions, including the rite of circumcision and the keeping of the Sabbath. It was what defined them, and for that reason their faith was perhaps stronger than among many of those left behind.

Persian kings next came on the scene and, unlike the Babylonians, they allowed their subject peoples to continue with their own traditional culture and religion. The Temple was restored in Jerusalem, the city walls were rebuilt and under Nehemiah as governor some of the exiles were brought back. The foremost priest in the Temple of Jerusalem became the High Priest of all Israel and a subsidiary class was developed, the Levites, from among those formerly running local cults. The priestly class gained a degree of importance and influence that it had not had previously. There was now one center of collective worship and religious authority for the whole of Israel, and for Israelite descendants keeping the faith while dispersed into foreign lands.

Palestine next fell into the hands of Alexander the Great's Macedonian Empire in 332 BC. More than a century later, this empire divided and Palestine then came under the rule of the Seleucids, or Syrian Greeks, a dynasty that ruled Syria and a large part of western Asia from 311 to 63 BC. The two halves of the empire, Egyptian and Syrian, continued in conflict with each other and with the Romans, another rising power.

Over a period of centuries, the books of the Old Testament which combined history, myth, prophecy and law were developed as the sacred books which the priestly class interpreted and maintained. But in religion, as in politics, there was a constant interplay between unifying and fragmenting forces. About the time of Alexander, the Israelite Samaritan community separated from the other tribes. The inhabitants of Samaria developed their own cult center, based at Mount Gerizim, and followed their own form of Judaism. The Judaeans, who had arguably suffered less from enforced exiles inflicted by successive conquerors, regarded the Samaritans as less racially pure, and therefore "unclean", because they had fraternized with and intermarried with the foreign ruling classes. Hostility between Jews and Samaritans simmered on for over 300 years, down to the time of Jesus.

Seleucid rule was weakened by external conflicts, particularly with the Romans, and became harsh and unstable. The point of greatest brutality came under King Antiochus IV who showed complete contempt and insensitivity towards local traditions, installing at whim High Priests in Jerusalem who were not of the priestly lineage. Strapped for cash, he took the Temple valuables and entered and so defiled the inner sanctuary. He allowed the city to be looted and set up a fortified area within it, with a permanent Seleucid garrison. Finally, Antiochus prohibited all Jewish religious observances and feasts, had Jewish holy books destroyed and set up new Greek-style religious cults. In this way, the rights of the people to live by their own customs, which had been introduced under Persian rule and which had persisted for almost three centuries, were suddenly swept away.

Seleucid officials were sent around from town to town to enforce the edicts prohibiting the Jewish religion and establishing pagan sacrifices. With the whole nation seething with fury, it needed just one small spark to ignite a revolution. That came in the small town of Modein, in the territory of the tribe of Joiarib.

Because the base of Seleucid power was crumbling under the forces of internal neglect and external threat, and because the power of the Romans was not yet fully fledged, this left a small time gap for the flame of independence once again to survive. Second time around, it took the Israelites almost forty years of struggle to reestablish independence under a monarchy. But this independence lasted only a further sixty years.

CHAPTER 7

FREEDOM

"You saw, O king, and behold, a great image. This image, mighty and of exceeding brightness, stood before you, and its appearance was frightening. The head of this image was of fine gold, its breast and arms of silver, its belly and thighs of bronze, its legs of iron, its feet partly of iron and partly of clay. As you looked, a stone was cut out by no human hand, and it smote the image on its feet of iron and clay, and broke them in pieces; then the iron, the clay, the bronze, the silver and the gold, all together were broken in pieces, and became like the chaff of the summer threshing floors; and the wind carried them away, so that not a trace of them could be found. But the stone that struck the image became a great mountain and filled the whole earth.

"This was the dream; now we will tell the king its interpretation. You, O king, the king of kings, to whom the God of heaven has given the kingdom, the power, and the might, and the glory, and into whose hand has he given, wherever they dwell, the sons of men, the beasts of the field, and the birds of the air, making you rule over them all– you are the head of gold. After you shall arise another kingdom inferior to you, and yet a third kingdom of bronze, which shall rule over all the earth. And there shall be a fourth kingdom, strong as iron, because iron breaks to pieces and shatters all things; and like iron which crushes, it shall break and crush all these. And as you saw the feet and toes partly of potter's clay and partly of iron, it shall be a divided kingdom; but some of the firmness of iron shall be in it, just as you saw iron mixed with the miry clay. And as the toes of the feet were partly iron and partly clay, so the kingdom shall be partly strong and partly brittle. As you saw the iron mixed with miry clay, so they will mix with one another in marriage, but they will not hold together, just as iron does not mix with clay. And in the days of those kings the God of heaven will set up a kingdom which shall never be destroyed, nor shall its sovereignty be left to

another people. It shall break in pieces all these kingdoms and bring them to an end, and it shall stand for ever; just as you saw that stone was cut from a mountain by no human hand, and that it broke in pieces the iron, the bronze, the silver and the gold. A great God has made known to the king what shall be hereafter. The dream is certain, and its interpretation sure."

Daniel 2:31–35

And the king [Antiochus] sent letters by messengers to Jerusalem and the cities of Judah; he directed them to follow customs strange to the land, to forbid burnt offerings and sacrifices and drink offerings in the sanctuary, to profane Sabbaths and feasts, to defile the sanctuary and the priests, to build altars and sacred precincts and shrines for idols, to sacrifice swine and unclean animals, and to leave their sons uncircumcised...

Then the king's officers who were enforcing the apostasy came to the city of Modein to make them offer sacrifice...

But Mattathias answered and said in a loud voice: "Even if all the nations that live under the rule of the king obey him, and have chosen to do his commandments, departing each one from the religion of his fathers, yet I and my sons and my brothers will live by the covenant of our fathers. Far be it from us to desert the law and the ordinances. We will not obey the king's words by turning aside from our religion to the right hand or to the left."

When he had finished speaking these words, a Jew came forward in the sight of all to offer sacrifice upon the altar in Modein according to the king's command. When Mattathias saw it, he burned with zeal and his heart stirred. He gave vent to righteous anger; he ran and killed him upon the altar. At the same time he killed the king's officer who was forcing them to sacrifice, and he tore down the altar. Thus he burned with zeal for the law, as Phenehas did against Zimri the son of Salu. Then Mattathias cried out in the city with a loud voice saying: "Let everyone who is zealous for the law and supports the covenants come out with me!" And he and his sons fled to the hills and left all that they had in the city.

Maccabee 1:44–49, 2:15, 19–27

When the Assyrians conquered Palestine, Judah remained as a vassal state until finally it was destroyed too with the fall of Jerusalem in 587 BC. The subject and the dispersed Israelites longed for a time when their Kingdom and their power would be restored. It was expected that the land promised by Yahweh to Abraham and his descendants would be restored, and to do this a new king would arise, "a Son of David" or "a king like David".

A number of the Psalms and books of the Old Testament, including Isaiah, Ezekial and Jeremiah, conveyed this message.

So the era of the Kings and particularly of David was looked back on as a golden age. At that time, the priests were merely royal officials. The king's power was primarily political, although he also had a role as Guardian of the sacred Ark and the monotheistic religion of the Israelite tribes. The old kings did not, however, for the most part provide role models for a religious way of life.

David, for example, was revered for his military brilliance, especially his achievements in defeating the Philistines and other enemies. He succeeded in welding the nation together and in building an empire, both by gaining territory and exerting power over neighboring states. But it would seem that he was a cruel man, as well as ruthless. He had two thirds of a captive Moabite army killed, visited mass slaughter on the unfortunate Edomites (Idumaeans) and was not above serving as a mercenary for the hated Philistines at the start of his career. But for the objections of some of the Philistine commanders, he would have entered into the fray with the enemy against his own people. He stood by while his predecessor Saul was defeated by the Philistines.

David's most odious act, as described in the second Book of Samuel, may have been to take a woman adulterously and then, when she fell pregnant, have her husband abandoned in the forefront of the battle and thereby killed. That was the unfortunate fate meted out to Uriah the Hittite, husband of the beautiful Bathsheba who was taken as one of David's wives.

To begin with, then, the Messiah that the scattered tribes of Israel longed for was primarily a warrior king who would deliver them out of the hands of their enemies, restore the kingdom and save them from exile. A strong leader was needed, but not necessarily a godly man. The word Messiah derives from the Hebrew for an "anointed one", according to traditional practice of anointing someone for high office, as a king maybe or later as High Priest.

In the face of the afflictions successively faced by the peoples of Judah and Israel, deliverance progressively came to be seen as religious as much as political. Old Testament writers and prophets came to terms with defeat and enslavement by seeing these conditions as punishments for transgressions against the will of Yahweh. The consolation was that their enemies were merely pawns in God's greater design. He would ultimately deliver them. The expected Messiah was to be an agent of Yahweh, restoring his kingdom on earth more by divine deliverance than by military prowess.

This was more or less the position taken in the Book of Daniel, in which the prophet is described as interpreting the visions of the Babylonian King Nebuchadnezzar. Four kingdoms would arise, first the Babylonian, then the Medean, Persian and finally Greek empires. The four kingdoms are symbolized by the metals gold, silver, bronze and iron.

But the last of the four would be a divided empire, made of parts which do not mix–like iron and clay–and it would ultimately fall to a never-ending kingdom established by divine intervention. This is the origin of the phrase "feet of clay", a metaphor for those who seem powerful, but suffer from some fatal defect.

It was, of course, all very good prediction since the author of the Book of Daniel wrote in the second century BC, after all of the events had happened except for the final divine intervention!

Daniel was writing at a time of terrible persecution and injustice, which included proscription of the Israelites' religion, instigated by Antiochus IV. Idols were instead set up for worship, including one for burnt offerings in the Temple in Jerusalem to the Greek god Zeus. To add to the insult, a new gymnasium was constructed in Jerusalem for Olympian-style naked athletic events.

These acts provoked a reaction, although it was not the apocalyptic judgment which Daniel had anticipated. It was a rebellion by one of the lesser tribes, which was not from the house of Zadok believed to be in the line of descent from the priests appointed by King David.

When the Seleucid official came in 166 BC to Modein to enforce the pagan sacrifices, he was struck dead by the outraged Mattathias, a member of a priestly family of the house of Joiarib. With no forces at first to organize armed resistance, Mattathias and his followers were then compelled to withdraw into the desert and conduct a type of guerrilla resistance. The core family group called themselves Hasmoneans after one of their ancestors, Hasmon, but they also became known as Maccabees from the nickname of one of Mattathias' sons, Judas Maccabeus (Judas the hammer).

At first, there were minor skirmishes, surprise attacks and assassinations. But the rebels became more confident as their numbers grew, along with military successes against an enemy diverted by internal conflicts and other external challenges. Judas succeeded in defeating the enemy forces in two pitched battles and regained control of the most of the territory of Judah and the city of Jerusalem, apart from the fortified stronghold, the Akra.

When Judas was killed, his younger brother Jonathan took over and succeeded, by playing off rival contenders, in gaining concessions including the office of High Priest in Jerusalem and the status of subject king under Seleucid rule. This dangerous politicking ultimately cost Jonathan his life to one Seleucid rebel faction, but allowed a third brother Simon to take over and gain further ground by helping the Seleucid king.

Simon gave himself the official title of "great High Priest, general and leader of the Judaeans", so formalizing a merger of the highest religious and secular roles.

He took over the fortified garrison, the Akra, and enlarged his province which was by now virtually autonomous. When Simon was murdered by his son-in-law, his own son John Hyrcanus took over. John Hyrcanus effectively became the king and religious head of an independent Judah, as Seleucid power declined still further amid quarrels over succession to their throne. This was in 128 BC, just 38 years after his grandfather Mattathias had roused people to follow him with the defiant words, "Let everyone who is zealous for the law and supports the covenants come out with me!"

Because of the crass and callous actions by Antiochus IV, who thought suppression was the best means to bring compliance, there was no shortage of supporters to help the Hasmoneans in the struggle to gain power.

Subsequently, the term "zealot" was applied to those seeking to restore the kingship in Israel and with it political independence. But, unlike the Pharisees and Sadducees which were identifiable religious groupings among the priesthood, there does not seem to have been an equivalent "zealot" grouping, continuous over time.

The Sadducees were apparently the main priestly class who in practical terms organized religion, collected the Temple taxes and managed the sacrificial ritual. They were often wealthy, aristocratic, aloof from ordinary people but prepared to do business with political rulers, including the Hasmoneans and then in turn the Roman authorities.

But the necessities of dealing with foreign occupiers, like the Romans, at times caused strain and division over the extent to which it was appropriate to cooperate and collaborate.

The Pharisees as a group arose later in Jewish history at around the time of Antiochus.

They were concerned scrupulously to uphold the laws of the Old Testament (Torah) in meticulous detail and they were often obsessed with matters of ritual and purity. They differed from the Sadducees over what constituted the Law, being prepared to allow a much wider definition including oral as well as written tradition. Originating perhaps from those who called themselves "the pious", they were primarily concerned with the freedom to practice their religion and looked forward to a final apocalyptic deliverance by Yahweh, of the kind envisaged by Daniel, rather than political deliverance. So they were opposed to the political intrigue of the

Hasmoneans and became more so as Hasmonean rule degenerated into a messy and oppressive conflict.

The so-called Essenes (who never described themselves by this term) comprised a group or groups which likewise objected to the secularization of Judaism under the Maccabees but retreated to their own self-contained communities. Many of these were located in the "wilderness", as for example at Qumran, but there were also some in towns.

There was certainly a strong basis of support among the people as a whole for the Hasmonean dynasty because, whatever the shortcomings, it meant freedom from foreign rule.

John Hyrcanus thus had the backing to consolidate power in Judah and, with the aid of mercenaries, make territorial gains in Samaria and the old Kingdom of Israel. But, when he died, in 104 BC, there was a long struggle for succession.

One of his sons, Aristobulus, seized power and imprisoned three other brothers, before murdering a fourth. But, after a year, he died and was succeeded by a brother Jonathan, who became known as Alexander Jannaeus. This Hasmonean ruler devoted his time to waging war on surrounding peoples and expanding his territory to include the whole of Palestine. But his power was based on terror, lacked popular support and had no stable basis. As he moved on to put down a revolt in one area, power began to crumble in the areas he had just left.

When Alexander Jannaeus died in 76 BC, his wife Salome took control with her son John Hyrcanus II installed as High Priest. Nine years later, she died leaving her two sons John Hyrcanus II and Aristobulus II to fight over the succession in a bitter, fratricidal civil war.

Aristobulus succeeded to begin with, but then the second John Hyrcanus managed to secure for himself powerful allies. Antipater, governor of Idumaea, persuaded him to seek protection from Aretas, the Nabataean king. The price which Aretas exacted for military support was the surrender of a large swathe of territory east of the Dead Sea which had been taken by Alexander Jannaeus.

Aretas' forces swiftly defeated Aristobulus who was forced to retreat and remain under siege in the sanctuary offered by the city of Jerusalem, following which many of his own Judaean troops went over to the enemy.

The restored monarchy under the Hasmoneans had clearly lost its way, only a matter of 60 years since the first John Hyrcanus restored freedom to Judah and took the offices both of king and High Priest. The monarchy was unpopular with ordinary people, had antagonized some of the priestly class and had become embroiled in an internal power struggle which it could not resolve without outside, foreign help. It had in fact only survived for so long because of the temporary power vacuum left by the decline of Seleucid power on a wider international stage. That power vacuum was beginning to be filled by the rapidly expanding influence of the Romans. Lacking unity and so unable even to rule itself, the land of Israel was fated to become part of the next great empire.

CHAPTER 8

ROMANS AND HERODIANS

See, Lord, and raise up for them their king, the Son of David,
to rule over your servant Israel in the time known to you, O
God.
Undergird him with the strength to destroy the unrighteous
rulers, to purge Jerusalem from Gentiles who trample her to
destruction;
in wisdom and in righteousness to drive out the sinners from
the inheritance,
to smash the arrogance of sinners like a potter's jar;
to shatter all their substance with an iron rod;
to destroy the unlawful nations with the word of his mouth. ...
And he will purge Jerusalem and make it holy as it was from
the beginning,
for nations to come from the ends of the earth to see his glory,
to bring as gifts her children who had been driven out,
and to see the glory of the Lord with which God has glorified
her.
And he will be a righteous king over them, taught by God.
There will be no unrighteousness among them in his days, for
all shall be holy,
and their king shall be the Lord Messiah.

  Psalms of Solomon 17:21–24, 30–32

The expansion of the Romans in the eastern Mediterranean was one of the reasons for the decline of the Seleucid state, but this growing power did not at first impinge on the Hasmonean dynasty in Israel. Then in 65 BC the Roman general Pompey decided, on the crest of a number of victories, to wind up the decayed Seleucid state. He sent his legate

Aemilius Scaurus to Syria, where Seleucid power was based. Scaurus went to Judaea, having heard about the conflict there, and arbitrated on the side of the besieged Aristobulus II. The Nabataean King Aretas was forced by threat to raise the siege and withdraw.

Aristobulus II was confirmed in his previous offices of king and High Priest, except that now it was on the indulgence of an emissary from Rome.

When Pompey himself went to Damascus, he was confronted with representatives from Aristobulus II who wanted to keep his position, Antipater pleading on behalf of John Hyrcanus and envoys from the Pharisees who wanted to see Hasmonean rule abolished completely and the old position of the priesthood restored.

The danger inherent in appealing to outside powers soon became all too evident.

Pompey took exception to Aristobulus' independent and rebellious stance and pursued him with an army towards Jerusalem. While some of the inhabitants gave up and opened the city gates to the Romans, a minority decided to hold out in the fortified Temple area. After a siege lasting months, the defenders were massacred and Aristobulus II was taken in chains to Rome to be displayed along with other prisoners in a triumphal procession.

The whole of Syria and Palestine was now reconstituted as part of the Roman Province of Syria and Scaurus was rewarded with the position of its first governor.

Israel was effectively partitioned. John Hyrcanus II was reinstated as High Priest but he was not given back the title of king. That office was now abolished. Furthermore, his power was limited to the old province of Judah, Peraea and Galilee. Samaria was separated from Judaea and allowed to continue with its own religious cult centered on Mount Gerizim. Judaea's coastal cities were also detached from it, as were the Decapolis, ten cities in the land east of the Jordan.

Although this was the end of independent Hasmonean rule, it was not the end of the infighting and intrigue. This rumbled on for another twenty of so years until Herod, the son of Antipater who had mobilized support for John Hyrcanus II, secured power for himself under Roman patronage in Judaea.

Somewhat surprisingly, Aristobulus II had managed to escape from imprisonment in Rome and took up arms with his sons against Hyrcanus. Meanwhile, Pompey became involved in a struggle for control with Caesar and was forced to withdraw to the eastern half of the empire before being defeated and killed. Aristobulus II saw an opportunity and took Caesar's side, but he and one of his sons were murdered by Pompey's supporters.

Antipater and John Hyrcanus II lost no time in currying favor with the new order in Rome, to the extent of sending troops to give Caesar direct assistance in battle.

John Hyrcanus was rewarded by being confirmed in the hereditary title of High Priest and given the largely honorary title of "Ethnarch". However, real power at local level passed to the Idumaean Antipater who was made procurator of Judaea. Antipater gave his elder son Phasael the administration of Judaea and Peraea and his younger son Herod control over Galilee.

This was by no means the end of division and dissension. As a portent of things to come, John Hyrcanus was involved in a clash with Herod who had executed a group of rebels under Hezekias in Galilee. John Hyrcanus summoned Herod before the Sanhedrin, the highest court of justice in ancient Jerusalem, and accused him of contravening its authority. Herod managed to bluster it out, confident that he had the support of the Roman governor of the province, based in Syria.

After Caesar's murder, power in Rome passed to Anthony who had to face the challenge of the Parthians (from southeast of the Caspian Sea in present-day Iran) who invaded and occupied Syria in 40 BC.

Antigonus, the surviving son of Aristobulus, had in the meantime gathered an army to invade Galilee but had been repelled by Herod.

The Parthian invasion provided Antigonus with the chance he needed finally to wrest control of Judah, Peraea and Galilee from his uncle, John Hyrcanus II. He secured the help of the Parthians who brought their forces to Jerusalem and captured Phasael and John Hyrcanus. The Parthians then installed Antigonus as High Priest and king over Judaea.

Antigonus eliminated the possibility of John Hyrcanus ever becoming High Priest again by the simple expedient of cutting off his ears. The sick, disabled or disfigured, it will be recalled, were regarded as ritually impure and so barred from the Temple in Jerusalem. Herod's brother Phasael, the ex-administrator of Judaea who had supported John Hyrcanus, committed suicide.

Herod, still the administrator for Galilee, was forced to take measures to protect himself. He installed his family in the safety of his palace, on the fortress rock of Masada, near the southeastern shores of the Dead Sea. Then he went to seek help in Rome.

The Roman Senate responded by making Herod king of Judaea in 40 BC. Now all Herod had to do was take the kingdom, which was not in fact at that time under his control.

Herod was helped by the fact that the Roman governor of Syria had managed to drive out the Parthians. With the help of the Romans, Herod managed to take Samaria, then most of Judaea and finally Jerusalem in 37 BC. Antigonus was captured and beheaded by the Romans at Herod's request.

Antigonus' rule, by courtesy of the Parthians, had lasted just three years.

Herod, by contrast, would rule over the whole Kingdom of Palestine as a confederate king under the Romans for more than 30 years, until his death in 4 BC.

Like his father Antipater before him Herod was, besides being thoroughly brutal and amoral, an astute politician acutely aware of the need to secure the favor of whoever was in control at the time. When Mark Anthony was defeated by Octavius (Augustus Caesar) in a battle for power and shortly afterwards died, Herod managed to ingratiate himself with the successor. As a result, he was given back the coastal cities and other territory which Anthony had given to Cleopatra. Apart from the free cities of the Decapolis, Herod then ruled over all of Palestine.

But, just as they did under the rule of the hated Antiochus IV, the Israelites yearned for freedom from domination by the Romans. The anticipation of deliverance was expressed at the time of Antiochus by the Book of Daniel and, at the time Jerusalem fell to Pompey in 63 BC, by the Psalms of Solomon. Although attributed to the time of Solomon about a thousand years previously, the psalms were written at the time of the Roman occupation, probably by priestly scribes from one of the main religious groups.

The clearest indication of what was expected is given in psalm 17, quoted above. Instead of an apocalyptic deliverance by divine intervention, the expectation is now more for a warrior king who would be both strong and righteous.

In neither case, did the millennial expectations come to fruition. Daniel looked to divine deliverance and instead got the divided and degenerate Hasmoneans. The Psalmist looked for a mighty "Son of David" to defeat the ungodly, but instead got Herod who was to gain a deserved reputation for cruelty and brutality.

Herod, it should be remembered, was not a Jew by blood but an Idumaean, from a kingdom to the south linked perhaps racially but not by religion. His grandfather Antipater was a wealthy and powerful Idumaean who, like others in their community, was forced to be circumcised by the first John Hyrcanus and adopt Judaism.

His father, also called Antipater, exploited the opportunities provided by civil war, backing one side and gaining the position of procurator or governor of Judaea under John Hyrcanus II. Herod displayed the same talent for political intrigue, eventually gaining control over the whole of Palestine through his careful dealing with Roman power.

He ruled as a confederate king under the Roman system of government until his death in the year 4 BC. During this time he embarked on a number of prestigious construction enterprises, including the large-scale restoration of the Temple in Jerusalem, work that continued many years after his death.

He rebuilt a small seaport, naming it Caesarea in honor of Augustus Caesar, and also reconstructed the city of Samaria. He built numerous fortresses as a means of defending his power.

But these immense building works were costly and funded by heavy taxation. He dealt ruthlessly with any opposition and employed a network of spies to maintain control, a factor which contributed to a climate of fear. For all these reasons, and the fact that he was a Roman stooge and not a Jew, he was disliked by most of the people, except perhaps those who gained from his patronage.

He had numerous wives and concubines and lived a lavish lifestyle without much pretense of religious observance. He was therefore detested by many in the priesthood too.

Herod was, as an unpopular ruler, obsessed with threats from rivals for the throne of Israel, either from descendants of the Hasmoneans or from others claiming to be "Sons of David".

The summary execution of Hezekiah and his followers, though dismissively described as "bandits" by the Jewish historian Josephus, may well fit into this context. John Hyrcanus II sought to bring Herod to judgment before the Sanhedrin, so it may be that Hezekiah was someone of real importance, perhaps of royal descent.

In an effort to cement his claim to the kingship, Herod married Miriamne (or Mary) the granddaughter of John Hyrcanus II. Now king, and related to the Hasmoneans by marriage, Herod presumably believed that the birth of an heir–someone with a real claim to the throne by descent–would improve his popular position.

It didn't work and Herod's paranoia grew. When Miriamne's sixteen-year-old brother Aristobulus came of age, Herod made him High Priest. But the warmth of the people towards Aristobulus at his inauguration made Herod jealous. So he had the young man drowned while swimming in a pool at Jericho a short time later.

With no other serious Hasmonean contenders left, Herod finally had the aged John Hyrcanus strangled. Unable to brook any form of rivalry, he finally turned his attention to his own family and executed his wife Miriamne and their two sons. Once the hoped-for means of ingratiating himself with the Jews, even they came to be seen by him as rivals for the throne.

As an indication of just how odious a tyrant Herod was, the historian Josephus relates how Herod, when close to death, ordered senior members of all the important families in Jerusalem and surrounding areas to be rounded up and held in a great stadium. When Herod died, they were to be executed to ensure that there would be mourning at his death throughout the country.

But on Herod's death they were in fact promptly released. Herod's successors realized that such an act would have caused widespread public disorder and that they, not the dead Herod, would have been blamed.

There is no corroboration elsewhere for the account in the Gospel of Matthew (2:16), that Herod had all the Jewish children under two years old murdered in Bethlehem, in an effort to destroy the expected Messiah. This story owes much to the Old Testament story of Moses and may be a reflection of what the egomaniacal ruler actually did to his own sons. As with the other Nativity stories, there seems to be a degree of myth and embellishment which needs to be taken into account.

But all the other evidence, particularly as related by Josephus, indicates that Herod, even if he did not do it, would have been capable of an act like this.

It is no wonder that, when Herod died, rebellion broke out all over Palestine. It was a reaction not just to foreign rule, but to cruel and oppressive domination—just like the situation 162 years previously when Mattathias took up the cause and killed the agent of the hated Seleucid ruler Antiochis IV.

The difference this time, of course, was that the people of Israel were not facing an empire which was crumbling and leaving a power vacuum to fill. They had to deal with the Romans who were organized, dynamic and increasing in strength.

There were not one but three simultaneous rebellions in Palestine under different leaders, all potential deliverers and Messiahs of different kinds for their people.

In Galilee Judas, son of the Hezekiah that Herod had executed, took over Sepphoris and armed his followers from the Roman armory there. Simon, a former slave of Herod's, operating from Peraea east of the Jordan moved in with an armed band to plunder the royal palace at Jericho and proclaimed himself king. In Judaea, Athronges ("a mere shepherd" according to Josephus) had the temerity to do the same and, with his brothers, managed to wage a sustained and initially successful campaign.

It took the intervention of three Roman legions and numerous auxiliary troops to quash the unrest. Many hundreds were killed and 2,000 prisoners taken alive were crucified throughout Palestine. Suppression on this scale, following on from the harsh years of Herod's rule, must have created an immense legacy of anguish, hatred and bitterness. So many families had lost loved ones; so many children had been orphaned.

This, then, was what was happening when Jesus was in his infancy. It was not the Palestine of sunny, bible-sticker fields of waving corn but a place seething with discontent. The land was still riven with Herodian spies, its people were oppressed by Roman taxes and they nurtured the memories of their martyrs. They were looking for deliverance. It needed just a spark to produce a reaction, and such a reaction did often happen.

History probably doesn't record all the acts of insurrection, especially minor revolts put down with comparative ease. The main source for events at this time was Josephus, a Jewish general in Galilee during the first uprising against Rome between AD 66 and 70, who became a turncoat and supported the Romans thereafter to save his own skin. Josephus devoted a lot of space in his writings to major conflicts but was less interested in localized disturbances.

Another source, the Roman historian Tacitus, stated that under the Emperor Tiberius (AD 14–37) "all was quiet". But what he meant was there were no rebellions during this time requiring the intervention of the Roman legate in Syria backed by two or more army legions. Revolts necessitating this level of intervention happened in the uprisings after Herod's death in 4 BC and then later under Caligula in AD 41, Claudius in AD 52 and finally under Nero at the start of the first Jewish War in AD 66.

These major events around the time of Jesus' life are an indication of the level of underlying tension and discontent.

After Herod's death, three of his sons were appointed by the Romans as rulers in different parts of Palestine. While two, Herod Antipas in Galilee and Philip in northern Palestine, remained in place for many years, Archelaus in Judaea and Samaria was so inept and brutal even by Roman standards that he was soon deposed in AD 6. A deputation of his subjects went to Augustus Caesar to complain and the Emperor responded by banishing Archelaus and putting a Roman procurator in his place.

Thereafter, during all of Jesus' adult life, Samaria and Judaea were under direct Roman rule. The jurisdiction of the Sanhedrin, a council of 70 priestly elders, was recognized in most matters but only the Roman procurator had the right to pass and carry out the sentence of death.

The procurator was also responsible for gathering taxes. Following the institution of direct rule in AD 6, the Roman governor of the Syrian province Quirinius carried out a census in Judaea to help reorganize the system of taxation.

Jesus was born not at the start of the Christian era, a date which is the product of an early mathematical miscalculation, but around the year 6 or 5 BC. So, although Herod died in 4 BC, his purge of the newborn to try and eliminate the rumored newly born Messiah could still have taken place. As I've argued, this is more likely to have been fable rather than historical fact, an illustration of Herod's character derived from the Old Testament story of the infant Moses–and maybe even reflecting the fate that he inflicted on some of his own children.

When the census was carried out, Jesus would have been about thirteen years old. So Luke's story of Mary and Joseph traveling from their home in

Nazareth to Bethlehem to record the birth for the census was an after-the-fact invention to fit with the Old Testament prophecy of Micah, that the future ruler of Israel or Messiah would be born in Bethlehem. That this was a material consideration is indicated by the report in John (8:40–51) of Jesus later preaching at the Feast of the Tabernacles. Some in the audience argued that his teaching and manifest wisdom demonstrated that he was the expected Messiah. Others pointed out that, according to the scriptures, the Messiah would come from David's village of Bethlehem and Jesus was clearly from Galilee. "Search and you will see that no prophet is to rise from Galilee," they said.

That was, of course, the moment for someone, anyone, to stand up and stay, "Well, actually ... ", and point out where Jesus was "actually" born, that is as supposed by Luke in Bethlehem. They didn't of course because the story in Luke was invented later to deal with just this sort of difficulty. Not every aspect of Jesus' life could be made to fit with Old Testament prophecy, though the gospel writers did their best.

The Roman authorities, faced with difficulty enough in carrying out an unpopular census for the purpose of raising an unpopular tax, would never have added to their problems by requiring that everyone return to his or her ancestral home, however that could be defined.

So Jesus was almost certainly not born in Bethlehem. It is also quite likely that he was neither born nor brought up in Nazareth.

There is no independent historical confirmation that the settlement of Nazareth even existed at the time Jesus lived. It is possible that Nazareth derives from Lake Gennesareth, or the Sea of Galilee as it was known, the general area where Jesus as a Galilean would have come from. Other possibilities are that Jesus was originally described as a Nazirite, derived from the Hebrew for consecrated or set apart, or Nazoraean, derived from the Hebrew for keeper, meaning keeper of secrets or the covenant.

There were no open rebellions then requiring the intervention of legions from Syria, but all was far from "quiet" as Tacitus described it, in Palestine during Jesus' lifetime.

At the time of the census in AD 6, the historian Josephus describes a movement arising in opposition to the census, and the tax which would arise from it, under the slogan "No Lord but God". It was led by someone called Judas, the Galilean, apparently not the same Judas who led the attack on Sepphoris at the time of Herod's death some ten years or so previously. Josephus describes this resistance to paying tribute as a movement for independence. Its adherents subscribed to the same views as the Pharisees, according to Josephus, but differed in being prepared to take action and if necessary suffer death.

It is unclear whether the Judas' followers took up arms or proceeded by passive resistance in refusing to pay tax; it is likely the Romans would have dealt with it just the same. What precisely happened to Judas is not recorded by Josephus, though it appears that he was killed. The Acts of the Apostles (5:37) records that, "Judas the Galilean arose in the days of the census and drew away some of the people after him; he also perished and all who followed him were scattered."

Like the Maccabees in belief and inclination, the followers of Judas could well have been, and indeed were described as, zealots. There may well have been a claim to kingship based on descent.

James and Simon, described as sons of this Judas, were later considered such a threat that they were executed around AD 46, when the whole of Israel had come under direct Roman rule. Later still, another descendant of Judas, Menahem, with messianic claims, led a group which captured Masada and participated in the first Jewish revolt against Rome. These rebels included a group described by Josephus as sicarii, so called because of the short daggers or "sicae" which they carried beneath their cloaks and used to assassinate opponents. These sicarii were arguably "zealots" by another name, distinct only in their urban basis and their methods of operation which included kidnap and assassination.

When Menahem was then killed in the conflict between the forces struggling for supremacy in Jerusalem, the sicarii retreated to Masada under Eleazar, another descendant or relative of Judas. Here, they committed mass suicide as the Romans prepared to take the fortress, after a long siege at the end of the war.

Throughout the time that Jesus lived, there appeared then to have been a parallel group with messianic claims, also based in Galilee, and prepared to take passive or active steps to resist Roman rule. It is an odd coincidence that the names of Judas the Galilean and his sons James and Simon correspond to the names of three of Jesus' brothers. Since the Joses or Joseph named as a son of Mary and Cleophas disappears from subsequent records, and may thus be a reference to Jesus himself, the coincidence could indeed be exact. So there is a possibility that the historical record has been muddied, separating the political from the religious aspects of one resistance movement. Jesus could be seen as presenting the religious challenge, reinterpreted by later writers to be against Judaism, while the challenge to Rome is delegated to Judas and his sons, James and Simon.

The problem with time scales and possible conflation of events will be looked at later. Suffice to say that Menahem in AD 66 is described by Josephus as a "son" of the tax rebel Judas, which he is unlikely to have been given that his father, presumably in his maturity, was leading a revolt 60 years previously.

One possible explanation is that Josephus made a mistake and should have said "grandson". Another, even more interesting possibility which will be developed later, is that the genealogical description was right but the timetable of events mistaken or falsified.

There were also other recorded incidents of conflict at this time. When Pontius Pilate became procurator of Judaea in AD 26, he insensitively allowed Roman standards with embossed medallions of the emperor to be taken into Jerusalem, even though such images were considered by the Jews to be idolatrous. This resulted in a mass protest outside Caesar's palace in Caesarea which went on for five days and nights. When Pilate threatened the protesters, they offered to die rather than back down. Faced with the prospect of having to massacre so many, Pilate gave way and had the offending standards removed.

The Roman procurator also provoked popular outrage for using Temple funds to bring water by an aqueduct to improve the supply for Jerusalem. This led to a popular demonstration in the city.

Pilate had soldiers dressed as civilians and carrying hidden clubs infiltrate the protesters, with the aim presumably of causing panic and dispersing the crowd. Not surprisingly, a lot of injury was caused both to bystanders and peaceful protesters and this led to considerable resentment.

Pilate eventually overstepped the mark in AD 36 by sending a detachment of cavalry and heavily armed infantry to deal with what was apparently a peaceful gathering of Samaritans at their holy site of Mount Gerizim. It seems a man had appeared claiming to be the messianic figure expected by the Samaritans, the "Taheb". The crowd had gathered to follow this man up the mountain to find sacred vessels, reputed to have been hidden in ancient times on the mountain. Many of the Samaritans were killed by the Roman troops and Pilate had some of their leaders subsequently executed. But the Samaritan authorities appealed to the Roman legate of Syria, Vitellius. He found in their favor and had Pilate removed from his position, either late in AD 36 or early in the year AD 37.

Since Jesus was crucified while Pilate was governor, the latest date for his Crucifixion would have been the Passover Feast in the Spring of AD 36. This seems to fit in with other evidence. The reason for John the Baptist's imprisonment was ostensibly his criticism of Herod Antipas who had divorced his wife, daughter of King Aretas of Peraea, in order to marry his brother Philip's widow. Philip died in AD 33 or 34, so the marriage must have taken place in AD 34, and John was executed the following year. This was before a battle with King Aretas in which Herod was heavily defeated.

The gospels report that Jesus was baptized by John the Baptist and began his preaching and healing ministry following John's death. So, by this calculation, the trial and Crucifixion of Jesus would have taken place in the last full year of Pilate's administration in AD 36.

Pilate's ferocious reaction to the Samaritan messianic claimant must then have happened a matter of weeks or months afterwards. This suggests that there may have been a culmination of successive misjudged situations leading to the procurator's downfall.

The last years of Pilate's rule were then certainly marked by increased tension. The census, for the purpose of carrying out the deeply resented poll tax, took place every fourteen years and the year AD 34–35 was a census year. Hence the significance of the question put to Jesus, preaching in the Temple, as to whether the tax should be paid to Caesar.

References in Acts and by Josephus suggest that the tax rebel Judas the Galilean and his followers represented a distinct opposition movement. Both sources, the Acts of the Apostles almost certainly following Josephus, date this to the time of the census instigated by Quirinius in Judaea in AD 6. There are difficulties however with the time scale involved, particularly when it comes to placing another rebellious son of Judas, Menahem.

While Judas the Galilean had advocated a direct refusal to pay tax, Jesus adopted a more subtle approach. According to the Gospel of Matthew, he dealt carefully and brilliantly with a question about the Roman tax.

The issue was put to him: was it lawful to pay the tax? Jesus demanded to be shown a coin and asked whose likeness and inscription were on it. "Caesar's" was the reply.

To which came the famous rejoinder, "Render therefore to Caesar the things that are Caesar's and to God the things that are God's".

Jesus thus safely distanced himself from those who might have been advocating a tax rebellion. But he did so in a way which made clear to Jewish listeners his scorn both for material concerns and the temporal power of the Roman authorities. Moreover, he also managed a dig at imperial pretensions. There are things that are God's and Caesar whatever he might think, Jesus implied, was not a God.

Jesus was preaching, as will be shown, a spiritual kingdom on earth. Others were advocating more overt political resistance. Were there two different approaches to the same issue at around the same time, or were these just two sides of the same coin? This is a question which will be worth pursuing.

Judas perished. It may be that the Romans executed him. Jesus was crucified.

This was certainly a time of great tension and danger, with periodic misjudgments by the Roman rulers of Palestine and outbursts of popular unrest, often met with harsh repression. Pilate, despite the gloss put on him by gospel writers, operated within the framework of Roman rule and would have had little sympathy for someone treasonably claiming to be king over his territory. Indeed, Pilate's harsh response to followers of a Samaritan messianic claimant shortly afterwards suggests that he could well have responded to Jesus in much the same way.

Pilate was not pushed by the Sanhedrin into crucifying Jesus, as the gospels would have it. He was a man caught in a difficult position, not entirely in control of events but dealing with the situation as best he could and by his own standards.

CHAPTER 9

THE POOR

In his time [that of Coponius as procurator] a Galilean named Judas tried to stir up the natives to revolt, saying that they would be cowards if they submitted to paying taxes to the Romans and, after serving God alone, accepted human masters. This man was a rabbi with a sect of his own, and was quite unlike the others. Among the Jews there are three schools of thought, whose adherents are called Pharisees, Sadducees, and Essenes, respectively.

The Jewish War, Josephus 2:117–118

As for the fourth of the philosophies, Judas the Galilean set himself up as leader of it. This school agrees in all other respects with the opinions of the Pharisees, except that they have a passion for liberty that is almost unconquerable, since they are convinced that God alone is their leader and master. They think little of submitting to death in unusual forms and permitting vengeance to fall on kinsmen and friends if only they may avoid calling any man master. Inasmuch as most people have seen the steadfastness of their resolution amid such circumstances, I may forego any further account. For I have no fear that anything reported of them will be considered incredible. The danger is, rather, that report may minimize the indifference with which they accept the grinding misery of pain. The folly that ensued began to afflict the nation after Gessius Florus, who was governor [AD 64–66], had by his overbearing and lawless activities provoked a desperate rebellion against the Romans.

Jewish Antiquities, Josephus 18:23–25

Looked at even in their own terms, the gospels do not show Jesus as he is now portrayed. He was human, not faultless. He had a family, a mother and father and brothers and sisters. He was most probably married, following the social obligations and customs of his time.

The evidence is there in the gospel writings, with all the omissions and overlays intended to obscure but actually highlighting what took place.

Not divine, nor even claiming to be divine, what Jesus claimed if anything was to be the Messiah, the expected king of his people, through a line of descent bound to be vague and tenuous after centuries of conquests, expulsions and exile. He was by no means the only claimant in the period which followed the death of the despot Herod.

He is presented as a religious teacher and a faith healer. But the gospel miracles do not appear to have been divine acts, overturning the laws of nature. Some are based on misinterpretation or mistranslation while others reflect Jesus' acute insight and understanding.

This is what the evidence in the gospels actually shows. As I have indicated, the motivation of gospels writers and later editors in concealing some aspects of Jesus' character and life were to do with the effort to separate Christianity from Judaism.

Jesus had to be separated from his family, his social context and apparently set against Jews and Jewish society, so as to repossess him for a wider Gentile religion, identify him with its deity and, more immediately, make him acceptable to the Roman authorities. This temporal power provided the context in which the gospel writers and makers had to operate and survive.

The reality, however, is that Jesus was a fully practicing Jew and, like most of his fellows, opposed to both rule by a foreign power and those it appointed to exercise power, including the High Priest and his followers. Jesus claimed the kingship for his people.

The first kings of Judah were the guardians of their religion and even exercised a priestly role, for example in the dedication of the Temple and the care of the Ark of the Covenant. A complex organization of priests evolved to take care of religious functions in Jerusalem. These priests, as royal officials, were responsible to the king. There were also other religious centers existing separately with their own local priests in other parts of the Kingdoms of Judah and Israel.

The center of ritual observance at Jerusalem eventually came to be recognized as paramount and associated with the office of High Priest over all the tribes, encompassing both Judah and the old Kingdom of Israel. The local centers were then abolished. With the Temple at Jerusalem now serving as a focus of worship for the nation as whole, religious and political functions were at this point separated.

Under Solomon, Zadok was made High Priest as a reward for his loyalty and service to the king and, from then on, the office was passed to the descendants of Zadok. The rulers of Israel, for centuries subject to foreign power, made new appointments whenever a vacancy arose and could sack and replace existing incumbents.

At the time of Jesus, the Sadducees, whose name possibly derives from "Zadok", were the dominant priestly group within the ruling council or Sanhedrin. Within their ranks was a powerful clique consisting of the High Priest and his supporters.

The Hasmoneans, as they began to wrest back Israel's independence, assumed the office of High Priest as well as the mantle of kingship. First Jonathan, and then his brother Simon, took on the joint role of ruler and religious head of Israel. The Hasmoneans were from a minor priestly family and therefore, in the eyes of many Jews, not entitled to do this.

After Herod became king of Judaea and then ruler of most of Palestine, High Priests were selected from one of four priestly families which were also not of the Zadokite lineage. Appointments were either made by Herod, and later by members of his family inheriting part of the kingdom, or by the Romans directly.

The Pharisees developed around about the second century BC as a group devoted to the observance of Jewish religious tradition and law. As long as freedom of religious expression was maintained they were not, however, concerned with the overthrow of foreign rule. This, they believed, would ultimately come about through divine intervention. It was left to the Sadducees to make the compromises necessary to accommodate to the political reality of working with an occupying power and administering Temple life.

One group, the Essenes, withdrew from the mainstream and set up fairly self-contained communities at Qumran by the Dead Sea and elsewhere. Their origins are unclear. But they may have broken from the Sadducees in order to preserve what they believed were Judaism's true religious ideals. The discovery of the Dead Sea scrolls, which the Essenes had hidden just before the destruction of Qumran by Roman forces in AD 68, provides an insight into this group and Jewish society as a whole at around the time that Jesus lived.

Some of the writings consist of rules for the community and there is also a body of biblical commentary. The sect interpreted the Old Testament prophets in ways which provided legitimacy and justification for their own beliefs.

They saw themselves as the righteous and as a refuge for seekers after righteousness in a world of wickedness.

One prominent figure is the "teacher of righteousness" who may have been the person who initially took followers into physical separation from what was seen as the decadence of the ruling Hasmoneans. Opposed to him was the "wicked priest" or the "spouter of lies".

The Essenes, "the poor" or "the men of the Community" or "men of the new covenant" as they variously described themselves, objected to the Hasmonean kings usurping the office of High Priest, without having the right religious credentials. It may be that the wicked priest was Jonathan, one of the sons of Mattathias. Jonathan's crime, in the eyes of "the poor", was to accept the office of High Priest through the hands of a foreign ruler, Alexander Balas, a usurper of the Seleucid throne, even though he had no entitlement to it. His brother Simon, who succeeded him, made matters worse by taking on the combined priestly and kingly role as if it were hereditary.

After the wicked priest came the "last priests of Jerusalem", more Hasmoneans, whose fate was to be meted out to them by the "kittim" or Romans. The Essenes left behind a "war scroll" which provided elaborate description of preparations for a final battle against the rulers of the world, the kittim. It may have been more a symbolical and theological work than a manual of warfare which would have been useful in a real conflict.

However, the documents show that the Romans were the enemy in the eyes of the Essenes, as with most of the Jewish people, and it gives a declaration of interest if not of intent in fighting them. It is also likely that many of the zealots who took part in the uprising against Rome came from Qumran and similar communities. Josephus describes one Essene, John, as a commander who took part in the revolution and fell in battle. The Romans took time during the siege of Jerusalem to attack and wipe out the settlement by the Dead Sea at Qumran.

The scrolls, the library of the community, were almost certainly hidden just before the attack. They remained there untouched for 1,900 years because no one came back for them. No one came back, of course, because the Romans had done the job thoroughly. Some inhabitants may have managed to flee to Masada but there they also subsequently died. No one survived.

The community at Qumran may well have been the religious center for groups loosely confederated throughout Israel, all following a similar code.

The Essenes devoted themselves to the observance of "perfect holiness" in a regime that included ritual cold bathing, bible reading, solemn meals and frequent assemblies. They bound themselves by stricter rules than their fellow Jews, in a strictly hierarchical society. While the bulk of members, "men of the covenant" were free to marry and own property, the upper tier, members of the "Council of the Community" surrendered their possessions to communal ownership and, it would seem, either aspired to or practiced celibacy.

There are similarities here with the primitive religious communism practiced among the early Nazoraean community in Jerusalem, as described in Acts, where followers were encouraged to give up their possessions to the Apostles. There are suggestions too in the gospels that the followers of Jesus should ideally be without family ties.

Like the Essenes, the Nazoraean followers of Jesus also practiced baptism by immersion and advocated strict adherence to Jewish Law. The root meaning of the Hebrew word Nazoraean describing them is "keeping", usually associated with keeping the law or the covenant or observing the customs of the ancestors. The Essenes were also keepers of the covenant or community law.

In the gospel writings of Mark and Luke, the Hebrew title "Nazoraean" became "Nazarene" in Greek translation and transposition, in an apparent attempt to associate Jesus with a place, Nazareth, rather than the idea of adhering to Jewish Law. The original meaning was not something that the gospel writers were keen to emphasize; indeed they sought to represent Jesus as opposed to Judaism for the reasons already suggested. They were laying the foundation for a wider religion appealing to Gentiles and followers of Hellenistic mystery cults, and associated with sacrifice, salvation, mystical communion and identification with the deity.

There is no record of a town or village of Nazareth at the time Jesus lived. Josephus lists all the places in Galilee which were defended or fortified under his control as military commander against Roman military attack. But Nazareth is not among them and indeed is nowhere mentioned in his extensive writings. Other sources apply the term Nazoraean to the early followers of Jesus and this would appear to be the accurate designation.

As was noted early, the Essenes did not describe themselves by the title ascribed to them but used descriptions such as the "meek" or the "poor". This latter self-designation significantly is shared with the early Nazoraeans and with another group, the Ebionites, whose name means "the poor" and who maintained the Nazoraean tradition following the destruction visited on the Jewish nation during and after the first Jewish War (AD 66–70).

From a distance of almost 2,000 years, and with limited written evidence produced for the most part to serve a particular political and or religious purpose, it is difficult to gain a sense of how society fitted together at the time Jesus lived.

One pitfall to avoid is taking descriptions that applied then and using them in the same way as labels are applied to discrete and well-defined groups now.

Josephus, the Jewish zealot commander in Galilee who surrendered to the Romans and became a kind of tame historical commentator for them, described three schools of Jewish philosophy: Pharisees, Sadducees, Essenes and then a fourth school, under the leadership of Judas the Galilean. This latter approach was, according to Josephus, identical with the Pharisees except for their refusal to accept anyone except God as their master. So, while the Pharisees were apparently content to practice their pure religion in the expectation of eventual divine deliverance, Judas the Galilean and his followers sought liberation in the here and now.

Josephus also describes how he had spent time as a member of each of the three main groups in order to gain personal experience and decide which was the best. He also claims to have spent time with one "Banus", in the wilderness under a regime that included the frequent taking of purifying cold baths. The use of an apparent pseudonym Banus, which is probably derived from the Latin for bathing, indicates some reticence on Josephus' part. Under the patronage of the Romans and having been spared after being captured by them in the early part of the uprising, he would not have wanted to emphasize his revolutionary past.

But Banus is likely to have been a radical figure in the mold of John the Baptist, perhaps the leader of a zealot group, possibly even the leader of a radical Nazoraean community like James, the brother of Jesus. That Josephus could have moved easily between these groups is an indication perhaps of a degree of fluidity in their boundaries. Josephus describes various people as "bandits", "zealots" or even "Essenes" according to the point he is trying to make, or the power group he needs to placate.

The mass of the ordinary people were Jews, opposed to Rome and in varying degrees prepared either to acquiesce for the time being or react. The ruling priestly caste comprised the Sadducees (Zadokites), while the Pharisees set themselves apart as being more pious. Some took this to the point of physical separation at Qumran and elsewhere in "assemblies of the camps" and "assemblies of the towns". These were "the poor" as they described themselves, or the Essenes as others described them.

There appears to have been an enormous amount in common in terms of practice and organization, as well as ideology, between the Essenes and the early followers of Jesus, the Nazoraeans. It would have been difficult for a tight central authority to be imposed on the various assemblies, even if it had been desirable. What linked the various groups was a community of approach and belief.

It is a fair to ask then how "the poor" at Qumran would have seen their fellow Jews, the Nazoraeans, practicing a similar way of life in their own assemblies just fourteen miles or a morning's walk up the valley from the Dead Sea at Jerusalem? Not as fellow "Essenes", because that is both to ask and answer the wrong question, but perhaps as part of a fellowship of some kind.

As Josephus pointed out, the rebels under Judas the Galilean opposing the census and payment of taxes to Rome were not a secular, irreligious group.

They were followers of Pharisaic ideals, differing only in their preparedness to take action and if necessary sacrifice their lives.

The High Priest was selected from core families among the Sadducee class, first by the Herodians and then by the Romans. It was, as such, a political office as well as a ceremonial religious office. The loyalties of some of the Sadducees might well have been stretched by this arrangement, while others willingly accepted the patronage which went with the High Priest's office. In a sense, the High Priest with his supporters and followers comprised a separate faction with decisive political power within the ruling Sanhedrin and within Jewish society as a whole.

The historical Jesus fitted into and was part of this mosaic of cliques and factions, within a sea of suppressed and sometimes not-so-suppressed resentment against the Roman occupation and also the Sadducean priesthood, enjoying as it did the favor and the patronage of Rome.

There are few references to Jesus outside of the gospels, including only a passing remark in the copious works of Josephus and another reference by the Roman writer Tacitus. At the time, Jesus may have appeared to his contemporaries as less important than the movement of which he was a part. There was no "Christ" religion based on a charismatic figurehead, just Law-upholding Jews, believing variations on a common theme.

It may also be that Josephus wrote out Jesus from his book *The Jewish War* and later work *Jewish Antiquities* because the episode was an embarrassment to the Romans and a reminder of the nationalism and messianism which were the fundamental reasons for the revolt. Since Josephus was a turncoat Jewish commander, dependent on the Romans for his life and living, he also had an interest in playing down the messianic element in his own former role.

Among a wide coalition of Pharisaic or Esssenic "pious" believers were the Nazoraeans. Beside the normal orthodox Jewish beliefs, they held the view that one of their number had been the Messiah, who had been brought back to life after Crucifixion and would one day return.

The brothers of Jesus, as has been shown, were among his Apostles. So instead of standing on the sidelines, or actively disapproving, provoking Jesus to repudiate his own family–the picture painted in the gospels–they were actively involved in Jesus' movement, or rather it should be said their movement.

The slant provided in the gospels and in letters written by Paul which predated them, is of a religion opposed to Judaism and based on faith and communion rather than the requirements of Judaism. Those who accept this have to deal with the uncomfortable historical fact of the early Nazoraean Church which was fully Jewish in its practices and beliefs. Not only that but James, the brother of Jesus, was the first leader of this Church and is also depicted astonishingly as holding the office, or having the attributes, of the High Priest! After James was stoned to death, he was succeeded as "bishop" by Simon or Simeon, son of Cleophas, who was another of Jesus' brothers.

Though there are few historical references to Jesus outside of the gospels, there is plenty of independent evidence on the first Church of his followers, the Nazoraeans, in Jerusalem. This can be found in the writings of Early Church historians and even, reading between the lines, in Josephus who began to publish his work around AD 70.

The way that all this is usually accommodated is by suggesting a form of recidivism, with the Early Church "sliding back" into the ways of Judaism, leaving it to the Apostle Paul to struggle valiantly to bring the Church back to Jesus' "true" message.

This is such an improbable scenario that it has to be discounted. It requires the Apostles and the brothers of Jesus to be so dim-witted, that they forgot within a matter of months what it is that they had believed and had been doing. It is also contradicted by the Acts of the Apostles, believed to have been written by the author of Luke, and the letters of Paul which detail a struggle over doctrine between Paul and the Early Church leaders in Jerusalem. As will be seen, this evidence suggests that it was Paul who was seeking (and ultimately succeeding) to break a Jesus-based religion away from its foundation in Judaism, rather than the other way round.

It is also so much more likely that Jesus and his brothers were like other similar groups in Jewish history, such as the Maccabean sons of Mattathias, and worked together within a common ideological framework and towards a common purpose.

In looking at the character of Jesus in earlier chapters, especially those attributes which were supposed to mark him out as divine, the framework of the gospels was taken for granted. Analysis of internal inconsistencies and contradictions revealed bias, rewriting or concealment. Text going against the trend of bias deserved more weight since it was included in spite of, rather than because of, the author or editor's motivations. Some material simply escaped the editor's attention because of the fact that one alteration may require many supporting changes, and not all of these could be or were tracked down.

Now, however, the analysis can be taken a stage further. Other historical writings show a different picture of the Early Church from what would be expected according the gospel view of Jesus and his followers. The efforts of the Apostle Paul, self-appointed after a vision on the way to Damascus, were to create a different kind of Church from the one formed by those who had actually met and in many cases had known Jesus well. Paul's proselytizing and his letters to early "Christian" communities happened before the gospels were written and appear very much to have influenced them.

The Nazoraean movement led by James in the 40s and 50s AD was essentially Pharisaic, fiercely upholding Jewish Law including the requirement for circumcision, both for those born into Judaism or converted to it. Jews were required by custom to abstain from certain kinds of meat. They could only eat meat from permitted animals which had been ritually killed by having the blood drained away.

James himself took these prohibitions even further. As the fourth century Church historian Eusebius stated, quoting from an earlier writer Hegesippus (whose works are now lost), "He [James] drank no wine or strong drink, nor did he eat meat. No razor came near his head, nor did he anoint himself with oil, and he did not go to the baths."

As the quote indicates, James was as a vegetarian and he denied himself the pleasures of the Roman hot baths. According to another writer Epiphanius, he also practiced "life-long virginity", that is he abstained from sexual activity.

These and other writers note that he did not wear wool but only linen. While consistent with a practice of avoiding animal products, this also marks him out in his role as a priest.

He was known as "James the Righteous", renowned for his devotion and piety to the extent that his knees were hardened through constant praying. The Church father Jerome reported that "He alone had the privilege of entering the Holy of Holies, since indeed he did not wear woolen garments only linen, and he went alone into the Temple and prayed on behalf of the people, so much so that his knees were reputed to have acquired the hardness of camels' knees."

There are several other similar quotes. Epiphanius stated that "To James alone it was permitted to enter the Holy of Holies once a year because he was a Nazirite [one separated or apart] and connected to the priesthood."

The earliest quote is of Hegesippus related by Eusebius:

He alone was allowed to enter the Place of Holiness, for he did not wear wool, but linen, and he used to enter the Temple alone, and was often found upon his bended knees, interceding for the forgiveness of the people, so that his knees became as callused as a camel's, because of the constant importuning he did and kneeling before God and asking forgiveness for the people.

The references to entering the Holy of Holies alone and wearing only linen refer to the Day of Atonement (Yom Kippur), when the High Priest was permitted to enter the Holy of Holies once a year to supplicate God for forgiveness for the sins of the Jewish people. On that day, purity requirements were stricter than usual and the High Priest wore garments solely of white, coarse linen instead of wool and ordinary linen.

The important point is that James is consistently described as a priest. The significance of that can be appreciated when it is remembered that the "Christian" Church was yet to be invented, or rather was in the process of being invented among Gentile followers, largely through the efforts of Paul. The Nazoraeans were a sect fully within Judaism, differing only in one chief respect, their perception that the expected Messiah (anointed one) or Jewish king had already come. So James was not in any sense a Christian minister. But, on the evidence, he certainly did have the status of a Jewish priest. He was the religious leader of a sect within Judaism.

Could James have really held the highest office of High Priest? Not on the face of it. The succession of High Priests is well documented, with Ananus being the incumbent at the time as recorded by Josephus and others.

But the way James is reported to have perished in AD 62 does throw some light on the matter.

When the Roman governor Festus died, the next holder of the office Albinus was appointed by the Emperor Nero and sent to Palestine to take up his position. But in the meantime, while Albinus was still on the way, Ananus called an assembly and had James and others brought before it on a charge of offending against Jewish Law (the Torah). Before Albinus could take up his office, James was stoned to death.

This was done without proper authority, since only the Roman authorities could confirm or pass the sentence of death, and since the action was taken by the High Priest and his followers, rather than by a properly convened Sanhedrin. Ananus was deposed as a result of this irregular action but it was of course too late for James.

The method of execution, stoning, was reserved for a number of offenses, but especially for blasphemy which is what it seems was James' alleged offense.

If James was not the High Priest, then he had no right to enter the Holy of Holies sanctuary, with the diadem of office, pray for the people's forgiveness and intone the forbidden name of God, as customarily happened once a year on the Day of Atonement (Yom Kippur).

Why would James have attempted something so seemingly rash and apparently doomed to failure? There was clearly a power struggle going on and it may have been evenly balanced. Ananus and his allies chose to kill James at a moment when there was no Roman governor, when they might be able to argue that they did need permission.

It should be remembered that the office of the High Priest and its incumbent were not at the time held in great esteem, given that he was an appointee of Rome. By contrast, James was a highly popular figure and his followers in Jerusalem, according to both Josephus and Early Church commentators, had grown to 5,000 or more. It may even be that the bulk of ordinary people supported him and so he was their de facto spiritual leader.

James had a power base, he was the people's choice and, again according to early sources, was well regarded by the Pharisees. He may have chosen or been impelled to intercede, not as the officially appointed High Priest but as the representative of the "poor", the "righteous", his Nazoraean followers, those upholding or "zealous" of the Law.

In so doing, he presented a challenge to the existing religious order based on collaboration–just as Jesus did in overturning the tables of the Temple money-changers. The real argument may well have been, as will be argued, something similar to do with the corruption of the Temple, as seen through the eyes of James and his followers.

It is interesting and significant that James and Jesus both, as their stories are related, presented the same type of challenge directly to the religious establishment and thus indirectly to the political order which appointed it. This is yet another factor which makes it much less likely that they differed significantly in their religious beliefs.

The new governor Albinus showed his displeasure with Ananus by replacing him, a relatively mild punishment in the circumstances. He then allowed subsequent Saducean holders of the office a free hand in persecuting opponents, called by Josephus "leaders of the multitudes of Jerusalem".

It was not the official High Priest, who was a Roman collaborator, but James who spoke for the mass of Jewish people in Jerusalem. He gathered a following which did not simply disappear, as will be seen.

The office of priesthood ran in families, not that every member of a family would necessarily become a priest. But this means that Jesus, brother of someone who acted as a priest, was part of a priestly family too, even if one of his possible fathers, Joseph or Cleophas, had been a builder (or carpenter) from the Greek "tectonis".

This puts into context the romanticized and it has to be said misleading gospel accounts of Jesus' origins. Far from being from a humble family, Jesus came from a family with priestly connections or origins, wealthy enough to afford a wedding feast judging by the surplus wine required for maybe two hundred guests. He was not born in a stable (more mistranslation), because "there was no room in the inn" but on the lower floor of a typical house, where the animals were usually kept, because there was no room on the upper floor where the family lived.

It shouldn't really come as a surprise that Jesus was from a priestly family. There are clues to this in the gospels which strike a chord with the sort of religious community which arose in Jerusalem after Jesus' Crucifixion.

Mary the mother of Jesus had a "kinswoman" Elizabeth, thought to be barren, whose husband was Zachariah, a priest serving in the Temple at Jerusalem. Though approaching old age, Elizabeth conceived and bore a son, who was named John and who would in some way have been Jesus' cousin.

If related in the male line, this would indicate a possible priestly background for Jesus. This is something which appears quite likely, given that his own brother James was later a priest, either exercising or claiming the highest office. That Elizabeth conceived late in life suggests that John would have been her only son.

John disappears from the scene, or at least from the record like Jesus, and reappears later on wandering, preaching and baptizing in the desert. He was killed by the ruler of the Roman province of Galilee, Herod Antipas, one of the sons of the tyrant Herod who was supposed to have instituted the slaughter of the firstborn in Bethlehem. The suggested reason in the gospels for John the Baptist's execution was John's disapproval of the Herodian practice of sexual relationships between close relatives, specifically the marriage between Herod Antipas and his half brother's wife, Herodias. More likely, as Josephus suggests, Herod Antipas had become alarmed at the following that John the Baptist had attracted, and decided to make a pre-emptive strike to prevent a possible uprising.

On the face of it, this would seem to have been unduly paranoid, unless there was some other good reason. The efforts that the previous Herod, Herod Antipas' father, had devoted to destroying possible Hasmonean contenders for the throne of Israel provide a possible parallel. John the Baptist, a cousin of Jesus, may have been able to make a messianic claim based on his family background. This could also explain why both he and Jesus suddenly appear on the scene as fully mature adults. Even if the massacre of the innocents did not actually happen as told, Herod's interest in eliminating possible rivals was a reality, and he would have been a threat to both Jesus and John. So they may have been kept out of harm's way until their adulthood.

When Herod died, the kingship was for the time being abolished and Israel was divided between governors responsible to Rome. The threat to possible messianic claimants diminished, providing they kept a relatively low profile. But that is precisely what John the Baptist failed to do, as he baptized people in the River Jordan, perhaps in this manner symbolically crossing into the Promised Land. He drew too much attention to himself and paid for it with his life.

Because John was probably, on the gospel accounts, the first and only son of elderly parents, any claims he had would have passed to his closest male relative in the male line.

The mantle all too evidently passed from John to Jesus. When John died, Jesus was immediately spurred into an exhausting preaching ministry, traveling miles across the country to address large crowds, healing the sick and gaining converts. He was at first cautious about making claims in order to avoid provoking the High Priest, and his party within the Sadducees, and also the Romans. But he did finally stake his claim to be the rightful Messiah, or King of Israel.

The Gospels, Luke and Matthew, contrast the habits of John and Jesus thus:

> *For John came neither eating nor drinking, and they say, "He has a demon"; the Son of man came eating and drinking, and they say, "Behold, a glutton and a drunkard, a friend of tax collectors and sinners!" Yet wisdom is justified by her deeds.*
> Matthew 11:18–19

The point apparently being made is that, for those unwilling to receive the message, it doesn't matter how it is wrapped up, whether in the asceticism and piety of John or in the more earthly qualities of Jesus.

The character and beliefs of John, such as his objection to some forms of marriage, certainly fits well with the ideology of the "poor" at Qumran and elsewhere, and the practices of James and others in the Nazoraean assembly at Jerusalem. It is pointed out in Mark's Gospel that John and his disciples fasted with the Pharisees, with whom they would also have shared a lot in common.

But, according to Mark, Jesus and his disciples did not. It would seem on the face of it that there were a cluster of groups and personalities, all existing at about the same time and all sharing similar values: John the Baptist and his followers, James and the other brothers of Jesus together with the Nazoraean community at Jerusalem, the "pious" Pharisees and "the poor" in their assemblies at Qumran and elsewhere.

Only Jesus, at some points in the gospels, is depicted as repudiating the teaching of Judaism or living a life at odds with its values.

Is this a fair portrayal, or is this part of the process, already seen in the gospel writings, of disassociating Jesus from his background to make him the central figure in a new religion?

Further examination of the gospel sources, while providing new insights into Jesus' teaching, suggests that he was well within the Pharisaic traditions of Judaism.

CHAPTER 10

KINGDOM ON EARTH

And one of the scribes came up and heard them disputing with one another, and seeing that he answered them [the Sadducees] well, asked him, "Which commandment is the first of all?"
Jesus answered, "The first is, 'Hear, O Israel: The Lord our God, the Lord is one; and you shall love the Lord your God with all your heart, and with all your soul, and with all your mind, and with all your strength.' The second is this, 'You shall love your neighbor as yourself.' There is no other commandment greater than these."
And the scribe said to him, "You are right, Teacher; you have truly said that he is one, and there is no other but he; and to love him with all the heart, and with all the understanding, and with all the strength, and to love one's neighbor as oneself, is much more than all whole burnt offerings and sacrifices."
And when Jesus saw that he answered wisely, he said to him, "You are not far from the Kingdom of God."

Mark 12:28–34

But when the Pharisees heard that he had silenced the Sadducees, they came together.
And one of them, a lawyer, asked him a question to test him. "Teacher, which is the great commandment in the law?"
And he said to him, "You shall love the Lord your God with all your heart, and with all your soul, and with all your mind. This is the great and first commandment. And a second is like it, You shall love your neighbor as yourself. On these two commandments depend all the law and the prophets."

Matthew 22:34–40

One Sabbath he was going through the grainfields; and as they made their way his disciples began to pluck heads of grain. And the Pharisees said to him, "Look, why are they doing what is not lawful on the Sabbath?" And he said to them, "Have you never read what David did, when he was in need and was hungry, he and those who were with him; how he entered the house of God when Abiathar was High Priest, and ate the bread of the Presence, which it is not lawful for any but the priests to eat, and also gave it to those who were with him?" And he said to them, "The Sabbath was made for man, not man for the Sabbath; so the Son of man is lord even of the Sabbath."

Mark 2:23–28

In looking at the gospel records it needs be remembered that, with the possible exception of an early version of Mark which is no longer extant, they come relatively late in the chronology of available sources. Paul's letters to some of the Early Church communities he was seeking to establish were written from about AD 50. Josephus wrote his first work, *The Jewish War*, between AD 75 and 79. The first version of Mark's Gospel may have been written at about this time, or a few years earlier.

Scholars agree that the other synoptic Gospels, Matthew and Luke, were written a few years after this in the nineties. But John's Gospel and the Acts of the Apostles, written by the author of Luke, both date from the early second century AD.

There is a strong presumption that one of the first documents circulated was a collection of sayings attributed to Jesus, the *Sayings Gospel Q*, which was used as a source by Matthew and Luke. Another early gospel dating from about AD 50, not included in the New Testament, is the Gospel of Thomas. This also consists of a collection of sayings attributed to Jesus and provides a very useful comparison with the material found in Matthew and Luke.

It should also be recognized that not one of the documents survives intact in the form in which it was originally written. Copying invariably involved amendment and editing. As has already been seen, the gospels were edited to minimize or eliminate Jesus' family connections and put him in opposition to his own religion, Judaism.

The story of the "passion", Jesus' confrontation with the Jewish religious authorities and equally or consequentially the Roman authority in Jerusalem, is found only in the gospels. The fact of Jesus' execution is mentioned only briefly in Josephus' *Jewish Antiquities*, dating from about AD 94, and by the Roman historian Tacitus, writing about AD 120. For the moment, therefore, the focus will be on what Jesus is claimed to have said or represent, rather than what it is claimed happened to him.

The author and historian John Dominic Crossan has conducted an analysis of the sayings attributed to Jesus, looking at a range of independent or derivative sources. He identified clusters where a given saying or story appears in two or more independent sources. The principle behind the analysis is this: while a single attestation could be the pure invention of the author, this is not likely with variants multiply attested by more than one author. Especially if the sources are early, such sayings are more likely to reflect the original and authentic teaching of Jesus himself.

The outcome suggests that Jesus was preaching a message of spiritual values, as against materialism, and arguing that wealth itself was a barrier to enlightenment and understanding. He appeared to represent the desperate and downtrodden. So, he said, "blessed are the poor", not meaning simply the less well off, but those absolutely destitute (from the Greek *ptochos*). It would be easier, he maintained, for a camel to go through "the eye of a needle" (the entry in a city wall just big enough for a person to go through) than for a rich man to enter the Kingdom of God.

It should be recalled "the poor" were what the Essenes, the Nazoraeans and Ebionites after Jesus called themselves and actually were, to the extent that they gave up or pooled their possessions.

In like manner, Jesus championed the hungry, the sad (those who mourned) and the rejected.

But the kingdom Jesus spoke of was something in the hear-and-now, rather than a state to be achieved at some point in the distant future. It was within people, in their moral lives, and also without in their relationships with others. As the Gospel of Thomas has it, Jesus said, "It will not come by waiting for it. It will not be a matter of saying, 'Here it is' or 'There it is'. Rather, the kingdom of the father is spread out upon the earth, and men do not see it."

It was, like a small seed, something that could grow into a great tree. Or it was like yeast which could expand dough into bread, something pervasive which (though this is unstated) the authorities, whether political or religious, could not check.

The kingdom, rather than a theoretical construct, was something to be performed and practiced. This is why Jesus told the wealthy young man, who had kept the commandments but was concerned what else he should do, to give up his riches and become one of his followers.

For those who followed the prescription, there was serene consolation based on stoic acceptance, virtue in having taken the right path and belief that, as with the ravens of the air and the lilies in the field, God would provide.

The kingdom was or was to be one of equals, with no distinction between male and female, and without the hierarchical divisions of the patriarchal family.

This latter prescription may then have been the basis on which Jesus is taken in the gospels to have rejected his own brothers and sisters.

In reality, as was argued earlier and can now be seen even more clearly, the Nazoraean community headed initially by Jesus' brother James represents a continuation of Jesus' teaching and mission. Far from hindering him, his brothers would have supported him and did indeed carry on from where he left off. It is indeed the creation of a subsequent Jesus-centered religion, Christianity, which makes it difficult to acknowledge the reality that Jesus was one figure in a movement, in which others were also important.

The teaching, as far as it can be ascertained, was certainly radical in the context of the male centered, patriarchal, hierarchical, property owning or property aspiring culture of the time.

Jesus and his followers lived an itinerant life, were not ashamed to be supported by "women of substance", did not have or gave up their settled occupations, praised poverty and advocated equality.

But there is really nothing in this which could be construed as a challenge to the Judaism of the time, certainly not to the Pharisaic view. It was not even a challenge to the Sadducees except those, the High Priest and his followers, who owed their positions to patronage, who exchanged collaboration with the Roman authorities for wealth and power and who became idle and corrupt.

As was argued in earlier chapters, the gospels which were accepted into the New Testament were written or edited and adapted to represent the position of the early Christian Church. In this reconstructed version, Jesus was represented as semi-divine, and to do this it was necessary to distort or omit his real familial relationships. This then was the introduced bias.

However, making changes in this way inevitably led to inconsistencies and left a host of other detail pointing to the original text or circumstances. In principle, the evidence found which goes against the known bias is likely to be from the earlier or original stratum, and more reliable.

The same method can be applied to Jesus' relationships with religious groups within his society, of which he too was a part. The Early Church had to coexist with Rome and indeed wished to expand its message throughout the Roman Empire. That meant hugely diminishing the role of the Roman authorities in the execution of Jesus, and as far as possible blaming the main Jewish religious groups or authorities.

This is the despite the one really definite group of historical facts. Jesus was executed by the Romans, on the orders of the Roman governor, in a manner which would indicate that his offense was considered political.

Acting on behalf of Rome, Pilate rather than the Pharisees or the Jewish people as a whole, was the authority responsible for what took place.

Not only was the passion sequence written or rewritten, as will be seen, to give an improbable impression of Roman innocence, but the gospel accounts throughout are interspersed with vitriolic comments and negative references directed against Pharisees and, in the case of John's Gospel, simply Jews.

This reaches its highest pitch in the ritual denunciations in Matthew, attributed to Jesus, for example: "Woe to you, scribes and Pharisees, hypocrites! for you cleanse the outside of the cup and of the plate, but inside they are full of extortion and rapacity."

Luke repeats some of the comments in another context but such sayings, following Crossan's principles, do not appear to have a degree of independent attestation.

If there were throughout the gospels a range of attributed sayings of Jesus and reported sayings and actions of the Pharisees which gave only negative portrayals, then it would have to be said that this probably represented Jesus' true relationship with this group. The Pharisees would be the enemy, against whom Jesus is presenting a counter philosophy.

But the gospels are in fact replete with examples which show the Pharisees as sympathetic to Jesus and as acting as his friend and helper, if not his ally. The same sort of pattern emerges as in the case of the denial of Jesus' family: it takes just a little scrutiny to find the evidence of the position as it was, before the insertion of bias.

For example, in Luke (13:31) Pharisees are reported as coming to Jesus whilst he was in Galilee to warn him to leave because the Roman-appointed ruler Herod Antipas was seeking to kill him. This would have been a real threat and possibility since this was the same Herod Antipas, son of the infamous King Herod, who had previously carried out a cold-blooding "precautionary" execution on John the Baptist.

Jesus is reported as eating at the table of Pharisees. Two prominent members of the group, Nicodemus and Joseph of Arimathaea, who were also members of the Sanhedrin, are described as his sympathizers. Nicodemus is also reported to have come to talk to Jesus at night; one wonders what precisely needed to be discussed at such a time and presumably in such great secrecy. Both men were involved in assisting immediately after Jesus was taken down from the cross. Joseph of Arimathaea, as Mark reports, asked Pilate to release the body to him.

The leader of the Pharisees at that time was Gamaliel. The gospels do not say what his relationship to Jesus was. However, not long after the Crucifixion, Peter and some of the other Apostles are reported in Acts as being arrested by the High Priest and some of his Sadducee followers. Their alleged crime was to continue preaching about Jesus, after having been told to desist.

They were then brought for trial for their lives before the highest Jewish authority, the Sanhedrin.

However, the Pharisee leader Gamaliel interceded on their behalf, arguing that they should be left alone; "for if this plan or this undertaking is of men, it will fail; but if it is of God, you will not be able to overthrow them. You might even be found opposing God!" (Acts 5:38–39).

Gamaliel's attitude, in the aftermath of Jesus' Crucifixion, could be described as one of at least positive neutrality. His diplomatic intervention ensured the release of these men who had known Jesus and were some his key followers. In view of which, it hardly seems likely that the Pharisees, whose leader was Gamaliel, had been Jesus' sworn enemies only a few months earlier.

The conclusion which I suggest should be drawn is this. The elements which indicate a friendly relationship between Jesus and the Pharisees, persisting despite the evident introduced bias in the gospels, are authentic and represent the more likely, true picture.

An indication of the way in which bias was introduced is shown in the two versions of a conversation reported between Jesus and a Pharisaic "scribe", whose role can best be described as a biblical lawyer concerned with the exegesis of scripture. These are quoted at the start of this chapter. For insight into these alternative descriptions of the same event, I am indebted to the analysis provided by Hyam Maccoby.

In the earlier Gospel, Mark, the conversation is described in definitely civil and friendly tones. The Pharisee appears motivated by curiosity and admiration "seeing that he answered the Sadducees well". Jesus gives a good response. The questioner responds in agreement, reiterating what Jesus says, and adds a comment of his own to the effect that love is greater than sacrificial offerings. Jesus replies with his own complimentary remark.

The second version, in the later Gospel of Matthew, is based on Mark's story. But the entire element of friendly exchange has now been eliminated. The Pharisees are no longer motivated by admiration; they get together and put forward one of their number to "test" Jesus, that is to try to catch him out. The passage ends with Jesus' first reply so that, rather than being shown as a meeting of minds, as in Mark, the response now appears as a put-down.

Indeed, nowadays many Christian interpreters read Jesus as substituting Jewish Law with his own philosophy. But, since the original version in Mark shows the Pharisees and Jesus in agreement on what the most central commandments in the Law are, that cannot be the case. In addition to which, the two injunctions put forward by Jesus, to love God and to love your neighbor, are actually verses quoted from Deuteronomy and Leviticus in the Hebrew bible and both are central principles to Judaism.

Putting these principles together may well have been Jesus' own original contribution, but it does not seem at all that he is advocating that the rest of the Torah should be disregarded. Indeed, there are references in the gospels which show Jesus as taking a very tough stance towards observing the Law, especially on the question of divorce. He argued that too many exceptions had been allowed to creep in so that "every one who divorces his wife, except on the ground of unchastity, makes her an adulteress; and whoever marries a divorced woman commits adultery." (Matthew 5:32).

In discussions with Jewish scholars, "scribes" whose whole occupation was biblical explanation, Jesus is shown in the gospels as thoroughly at ease and always able to deal with questions. This suggests that he had acquired a greater knowledge and understanding than would have been picked up by daily attendance at the Temple and in the normal course of his education. If Jesus was on an equal footing with those whose job was biblical interpretation after years of training, then this indicates that he also had spent some time studying.

There are other ways in which Jesus is said to have shown disregard for Jewish Law, for example by carrying out faith healing on the Sabbath. However, it was in fact a Pharisee doctrine that the saving of life took precedence over Sabbath observance and healing on the Sabbath was not in fact forbidden. So Jesus was merely carrying out in practice what the Pharisees allowed in theory.

The suggestions in the gospels (Mark 3:6) that the Pharisees starting plotting against him as a result of his Sabbath healing can only therefore be an editorial distortion, made to create the impression of a conflict between Jesus and the Pharisees which did not in fact exist.

The story of the disciples plucking ears of corn on the Sabbath, quoted from Mark's gospel above, provides further insight into the real position. Plucking corn on the Sabbath was forbidden, like other forms of work on this day, so Jesus and his followers were apparently breaking the Law.

But Jesus is quoted as giving in his defense a parallel example from scripture where failing to observe the letter of the Law was allowed in circumstances of extreme danger to life. Thus David and his soldiers, suffering from starvation and fleeing from Saul, were justified in eating the consecrated unleavened bread (shrewbread) which only the priests were allowed to eat.

But the clear implication from the argument put forward is that Jesus and his disciples were at that time in a similar state. This at first seems very curious, but there is really no other interpretation from the analogy which Jesus is shown to make.

If it is remembered that the times were turbulent and there were desperate struggles going on, which the gospels for the most part carefully avoid, then the text becomes very much clearer.

What appears superficially in Mark's Gospel as a Saturday afternoon stroll through the cornfields, a story out of context, is really something else. Jesus and his followers did have to make an escape to save their lives, as the incident in Luke involving the Pharisees' warning indicates. This provides, as Maccoby suggests, a possible context for the story. Fleeing from the might of Herod Antipas, who is concerned to stamp out another possible John the Baptist, they arrive in Judaea weary and hungry and pluck the corn to stay alive. According to an early manuscript, possibly generated by an Ebionite community maintaining the Nazoraean tradition, the state of starvation of the disciples was the reason and the legal justification for their action.

The Pharisees' question about the disciples eating corn, not at all hostile as it appears in Mark, is therefore met with a response which is sensible both in terms of the real situation and Jewish Law. Jesus ends by quoting a Pharisaic principle that "the Sabbath was made for man, not man for the Sabbath". So, in paraphrase, the Son of Man, meaning here humanity or mankind rather than Jesus himself, is lord even of the Sabbath.

What is intriguing about the corn-plucking story is that it lifts the lid a little to give a glimpse of the real picture of Palestine at the time. It was a place seething with discontent at foreign occupation, physical repression and extortionate taxation. The enemies, as far as ordinary Jews were concerned, were the Romans, the collaborating High Priest's faction and the still-wealthy Herodian extended family and their hangers-on. Jesus was on the side of the people and so, from time to time, he was a hunted man.

He had supporters who were there not just to help heal and preach but also to protect him. There are occasional references in the gospels which show that some of Jesus' followers carried weapons. It is quite possible that there was a core group who was permanently armed. Once again, the likely reality differs considerably from what is now the taken-for-granted gospel script.

Jesus was not, as these examples have shown, opposed to the Pharisees. On the contrary his thinking and interpretations of the Law and theirs were generally in accordance. So what is the point of the editorial overlay in the gospels suggesting that there was a conflict between them?

The object was simple. Jesus was really, like many other figures that arose at this time, a rebel against Roman occupation, though he directed his attention chiefly or possibly even exclusively to Sadducean collaborators with Rome. It would appear that he also sought to focus effort on generating a sort of spiritual empire, a kingdom of heaven on earth, a world of spirit and spiritual values which could exist notwithstanding and alongside the brutal reality of political domination, repression and power. Jesus knew the bible history of Israel's occupation by foreign powers. People of his parent's generation had experienced the terrible price paid by thousands of Jews in the revolts which happened after Herod's death, just a few years before. Jesus would have also have heard their testimony. So he was careful to avoid a confrontation with Rome that could not be won. As will be seen, the messianic movement had other faces. There were others less patient than Jesus, more anxious for action and prepared to engage in a political and even military battle.

Jesus alone among all the prophets, charismatic characters and messianic preachers became the object of a religion which, under the auspices of Roman rule, was directed towards converting the Roman world. So the gospel stories were written or rewritten to make the Romans not the point of conflict, but as far as possible blameless. This new religion furthermore had to be made separate from Judaism, even though Jesus and his immediate followers, the Nazoraeans, were conforming Jews. So Jesus was rewritten in the script as being opposed to the Jewish religion, which neatly resolved both problems in one go, even though surviving references show that the Pharisees were friendly and his allies.

It should be added that this is also in spite of the fact that the gospels and the Acts of the Apostles show Jesus and his followers worshipping with, and attending the same synagogues as, their fellow Jews. Jesus, as will be seen, may have had some help from a community of the "poor" in Jerusalem, who were also Jews. He would not have generated much popular support by attacking the fundamentals of Judaism, as opposed to the powerful though corrupt clique of the Rome-appointed High Priest.

It is possible to see why the distancing of Jesus from his origins and objectives happened. But how did it all come about?

The answer is that it happened largely as the result of the efforts of one man, the so-called "Apostle" Paul, saintly Church founder, self-created from the murderous persecutor of early followers of Jesus, known as Saul.

As outlined at the beginning of this chapter, Paul or Saul was active and wrote his letters to early Gentile "Christian" communities before the gospels were edited. These letters show a power struggle between Paul and the real followers of Jesus, the Nazoraeans, and also indicate how surprisingly little Paul's character had changed. Egotistical, devious, manipulative, power-hungry and amoral, Paul's claim to virtue lay in his Damascus-road revelation, if that ever happened.

He might have failed in his enterprise, had not the first Jewish uprising led to the Nazoraeans being all but wiped out. Following the suppression of that revolt, the Romans banned not Judaism itself but messianic groups like the Nazoraeans. They did so because they understood correctly that the basis of rebellion was the move to restore the Jewish throne. It was only seventy years later, after a second rebellion had been crushed, that a "Church" was reestablished in Jerusalem. But now all trace of its origins had been eliminated, because this new Church was a "Christian" establishment carrying out new practices and following beliefs which would have been anathema to the Jewish, Torah-observing Nazoraeans.

The story of the struggle between Paul and the Church of James, which led to the creation of a new religion, is written in the letters of Paul and in the Acts of the Apostles.

CHAPTER II

THE RELIGION OF SAUL

For all who rely on works of the law are under a curse; for it is written, "Cursed be every one who does not abide by all things written in the book of the law, and do them." Now it is evident that no man is justified before God by the law; for "He who through faith is righteous shall live"; but the law does not rely on faith, for "He who does them shall live by them." Christ redeemed us from the curse of the law, having become a curse for us–for it is written, "Cursed be every one who hangs on a tree"– that in Christ Jesus the blessing of Abraham might come upon the Gentiles, that we might receive the promise of the Spirit through faith.

    Galatians 3:10–14

What does it profit, my brethren, if a man says he has faith but has not works? Can his faith save him? If a brother or sister is ill-clad and in lack of daily food, and one of you says to them, "Go in peace, be warmed and filled," without giving them the things needed for the body, what does it profit? So faith by itself, if it has no works, is dead.

    The Letter of James 2:14–17

Now I, Paul, say to you that if you receive circumcision, Christ will be of no advantage to you. I testify again to every man who receives circumcision that he is bound to keep the whole law. You are severed from Christ, you who would be justified by the law; you have fallen away from grace. For through the Spirit, by faith, we wait for righteousness. For in Christ Jesus neither circumcision nor uncircumcision is of any avail, but faith working through love.

    Galatians 5: 2–6

When we had come to Jerusalem, the brethren received us
gladly. On the following day Paul went in with us to James;
and all the elders were present. After greeting them, he related
one by one the things that God had done among the Gentiles
through his ministry. And when they heard it, they glorified
God.
And they said to him, "You see, brother, how many thousands
there are among the Jews of those who have believed; they are
all zealous for the law, and they have been told about you that
you teach all the Jews who are among the Gentiles to forsake
Moses, telling them not to circumcise their children or observe
the customs. What then is to be done? They will certainly hear
that you have come."
"Do therefore what we tell you. We have four men who are
under a vow; take these men and purify yourself along with
them and pay their expenses, so that they may shave their
heads. Thus all will know that there is nothing in what they
have been told about you but that you yourself live in
observance of the law. But as for the Gentiles who have
believed, we have sent a letter with our judgment that they
should abstain from what has been sacrificed to idols and from
blood and from what is strangled and from unchastity."

Acts 21:17–26

The conventional picture of Paul, a major figure in the development
of the early Christian Church was that he was a Pharisee, studied
under the Pharisee leader Gamaliel and persecuted some of the early
"Christians" under the authority of the High Priest. He is recorded as
participating in the martyrdom of Stephen who was stoned to death. But
on a journey to Damascus, with the purpose of arresting more "Christian"
followers who had taken refuge there, he had a vision of Jesus. This
experience was so traumatic, by his own account, that he was temporarily
blinded.

He became, as a result of this, a follower of Jesus and set about the mission
of converting the Gentiles, that is those outside Judaism, to what he
described as "Christian" faith. He claimed that the truth was personally
revealed to him by Jesus in a series of visions; the essence of the message was
that Jesus was both human and divine, sent by God to earth to save
mankind, a mission achieved through the sacrifice of Jesus on the cross.

What was required for personal salvation was faith in these beliefs, as opposed to the emphasis in Judaism–as Paul would have it–on mere observance of religious rules.

For an exposition of Paul's views, there exist letters which predate the gospels and which were written by him to some of the Early Church communities. These are incorporated in the New Testament among a number of letters, including some probably wrongly attributed to Paul. There is also a later account, probably written by the author of Luke's Gospel, of some parts of Paul's life and his relations with the early Nazoraean Church in the Acts of the Apostles.

The problem with the conventional view of Paul, or Saul as he was known before his conversion, is that there are both internal discrepancies in this record and also discrepancies with what is known of Judaism and the early Nazoraeans at this time.

For example, it is confirmed from Ebionite sources that Paul originally came from Tarsus in Sicily. But these sources suggest that, far from being born a Jew, his parents were Gentiles and he was converted to Judaism. If he studied under the Pharisees, it could not have been with great effect because his writing does not appear to show a deep understanding of Jewish custom and religion. His quotes from the bible are all from the Greek translation, the Septuagint, rather than from the Hebrew original–which he would have known well, had he been a Pharisee scholar.

As Maccoby points out, Paul's arguments also appear to lack the logic and understanding of Pharisaic thought. Thus, for example, in the first of the passages quoted above Paul interprets a passage from Deuteronomy to suggest that anyone hanged on a gibbet is under a curse. In fact, according to the Pharisees, the curse came from leaving the body hanging overnight. The manner of a person's death, often being outside of the individual's control, did not of itself constitute a curse. Indeed, even in the case of a capital offense, the individual by undergoing punishment expiated his crime. In many instances, in Jewish eyes, there was no crime at all since the Romans crucified people who were highly regarded in the community. Paul's argument in this passage is a loose association of ideas not linked by any logic, and his manifest concern is to denigrate the Jewish Law or Torah.

The High Priest for whom Paul worked was a Sadducee and a pro-Roman appointee. Besides ceremonial authority in relation to the Jewish community in Jerusalem and Judaea, the High Priest had a lot of political clout deriving from his status in relation to Rome. He had his armed police force, presided over a police tribunal and operated a penal system for both civil and religious offenses. He could have offenders imprisoned or flogged, although the Romans retained jurisdiction for capital offenses.

The Pharisees, despite the distortions created in the gospels, were as has been shown broadly sympathetic to Jesus and his followers. Unlike the Sadducee High Priest's faction, they were also not at all hostile to the early Nazoraean Church under James.

So, on all these grounds, it is unlikely that Paul was genuinely a Pharisee. Rather, he got himself a position as a police enforcer attached to the High Priest's faction among the Sadducees, to which the Pharisees were opposed. Paul's role was to round up and have imprisoned those subject to the High Priest's disapproval; it was not exactly a job which would have made him popular among ordinary Jews.

Paul claimed to be a Roman citizen by birth, and in the Acts of the Apostles this is what saved him when he was threatened with an assassination plot. The Roman captain of the citadel in Jerusalem, on discovering that Paul was a Roman citizen, provided him with a huge escort of soldiers to take him to the Roman governor Felix. There are grounds for believing that Paul was part of the Herodian lineage, possibly tracing descent back to one of the many wives and concubines of Herod the Great. In which case, he did have a good case to be a citizen by birth. The Romans had bestowed citizenship on Herod and his offspring for the service rendered in bringing Israel under Roman rule.

If Paul had Herodian family links and was from the outset a Roman citizen, this provides a further reason why he would have found it hard to form an alliance with Peter, James and the other Apostles after his Damascus revelation. The Nazoraeans constituted a messianic movement within Judaism, and were as such opposed to the Roman occupation and the collaboration of the Herodian dynasty. James and the others were suspicious of Paul not merely because he had persecuted some of their number. They were also very wary of his connections and his highly personal and sometimes aggressive approach.

In a number of ways, Paul sought to aggrandize himself and diminish the Apostles. These were relatives, friends and confidants of Jesus who had actually known him during his lifetime. Paul, it should be emphasized, never met Jesus, except though the experience of a vision for which there is only Paul's word. He claimed direct divine revelation from Jesus and he claimed that Jesus was acting through him and in him, thus making himself also semi-divine.

Paul was quite unashamed about the fact that he dissembled about himself, whenever he thought it necessary. He put on whatever appearance he thought best suited to achieving his ends, and he was utterly and unscrupulously focused on getting his way.

In a revealing passage in a letter to the Corinthians (1 9:20–23), this is what he had to say:

To the Jews I became as a Jew, in order to win Jews; to those under the law

I became as one under the law–though not being myself under the law–that I might win those under the law. To those outside the law I became as one outside the law–not being without law toward God but under the law of Christ–that I might win those outside the law. To the weak I became weak, that I might win the weak. I have become all things to all men, that I might by all means save some. I do it for the sake of the gospel, that I may share in its blessings.

Paul adds, using imagery redolent of Olympian contest, that he did not "run aimlessly" or "box as one beating the air". He played to win, by whatever means.

The level of deception that Paul was prepared to practice is shown in the passages from his letter to the Galatians and from the Acts of the Apostles given at the start of this chapter. He was actually advocating abandonment of adherence to the Torah, Jewish dietary practice and the rite of circumcision in his contacts with, and letters to, the Gentile Churches he was in process of establishing. But at the same time he was also seeking to maintain a position within the framework of the apostolic community of Jesus' followers led by James–who were Jews firmly advocating strict adherence to the Judaic Law!

James and the other leaders would not have had before them copies of the letters Paul wrote (fortunately perhaps for Paul) but they had enough information to suspect strongly that he was speaking against circumcision and other aspects of Jewish custom and law.

So what they ultimately did was make him go through a purification ritual that amounted both to a public penance and declaration of allegiance. This would have helped counteract what Paul had been saying and make it easier for the Jerusalem community, in its own missions to the Gentiles, to correct the false doctrines that Paul had spread.

Paul underwent this humiliation because he still at that point wanted to maintain the continuity with Jewish tradition, albeit for his own purposes, and because he was under threat. As James is reported to have said, "they–the tens of thousands (myriades) of Nazoraean followers among the Jews–will certainly hear that you have come."

Luke, the author of the Acts, is motivated to make a bridge from the Jesus and the Apostles of the gospels through to the doctrines taught by Paul. He also wants to convey an impression of fellowship and unity. But he cannot disguise in his account the dramatic dissension between Paul and his followers and the Nazoraean community led by James in Jerusalem.

Paul was summoned before the Jerusalem elders and was forced to make a humiliating recantation. It is all there in the quote from Acts given above without any "take", apart from the gratuitous over-friendliness described at the beginning, before James launches into his accusations. It is not the image that the Christian Church has chosen to present of its founding father, Paul.

To go back to the start of Saul's second life as the "Christian" Paul, it seems that his objective as an agent of the High Priest was to try to kidnap and bring back for trial and imprisonment militant Nazoraeans who had fled to Damascus for safety. Because Damascus was not at that time under Roman rule, having been ceded to the Nabataean King Aretas, this was a highly dubious if not illegal activity. James and some of the other Apostles were according to Acts left unmolested, presumably because they held a more pacifist view.

So Paul went after the more militant of Jesus' followers. But, while he was on the road to Damascus, he had a vision of Jesus and was blinded. He then entered the city and was cured of his blindness by Ananias, one of the followers he had previously been intent on arresting.

Presumably because he was correctly perceived as an infiltrater infringing Nabataean rights and sovereignty, Paul had to escape from King Aretas, let down in a basket from the city wall. (II Corinthians 11:32–33).

He then went to James and the other Apostles in Jerusalem and allied himself with their cause. They must have viewed this sudden apparent transformation of their one-time dedicated foe with a considerable degree of unease and concern.

Paul chose to address his mission to the Gentiles, the wider non-Jewish world. But what he preached was effectively a fundamentally different religion. The Jerusalem community on the other hand regarded themselves as Jews, differentiated from their fellows only in their beliefs that Jesus had been the awaited Messiah, that is an earthly king, who would return to restore a kingdom on earth for the Jews.

Paul had a different idea of a "Messiah" which became in Greek translation the "Christ", a divine person sent by God, sacrificed for the salvation of the entire world. This was a type of figure familiar to the followers of Hellenistic mystery cults. But it would have been alien to the Nazoraean Jews and Jesus himself–when all the additions and alterations to his character in the gospels are stripped away.

It would seem that Paul wanted to maintain the link with Judaism in order to give the religion he promoted historical credentials going back in time, so increasing its appeal and credibility with the Greek-speaking and Roman worlds. He also wanted to avoid a damaging clash with those who in reality had a better claim, having known and worked with Jesus.

So that is why Paul became "all things to all men", telling his Gentile converts that they need not follow the Jewish Law whilst maintaining outwardly to the Nazoraeans an appearance as a Pharisee, still conforming to the Law.

Such inconsistent positions, and the deceptions that went with them, clearly could not be maintained indefinitely.

There was, as it happens, an already well-defined provision for Gentiles who wished to follow the precepts of Judaism. They could either become full converts, by being circumcised and accepting the full requirements of Jewish Law, or they could attain the status of "god fearers". To undertake the latter, they were required to follow laws believed to have been given to Noah by God forbidding idolatry, blasphemy, murder, robbery and fornication, that is sexual activity regarded as unlawful. In addition, there was an injunction not to eat meat with blood in it and to make provision for a justice system to administer these laws.

By following these prescriptions, Jews believed that the rest of mankind, that is the Gentile world, could also attain a state of righteousness.

The rules which Jews had to follow were more detailed and onerous, especially with regard to dietary law. Certain types of meat, such as rabbit and pork were proscribed, as well as all meat from which the blood had not been drained. This meant that Jews and Gentiles, whether "god fearers" or not, could not eat the same food. But they might possibly be able to eat at the same table, providing there had been no offerings to "idols" and providing the foods allowed to Jews and Gentiles were kept clearly separate and not mixed.

Word reached the Jerusalem community that Paul in his practice and teaching was simply ignoring any dietary restrictions. This was almost certainly the case because Paul, as shown in his letters, believed or maintained that the divine Jesus, as personally revealed to him, had abolished the distinction between Jews and Gentiles and the need to follow the Torah.

Paul, together with his close associate Barnabas, was thus summoned for the first time to go before the Apostles and elders in Jerusalem. There followed a discussion, described in Acts, of the status of Gentile followers, especially whether they should be obliged to become full converts to Judaism. The final ruling was given by James:

> *Therefore my judgment is that we should not trouble those of the Gentiles who turn to God, but should write to them to abstain from the pollutions of idols and from unchastity and from what is strangled and from blood. For from early generations Moses has had in every city those who preach him, for he is read every Sabbath in the synagogues.*
>
> Acts 15:19–21

These prohibitions present a shortened summary of the Noahide rules which applied to those among the Gentiles who wished to attain the status of god fearers. Some interpretation is, however, necessary. Blood had to be drained away so meat from animals which had merely been strangled would not be acceptable. The requirement for abstention "from blood", if not a repetition, presumably was a requirement to abstain from shedding blood, that is from killing or committing murder.

James also made the point that there were already enough people within the ranks of Judaism: the religion therefore did not need to recruit full converts from the ranks of the Gentiles to ensure its future.

So what was established by the meeting (often called the Jerusalem Council) was really a recapitulation of the existing position for Gentiles. The Nazoraean movement would follow the position for the Jewish religion as a whole. There would be a separate category of Gentiles believers, not full converts but nonetheless bound by certain laws.

It would appear that Paul, on the other hand, felt that he had achieved a dispensation to do much as he liked. By his account, in his subsequent letter to the Galatians, it had been agreed that he would have missionary authority to the Gentiles. He writes scathingly of "false brethren" sent to spy on his activities and describes, with scarcely veiled contempt, James and Cephas (either Simon Peter or Simon/Simeon bar Cleophas) and John as "reputed pillars" of society.

He claims that the only thing that had been required was that he "should remember the poor"–the very thing that he was eager to do. But what "the poor" meant here is not how a contemporary Christian Church might now define it, the intended recipients of money placed after the service in collecting boxes! "The poor" were the Jewish Nazoraeans, central and founding members of the sect. This was also, it will be recalled, the word that the Essenes applied to themselves.

James, as well as restating the Noahide rules for Gentile "god fearers" or associates (which Paul then ignored), wanted to remind Paul not to neglect their core constituency. Go after the Gentiles by all means, said James, but don't forget our followers.

Just what I was going to do, asserted Paul, and then he clearly omitted to do that too.

Paul's account of what had happened in his letter to the Galatians differs substantially from the one given in Acts and it would appear primarily to be Paul's effort at self-justification.

The Apostle Peter subsequently visited Paul at Antioch. At first all went well, until Peter realized that the Jewish rules on eating food were not being observed. Paul writes in Galatians that he opposed Peter face to face who, despite having known Jesus and worked with Jesus, was in Paul's eyes clearly in the wrong! Paul blamed James, as leader of the Nazoraean community, for sending people to spy on him. "For before certain men came from James, he [that is, Cephas/Peter] ate with the Gentiles; but when they came he drew back and separated himself, fearing the circumcision party." (Galatians 2:12)

The gulf was widening between Paul and the Nazoraeans. These were the real followers who had, in many cases, personally known Jesus and had a better claim to know his teaching. The culminating crisis came when Paul was again summoned before the Nazoraean elders in Jerusalem and made to undergo a humiliating purification ritual, reaffirming his full belief in the Jewish Law.

Paul was certainly under very real threat as James warned, "they will certainly hear that you have come."

At the end of his seven-day purification ritual in the Temple, Paul was spotted and dragged from the Temple by "Asian Jews" who objected to his teaching against the Torah. These were possibly people he had encountered in his missionary teachings in Galatia. But then Paul was rescued by the Roman police, whom he may well have summoned himself on the basis that he was a Roman citizen. He may also have had some sway through links with the Herodian family.

The use of his citizenship certainly saved Paul, but this may also have further damaged his already strained relations with the James and the Jerusalem community.

Acts now describes how the Roman commandant decided to bring Paul before the Sanhedrin to try to discover the facts behind the disturbance.

Paul there faced another enemy, the High Priest, under whose office he had been employed to root out Jewish followers of Jesus but instead had defected to the other side.

The High Priest would have seen Paul as a traitorously disloyal employee and a troublemaker.

Paul portrayed himself in his adopted role of pious Pharisee, winning the votes of the Pharisees on the Sanhedrin, and managed to get himself set free. It must be assumed that the members of the Sanhedrin were not aware of the views he had expressed in preaching to the Gentile proto-Christian communities, that the Torah was in effect a dead letter.

Next, came a failed attempt to assassinate Paul by a group of Jewish conspirators whom the author of Acts describes as associated with the chief priests, elders and council, that is the Sanhedrin. This may well not be all that precise since the Sanhedrin had just acquitted Paul. So this action was more likely instigated by the High Priest and his own faction within the council.

When the plot to kill to get Paul failed, the High Priest then proceeded to press charges against Paul before the Roman authorities. Paul was eventually taken to Rome and held for a while under some form of house arrest or protective custody. This is where the account in Acts ends in about AD 62, just before the death of James. It seems possible that Paul may then have returned to Jerusalem, reappearing again as Saul in the pages of Josephus.

There is no doubt about the bitterness of the dispute between Paul and the early followers of Jesus, which led to the final break and the creation of rival camps with different versions of the teachings of Jesus.

There are accounts among Ebionite sources, the *pseudoClementine Recognitions*, of an "enemy" intervening in a public debate in Jerusalem between James and the Apostles on the one hand and the High Priest Caiaphas and the other priests on the other. This person incited the priests to attack the Apostles, causing a riot. He personally attacked James, pushing him down the Temple steps, injuring James' legs and making him at least temporarily lame. In a marginal note to one manuscript, the enemy is identified as Paul. This is supported by a description of the enemy, presumably Paul, then securing authority and setting out for Damascus either to arrest or kill all those believing in Jesus. It was in just this way in Acts that Paul, before his conversion, embarked on his persecution of the Nazoraeans.

The difficulty is that it is hard to believe that Paul could have established friendly relations with the Nazoraeans, even for a time and even after a miraculous conversion, had he previously physically assaulted James and pursued some of the disciples including Peter to Damascus with murderous intent. According to Acts, it will be remembered, the Apostles themselves were left alone during a persecution aimed, it can be presumed, at more radical messianic elements.

The *pseudoClementine Recognitions*, which provide parallel evidence on the activities of Paul, are fictionally attributed, hence "pseudo", to a character called Clement of Rome. Clement lived towards the end of the first century and is portrayed in story form, again fictionally, as having accompanied Simon Peter on his missionary journeys.

The Ebionites were regarded as heretical by early Christians and their writings were suppressed. What survives suggests that they were aware of the tradition of the Crucifixion and resurrection and had access to a written source describing it, either the Gospel of Peter or something akin to it.

The Ebionites (in Hebrew, "poor ones") not only represented an intellectual continuation of the Nazoraean tradition; they were probably physically descended from the remnants of that movement following the collapse of the first Jewish rebellion, AD 66–70. They revered James, practiced circumcision and followed the Torah. They were hostile towards Paul, with probable good reason, whom they blamed for intervening in an interactive debate in which James and the other Nazoraean followers of Jesus were rapidly gaining converts among ordinary Jews. That intervention came, according to *Recognitions*, in the form of a riot and assault on James instigated by "a certain hostile man", generally accepted to have been Paul. In a passage, which echoes the description in Acts of James' following in thousands or even tens of thousands, *Recognitions* states:

For by the zeal of God we more and more were steadily increasing more than they. Then even their priests were afraid, lest by the providence of God the whole people might come over to our faith, to their own confusion.

In the same passage, the essential Jewishness of the Nazoraeans is reiterated with the comment that "only on this is there a difference between us, we who believe in Jesus, and those sons of our faith who do not believe."

Paul did certainly deceive and betray the Nazoraean Jews, followers of Jesus, for what Paul believed to be greater ends. He pretended to conform, while telling potential Gentile converts that they need not follow the Torah or Jewish practices including dietary restrictions and circumcision. He ignored provisions intended to maintain ritual purity for Jews eating with Gentiles. In these ways he acted secretly and surreptitiously to undermine the Nazoraeans' Jewish religion.

It can only be said that the evidence suggests that, far from being reformed, Paul's character–vain, deceitful, power seeking, manipulative and unscrupulous–remained consistent throughout his life. The conversion which he proclaimed happened on the road to Damascus did not lead to a fundamental personal change. Saul and Paul were the same person, except that, as Paul from then on, he used the Nazoraeans in a different and ultimately more destructive way.

Paul's philosophy of a divine savior prevailed because he associated himself with the Romans who were the source of power, because he ingeniously built on the roots of pagan beliefs, because he addressed a wider audience and a wider world and because the Nazoraeans were killed or dispersed and their messianism proscribed as a result of the subsequent Jewish uprising. He also had one advantage, a real one that he was not prone to boast about.

He was, it appears, related to the Herodian family and its network of power. There is a glimpse of this in Paul's letter to the Romans where he addresses a kinsman as Herodian or "little Herod". The implication is clear: if this person was a member of the Herodian extended family, then so too was Paul. Beyond this, there is the question of how Paul acquired his Roman citizenship; if by birth, then it would have been through his connection with the Herodian royal family.

Paul also was sufficiently important to be saved by the Roman Captain of the Temple Guard and provided with a substantial protective escort, which Acts describes with possible exaggeration as "70 horsemen, 200 soldiers and 200 spearsmen".

There was a character called Saul described by Josephus, operating at about the same time as the Saul or Paul of the New Testament, who was certainly related to the Herodian royal family and who was a man of some influence. This Saul first appears together with his brother Costobar, following the death of James, enjoying a degree of patronage because of their kinship with King Agrippa II. Josephus describes them as gathering a band of villains to "plunder the property of those weaker than themselves".

It is possible that this relates to the continuing persecution of some of the early Nazoraeans, in which the New Testament Saul had taken part. As described in Acts, Saul entered "house after house", and "dragged off men and women and committed them to prison". Plunder as payment does appear plausible in these circumstances.

Saul and Costobar, together with a cousin of theirs the Temple treasurer Antipas, next appear as the key figures in a delegation to their kinsman King Agrippa, inviting the king to intervene on the outbreak of the Jewish uprising in Jerusalem. Agrippa sent a considerable force of horsemen to bolster the Roman garrison, but the rebels gained control, killed the High Priest Ananias and massacred the garrison. Saul then went over to the Roman Commander Cestius Gallus and was then sent to Corinth to report to the Roman Emperor Nero on the situation in Palestine.

His disappearance from the text at this point fits in with the fate of Paul, who is believed to have been beheaded on the orders of the Emperor Nero in Rome around AD 68.

If Paul/Saul in Acts is the same person as Saul a little later in Josephus, this could clear up some difficulties. My suggestion is that there were two periods of clashes in which Paul was involved. The first, in which the young Saul or Paul took part, happened in the early days of the Nazoraean movement, as described in Acts. This was before Paul's conversion.

The second conflict took place after relations had utterly broken down between Paul and the Nazoraean community. It is beyond the time frame of Acts, and covers a period of years leading up to the Jewish revolt in AD 66, when I am presuming Paul had again returned to Jerusalem. The conflict involving Saul and Costobar is sketchily described by Josephus, but was I suggest once again a persecution of messianic followers of James and Jesus.

The *pseudoClementine Recognitions* include the crucially important detail of the "enemy" obtaining a commission from the Chief Priest Caiaphas with letters to take to Damascus in order to arrest believers in Jesus. This is precisely what the young Paul is described as doing in Acts (9:1–2). So *Recognitions* also describes the first conflict which took place, only a few years after the Crucifixion.

But *Recognitions* I suggest conflates this with a later assault on James leading up to his death, in which the "enemy" Paul may or may not have taken part.

Saul and Costobar were in place in Jerusalem, according to Josephus, using violence against the people and plundering the weak, just prior to the start of the Jewish revolt in AD 66. If this is the same Saul/Paul as in Acts, it suggests that Paul at the very least took advantage of the situation thrown up by the death of James arising from a confrontation with the Sadducean establishment. According to this scenario, he would have gone back to Jerusalem to exploit the power vacuum and confusion following the death of James and press home his authority on the Early Church. Then, at the beginning of the uprising, he went as part of a delegation to the Romans, seeking peace.

Saul went first to the Roman commander Cestius and then on to report to the Emperor Nero at Caesarea. This places the Saul of Josephus in contact with Nero at about the same time as Saul/Paul of the New Testament was executed. Paul's connections could not save his life during the persecution of Christians in Rome. But it may be that his Roman citizenship is what preserved him from the fate of being crucified or burned.

The analysis which I have given of Paul's relationship with James and the Nazoraeans, and his role in supplanting them with a different kind of Church, does not depend on the Saul in Josephus being the same person as Saul/Paul in the Letters and Acts. But there are a number of remarkable parallels and coincidences. These include the question of timing, character and behavior, relations with the Romans, connections with the Sadducee elite and a Herodian background. It does seem unlikely that there were two center-stage figures with such similarities, operating at the same time and sharing a not particularly common name. So my judgment is that the Saul described by Josephus may well have been the Saul who also appears in the New Testament.

If this identification is correct, then it only serves to underline how dangerous an adversary Paul was. It would also further explain how Paul and his followers had the power and influence subsequently to propagate a religion to suit the Roman world.

Paul's philosophy is certainly not that of the people who knew Jesus and were with him. Although Paul wrote his letters first, and so may have influenced what came to be written in the gospels, significant differences can be detected between what he advocated and what the gospel writers tell us were the teachings of Jesus.

Whereas Jesus' kingdom was going to be one of equals with hierarchical distinctions swept away, Paul constantly in his letters advocated adherence to the status quo. Slaves, he says, should obey their masters and wives their husbands. Jesus was an advocate and interpreter of Pharisaic thought while Paul by contrast saw Jewish Law as an encumbrance.

Like his brother James, Jesus saw actions as the key. He told the rich young men who had followed the commandments and wanted to know what more he should do, to divide his wealth among the poor. Paul by contrast advocated faith as the saving grace, and this was something he could use. Though it was faith in the risen Jesus, it was nonetheless faith in a version of Jesus mediated by Paul.

Some of the core values in Jesus' sayings can also be found in the letters. Jesus spelt out the twin principles of loving God and one's neighbor and Paul also places emphasis on the importance of love as well as faith.

But Paul nonetheless did was turn doctrines which were within the framework of Judaism into something else; he effectively by his own efforts invented Christianity. It should be remembered that his missionary work and his letters came first, before the gospels were widely disseminated.

A collection of the sayings of Jesus and a gospel source which no longer exists, but has been identified as a "*Cross Gospel*" (see chapter 10), may have been produced within a few years of the Crucifixion. But the canonical gospels that we now have were subsequently molded to follow the lead provided by Paul. These gospels were edited to distance Jesus from his Jewish origins and they continued the process of allowing the Gentile world to abandon the requirements of Jewish Law. Jesus became a divine figure, a savior sent to redeem all of mankind

But there are indications of an underlying reality that the editors and censors could not entirely disguise. As argued in the previous chapter, Jesus was a practicing Jew and in reality on good terms with most of his fellow Jews including the Pharisees. He would otherwise have had no following.

As was noted also in chapter two, Jesus is reported as saying (Matthew 15:21–28 and also Matthew 10:5–6) and that he was "sent only to the lost sheep of the House of Israel". That is because what he claimed to be was a Jewish Messiah, a king seeking to restore a Jewish kingdom on earth.

The way in which the Hellenistic religion created by Paul was written back into the gospel accounts of Jesus' life is nowhere better seen than in what has become the central ritual of Christianity, the communion meal or eucharist.

As it happens, there is no reference anywhere in the Acts of the Apostles to the followers of Jesus partaking of such a ritual meal. They had communal meals in which they "broke bread" together. In doing this, they were acting as Jews following the Jewish custom to initiate a meal where a loaf of bread is blessed, broken and pieces handed to those present. There is nothing in the Acts to indicate that there was a sacramental meal in which the body of Jesus, in the form of bread and his blood, in the form of wine, were mystically consumed. There is not even any mention of wine in any form.

Now this is odd, if it is believed that Jesus himself initiated for his followers a special ceremony in which he was to be symbolically consumed.

In fact, the earliest reference to such a ceremony comes in the writings of

Paul, in his first letter to the Corinthians:

> *For I received from the Lord what I also delivered to you, that*
> *the Lord Jesus on the night when he was betrayed took bread,*
> *and when he had given thanks, he broke it, and said, "This is*
> *my body which is for you. Do this in remembrance of me." In*
> *the same way also the cup, after supper, saying, "This cup is*
> *the new covenant in my blood. Do this, as often as you drink*
> *it, in remembrance of me." For as often as you eat this bread*
> *and drink the cup, you proclaim the Lord's death until he*
> *comes.*
>
> 1 Corinthians 11:23–26

It is clearly stated that this is not something which Paul picked up in conversation with other followers who knew Jesus. As with other aspects of his message, Paul claims to have received this directly "from the Lord", that is from Jesus himself. Since he did not meet Jesus in his lifetime, this can only mean that it was conveyed to him in one of the visionary experiences which Paul claims to have had. Paul in other words dreamed it or dreamed it up. There is no historical basis for the communion meal as something instigated by Jesus or his followers.

The gospels were written after Paul had written his letters and the gospel authors and editors would have had these letters available. But, more than that, by the time the gospels were written, it is likely that the Lord's supper ceremony had already become established among the Gentile "Christian" community arising from Antioch and split away from the Nazoraeans.

So the gospel writers merely justified what Paul had instigated and they followed what Paul had written. Paul is the source, based on his claimed or alleged vision. The eucharist, like the whole of the religion based on a divine savior, is essentially his invention.

What he did was take the elements of a normal Jewish meal in which bread would be blessed, broken and distributed and a cup of wine handed round and add the trappings of a mystery religion. The wine became the blood of the sacrificed God and the bread his body which the celebrants consumed. What he created, although it is the core ritual of Christianity, is a pagan sacrament.

In the Acts of the Apostles, an effort is made to portray the teaching of Paul as continuous with that of the Apostles and therefore of Jesus, but the very real conflict that occurred could not be disguised. The schism between Paul and the Nazoraeans, the followers of the Jesus, is confirmed by Paul's letters. Even the attempt in Acts to show Peter as wavering, adopting a half way position on the question of dietary prohibitions, fails. As Paul himself writes, Peter is shown to draw back when he realizes that the Gentiles at Antioch are not following the rules which the Jerusalem Council laid down.

History is largely written by the victors and the Romans were at this time the victors.

The new Christianity, as fashioned by Paul, advocated obedience of Rome. No longer the original Jewish messianic message of Jesus, this was a good religion for the empire to adopt. It was attractive to those formerly attached to pagan mystery cults and it had a long and respectable Jewish pedigree, courtesy of Paul's efforts to the last ditch to maintain such a link. But did it have another useful survival ingredient, a possible element of truth in the resurrection story which made it so attractive and initially caused "tens of thousands" to join the followers of Jesus under James?

Is there a chance that Rome did not have it all its own way and the Nazoraeans were not merely religious fanatics or "zealots" waiting for a miracle that could never happen? Was there a real Jesus who could have made another entrance, even though it never came?

The passion story, dismissed by some as pure invention and believed by others to be the gospel truth in every word, will need to be examined next.

CHAPTER 12

PASSION

And the soldiers led him away inside the palace (that is, the praetorium); and they called together the whole battalion. And they clothed him in a purple cloak, and plaiting a crown of thorns they put it on him. And they began to salute him, "Hail, King of the Jews!" And they struck his head with a reed, and spat upon him, and they knelt down in homage to him. And when they had mocked him, they stripped him of the purple cloak, and put his own clothes on him. And they led him out to crucify him.

And they compelled a passer-by, Simon of Cyrene, who was coming in from the country, the father of Alexander and Rufus, to carry his cross. And they brought him to the place called Gogotha (which means the place of a skull). And they offered him wine mingled with myrrh; but he did not take it. And they crucified him, and divided his garments among them, casting lots for them, to decide what each should take. And it was the third hour, when they crucified him.

And the inscription of the charge against him read, "The King of the Jews." And with him they crucified two robbers, one on his right and one on his left. And those who passed by derided him, wagging their heads saying, "Aha! You who would destroy the Temple and build it in three days, save yourself and come down from the cross!"

So also the chief priests mocked him to one another with the scribes, saying, "He saved others; he cannot save himself. Let the Christ, the King of Israel, come down now from the cross, that we may see and believe." Those who were crucified with him also reviled him.

And when the sixth hour had come, there was darkness over the whole land until the ninth hour. And at the ninth hour Jesus cried with a loud voice, "Eloi, Eloi, lama sabachthani?" which means, "My God, my God, why has thou forsaken me?" And some of the bystanders hearing it said, "Behold, he is calling Elijah." And one ran and, filling a sponge full of vinegar, put it *on a reed and gave it to him to drink, saying, "Wait, let us see whether Elijah will come to take him down." And Jesus uttered a loud cry, and breathed his last.*

Mark 15:16–37

———◦●◦———

Most people read the gospels as they stand, because it is by far the easiest course and also because that is all that they have readily available.

So I began the examination of the story of Jesus with a look at the gospels themselves to see what kind of man they showed Jesus to be. It very soon appeared that, on this evidence, Jesus was born in a normal way into a Jewish family in which he had several brothers and sisters. He had gifts for preaching and scriptural interpretation and he probably at some point studied to increase his knowledge. He was by no means perfect. He was a successful faith healer, and again it would seem he had gained some knowledge of the art of healing. A minority of the acts he carried out are portrayed as miracles, but this can be seen to be based on misunderstanding and misinterpretation.

He was almost certainly married.

Even on the evidence of material which had been written, or edited and rewritten, to make Jesus appear as divine and separate him from his family and origins, Jesus comes through as a character with a Jewish background and a mission directed to his own people. He may have claimed to be the Jewish Messiah, that is the anointed one, the Jewish king who would restore his people's kingdom on earth.

He did not claim to be or act as the divine personage created by early "Christian" writers who made him the God sacrificed to save, not just the Jews, but the whole of mankind.

An understanding of the historical context makes this clearer still. Jesus was one of several figures who staked a claim to be king, during a period under the oppression of foreign rule when the Jewish people yearned for their freedom.

His followers carried on after him in a community which operated fully within Judaism and fully adhered to Jewish Law and practices. They were led first by James and then by Simon, who were two of Jesus' brothers.

The gospels as edited made Jesus appear antagonistic towards the Pharisees with whom, as surviving references show, he in fact shared many beliefs and had a friendly relationship.

Jesus and subsequently his Nazoraean followers had a lot in common with groups at Qumran and elsewhere who called themselves the "poor", but who were described by others as Essenes, who shared or disavowed worldly goods.

Jesus advocated adherence to the Jewish Law and emphasized as central the twin principles of loving God and one's neighbor, both of which were key also to Pharisaic thought.

He espoused the cause of all the unfortunates in society: the destitute, the sick, those in mourning, the rejected, the hungry.

He believed practically in a kingdom that existed in its essentials in the present, that could be brought to greater fulfillment by individual acts and effort: the Kingdom of God on earth.

The Jewish "Messiah", anointed one or king, was translated into the Greek word "Christos", and given a different meaning–the God sacrificed for mankind. The "Christian" religion was invented for a wider world in which the Romans were dominant. For this reason, Jesus was separated in the gospels from his Jewish background and mission. The Jewish people, rather than the Romans who crucified him, were made to appear responsible for Jesus' death.

The self-appointed Apostle Saul or Paul created communities of followers based on Jesus' teaching. But Saul denied the new religion's Jewish origins by telling converts that they did not have to become circumcised or follow Jewish dietary restrictions. This led to a break with the Nazoraean community of followers who had known Jesus, led by his brother James.

The first mention of a ritual Lord's supper or eucharist, in which the body and blood of the sacrificed divine Jesus are symbolically or mystically consumed is by Paul–and he claims to have received knowledge from Jesus of this in a dream or revelation. Paul was largely the instigator of this new form of religion of Christianity, which was a term first applied to his followers at Antioch in Syria. It appears that, for good measure, he also invented the eucharist as the new religion's central ritual.

The great appeal of Christianity may have been precisely due to the continuity, which Paul and others created, with existing forms of Greek mystery religion. Its success also lay in the fact that, as it evolved, it offered no threat to Rome and was then later easily adapted as the empire's official religion.

But there were clearly other factors supporting the early growth of the movement. Before Paul came on the scene, the Nazoraeans as a sect within Judaism were by all accounts already immensely popular, with their thousands or possibly even tens of thousands of followers. It was a messianic movement. Jesus' followers offered their fellow Jews, still yearning for deliverance, a Messiah. They offered the message that Jesus had, following Crucifixion, been resurrected, was still alive and would return. They promised deliverance of a kind that was certainly spiritual and possibly, and more ambiguously, also political.

This was an appealing message and, because it was based on a promise and an interpretation of past events, it was one that was inherently hard to counter or disprove. But is it possible that there was something else, reappearances witnessed by many and passed on by word of mouth to many more? Was this the factor which cemented the appeal of the message with the need of the Jews, who heard it, into a compelling and popular doctrine?

The prime sources for the passion story, as for the sayings of Jesus and the tales of miracles, are the four New Testament gospels. It would appear, however, that the ultimate sources were different. The sayings, which came to be incorporated in Matthew and Luke's Gospel and possibly also the Gospel of Thomas, are believed to have come from a collection of sayings which were circulated very early on. This collection of sayings, whose independent existence is hypothetical rather than directly proven, has come to be known as the *Sayings Gospel Q*.

The passion narrative in the earlier Gospel of Mark was largely copied by the authors of Luke and Matthew. This in turn is believed to have come from an earlier source, which Crossan describes as the *"Cross Gospel"*, written within a few years of the death of Jesus.

Like the original book of sayings, there is no surviving *Cross Gospel*. There is a version in the later extracanonical Gospel of Peter which may be closest to it or, alternatively, the Gospels of Mark, John and Peter may all have used the *Cross Gospel* as a source.

Outside what may have been one original source, there is no independent historical evidence for the passion story other than brief references by Josephus in his *Jewish Antiquities* and by the Roman historian Tacitus in his *Annals*. Both refer to Jesus as having been executed. Later Christian editors may have added in some references to the resurrection which appear in Josephus' account. Their motivation would have been to increase the credibility of the resurrection, as an historical event, by having it authenticated by a contemporary Jewish historian.

There is a large amount of agreement on the passion story in the gospel accounts. However, it seems that Mark, followed by Luke and Matthew, provide an impossible timescale for all the events to happen leading up to the Crucifixion. They may have simply wanted to provide a précis of events. They may have also tried to disguise the fact that the Last Supper shared by Jesus and disciples, the Passover meal, did not take place on the day that it should have.

Since John's account leaves sufficient time, and also has the Passover meal on a day which in context makes sense, its timescale will be followed. The Gospel of Peter provides support for John, in that it has Jesus executed and taken down from the cross on the eve of Passover.

As far as the narrative is concerned, it needs to be recognized that only very limited reliance can be placed on actual words spoken. It was the custom at the time in historical writing for the narrator to supply speeches for what he thought the speaker would have, or should have, said in the circumstances. The gospels and for that matter other writings such as Josephus' description of the Jewish War are thus "pseudepigraphic".

So, to begin with, I shall give a summary of what I perceive to be the major elements in the narrative, minus most of the speeches. Then, I shall look at possible explanations.

Following the arrest and death of John the Baptist, Jesus began a preaching and healing ministry, wandering from place to place with a small band of followers or disciples, including at least two of his brothers. His mission began in Galilee and was extended to other areas including the country around Caesarea and also Judaea.

He attracted large crowds. To ease the burden of his ministry, he sent out some of his followers as Apostles to heal and preach upon his behalf.

On occasion, he asked those he had healed not to tell anyone what had happened, it would appear so as not to draw too much attention to his activities. He is also recorded by Luke as rebuking those he had healed of demons, that is mental illness, from attributing it as a work of God. This was for the same reason, so as not to appear to represent a challenge to the authorities.

But Jesus, in a roundabout way, told his disciples how he saw his mission. He asked them who other people thought he was and then who they thought he was. Peter replied "the Christ", for which read the Messiah or coming King of the Jews.

Jesus told them not to reveal this to anyone, again for presumably all the same reasons: claiming to be the Jewish king was a denial of Caesar's authority, an offense of treachery punishable by death.

Jesus is then reported to have told the disciples more than once that he would be killed but would rise again in three days.

Matthew describes how in Capernaum, a town that provided a base for Jesus in Galilee, Jesus and Peter discussed whether to pay the half-shekel Temple tax. Jesus claimed exemption as a son of the kings of the earth, that is the Messiah. But honor was satisfied by means of catching a fish to sell, specifically to pay the tax.

The Gospel of John describes how Jesus went to Jerusalem in October during the Feast of the Tabernacles and remained there after the Feast of the Dedication in December. This would have been, according to the timetable deduced for the trial and Crucifixion (see chapter 8), in AD 35. There is some support for this in the Gospel of Luke and in Mark, where there is a comment made by Jesus which refers to his teaching daily at the Temple.

Jesus left the area but returned, according to the Gospel of John only, to heal Lazarus who was Mary's brother and thus according to the analysis given earlier his brother-in-law. By the time Jesus arrived, Lazarus had been entombed, but Jesus is credited with raising him from the dead.

By this point, the High Priest Caiaphas and his followers felt that Jesus' activities would be regarded as seditious by the Romans and cause them to take military action against the Jewish nation as a whole. So they were looking for a way to have Jesus killed.

Jesus may then have returned to Galilee, following the synoptic Gospels (Mark, Matthew and Luke) or gone to Ephraim north of Jerusalem.

There was some speculation whether Jesus would attend the Feast of the Passover, the Jews' festival of liberation which commemorated Moses delivering his people from bondage in Egypt. The population of Jerusalem would be swelled by the arrival of hundreds of thousands of pilgrims. There may have been a plan to arrest Jesus to prevent any trouble.

But Jesus journeyed down through Jericho with a band of pilgrims. A blind beggar called after him as, "Jesus, Son of David", to heal him and Jesus obliged. This time, there was no move to rebuke the beggar for using a term which was in fact a messianic title.

According to the Gospel of John, Jesus arrived at Bethany where he had a meal provided at the house of Mary, who I suggested was his wife. Mary then anointed his feet with nard, or spikenard, a precious ointment reserved for ceremonies like the anointing of kings. This incident is described more elliptically in the Gospels of Matthew and Luke where an unnamed woman is described as anointing Jesus with "ointment".

By mingling with the pilgrims, Jesus was able to go from Bethany into Jerusalem unmolested and undetected, but with a protective band of followers. The Romans, who were used to large bands of followers arriving for the Jewish religious festivals, would have seen no cause to intervene.

According to the gospels, Jesus had arranged for an ass to be tethered and waiting so that he could ride into the city–apparently in deliberate fulfillment of the prophet Zechariah that the future King of Israel would arrive in Jerusalem in this way:

> *Rejoice greatly, O daughter of Zion!*
> *Shout aloud, O daughter of Jerusalem!*
> *Lo, your king comes to you; triumphant and victorious is he,*
> *humble and riding on an ass,*
> *on a colt the foal of an ass.*
>   Zechariah 9:9

The sign was recognized by the crowd who spread their clothes and palm leaves in the way for Jesus to ride over. There were proclamations both of Jesus as Messiah and the approaching restoration of the Kingdom of David.

Jesus did not, by any of the accounts, spend the night in Jerusalem in the week leading to the Feast of the Passover. He returned each night to Bethany with his followers while it was still light, to minimize the risk of being attacked by his enemies.

On the Monday before the Passover festival, Jesus went into the Temple and overturned the tables of the money-changers and the seats of those who sold the doves required for sacrifices. It was necessary, according to Jewish Law, to exchange the heathen coins stamped with the idolatrous images of Caesar for Jewish currency in order to buy the sacrificial doves and for other religious purposes. But the exchange rates, controlled by the chief priests, were artificially inflated so that they grew rich at the expense of the poor who found it ever harder to meet their obligations. According to the Gospel of John, which allows a more generous time scale, this event took place at a previous Passover Festival.

The following day, Jesus engaged in a debate in the Temple with representatives of the High Priest ("the chief priests and the scribes and the elders") in which they sought to trap him with loaded and difficult questions.

The Passover meal took place, according to John's Gospel, on the Wednesday evening. According to the time frame in the other gospels, it happened on the Thursday evening when in any case it would have been a day early. But then, in just a few hours, Jesus would have had to go to the Mount of Olives, wait, be arrested, interrogated and tried in the middle of the night by the High Priest, Pilate and Herod Antipas, shuttled back and forth and finally sentenced and executed on Friday morning. So it would seem that the timing of the Passover meal given in John's Gospel is the more likely.

As with the ass arranged to be waiting for his entry into Jerusalem, Jesus had made preparations. The disciples were sent to find and meet a man carrying a water jar who would taken them to a house with a large upper room, furnished and ready for their Passover meal.

At the meal, he told those present that one of the disciples would "betray" him. But the Greek word "paredideto" used here literally means to "hand over" and, while this could imply betrayal, it certainly need not. Jesus, according to John's Gospel, actually instructed Judas to go and do it. So Judas, far from being the synonym for treachery that he has since become, was most probably simply carrying out instructions. It should be noted that the word "betray" is almost universally used in translation from the Greek, when " hand over" would be more accurate and appropriate, as for example in the passage from Paul's first letter to the Corinthians quoted above (chapter 11).

There is a theory that there were not two Judases among the disciples, but that Judas Iscariot and Thaddeus/Judas, Jesus' brother, were one and the same. In which case, Jesus was entrusting his own brother with what would have been a delicate and possibly dangerous mission.

Jesus is recorded in Mark and Matthew as making an arrangement to meet the disciples in Galilee, after he had died and been "raised up".

After the supper, Jesus went with his disciples to the Garden of Gethsemane, on the Mount of Olives, where he waited in a state of great tension and stress while some of his disciples slept.

Judas then arrived with a party of the High Priest's men and Jesus was handed over.

According to John's Gospel, Jesus was first questioned by Annas, father-in-law of the current High Priest Caiaphas. He was then brought before Caiaphas. The testimony of the witnesses did not agree, while Jesus remained silent. But Caiaphas pressed on, asking Jesus if he were the Christ, that is the Jewish Messiah.

When Jesus agreed that he was, the High Priest's court decided he was guilty of blasphemy (for which the punishment should have been stoning) and condemned him. He was buffeted, struck and spat upon.

The whole council, the Sanhedrin, was then convened the next morning to rubber-stamp the decision. Jesus was then taken before Pilate. According to John's timetable, which does provide just sufficient time, all these and the following events took place on the Thursday before the evening of the Passover.

The High Priest's party made their accusations. Jesus for the most part remained silent, though admitting using a polite form of reply "you have said so" that he was King of the Jews. In Luke's Gospel, the form of words used by his accusers, "perverting our nation", "forbidding us to give tribute to Caesar" and "saying that he himself is Christ a king" made it clear that they were bringing against him charges of sedition. These are, it should be noted, the charges that could (and might well have been) brought against Judas the Galilean whom Josephus records as having led an earlier movement against the payment of the census tax, under the banner, "No Lord, but God".

In both Luke and John's Gospels, Pilate decided that he could find no fault with Jesus. By implication, this is also the case with Matthew and Mark. All four gospels have Pilate seeking to free Jesus according to a custom that the people could have one man of their choice released to them at the Passover Feast. This was apparently a sop by the Roman authorities to the Jews to help quieten unrest at Passover.

The people instead chose Barabbas, variously described as a robber, murderer and insurrectionist and demanded his release, rather than Jesus.

The name "bar abbas" literally means "son of the father or master". According to several early sources that provide alternative versions of the Gospel of Matthew, he was also called Jesus. But, while he may have been, there is no other indication from the gospels or any other source that he was related to Jesus.

Luke's Gospel has an interlude when Pilate, learning that Jesus was a Galilean, sent him to be interviewed by Herod Antipas, governor of Galilee, who was in Jerusalem for the Feast of the Passover. Jesus was once again silent, as he was mocked by Herod and his men.

In the end, Pilate is portrayed as giving way to Jesus' accusers, who were in effect the High Priest and his followers. If he released Jesus, who had made himself a king and set himself against Caesar, he would not in their words have been "Caesar's friend".

So Jesus was scourged, mocked once again and led away to be crucified. By this time, it was Friday morning. According to all the gospels except John, a passer-by who came from Cyrene in North Africa, was compelled to carry the cross.

Jesus was then offered wine mixed with myrrh or gall, a customary act of mercy with the intention of giving some protection against the pain of execution, but Jesus refused.

He was then crucified.

Pilate had posted on the cross the charge "The King of the Jews", and refused to alter it to "He said 'I am the King of the Jews'".

His clothes were divided up by lot among the soldiers.

Two other men were crucified on other side of him. They were described as robbers or criminals, though in John's Gospel their offense is unspecified.

Jesus was mocked again by passers by, the High Priest's followers or sympathizers.

There was darkness over the land.

Jesus called out and was given vinegar, via a sponge passed up on a reed or spear, after which he immediately uttered a cry and died. According to the Gospel of Peter, which with Mark appears to be based on an early source, Jesus was at this point given gall mixed with vinegar. Gall is a term used in the bible for bitter substances, such as hemlock or a derivative of the opium poppy. In this case it is unlikely to have been hemlock, which is a poison, but opium which could deaden pain and also the senses. The author of Peter, it will be argued, here got the basic fact right but made the wrong interpretation.

Next, Joseph of Arimathaea appears on the scene again, "a respected member of the council who was himself looking for the Kingdom of God", that is a member of the Sanhedrin as well as a messianic believer and secret follower of Jesus.

Joseph asked for the body of Jesus ("soma" in Greek which could refer to a living body) and Pilate replied that he could have the body (this time using "ptoma" which would refer to a corpse), having established with the centurion in charge that Jesus was already dead.

The body would have had to be taken down in any case since the Sabbath, which began at sunset on the Friday, was approaching. Under Jewish Law, bodies were not permitted to remain hanging on the cross on the Sabbath day.

John's Gospel gives a description of the procedure which would have been followed in such circumstances. Soldiers came round to break the legs of the crucified victims, an act which substantially hastened death. John reports that they broke the legs of the other two crucified victims but desisted with Jesus, on seeing that he was already dead. However, according to John, one of the soldiers pierced Jesus' side with a spear and blood and water flowed out.

Joseph of Arimathaea and Nicodemus took the body of Jesus, together with a very large bag ostensibly holding 100 lbs weight of burial herbs, and placed it in an unused tomb cut into the rock face in a garden where Jesus was crucified.

A stone was rolled over to seal the doorway to the tomb.

During Saturday, the Sabbath and this year also the day of the Passover Feast, the tomb was left alone. The Gospel of Matthew states, following the Gospel of Peter, that the tomb was guarded to prevent the disciples stealing the body and falsely claiming that Jesus was resurrected.

The body stealing charge was indeed later made by opponents of the Nazoraeans, so it may be that the detail of the Roman guard was inserted into the story to counter it.

On Sunday, the three women closest to Jesus went to the tomb with spices to anoint the body, having been effectively deprived of their traditional role in preparing the body for burial by the actions of Nicodemus and Joseph of Arimathaea. These women were his mother Mary, her sister Salome and Mary Magdalene. The latter, I have argued, must have been his wife and identical with Mary, the sister of Martha, whose family home was in Bethany.

They found the stone rolled away. Inside, according to Mark following the Gospel of Peter, was a young man they did not know dressed in a white robe. He told the women that Jesus was "risen" and to tell the disciples that Jesus was, according to what had been planned, going to meet them in Galilee.

According to the Gospel of Peter alone, the soldiers witnessed the stone roll away "of itself" when two men arrived and entered the tomb. Then later they saw three men coming out of the tomb with "two of them sustaining the other".

Two other gospels have variations for the person the women found left in the tomb. In Matthew, the man who spoke to the women was an "angel" with raiment white as snow. In Luke, there were two men dressed in dazzling apparel.

John has Mary Magdalene finding the tomb empty and then reporting back to Simon Peter and John-the-priest, the "disciple whom Jesus loved" and original source for John's Gospel. The two men raced to the tomb and found it empty, except for the burial cloths including the head napkin neatly folded. They returned home, leaving Mary weeping outside the tomb. At this point, Mary encountered the two "angels in white" and, turning round, saw Jesus whom she supposed at first to be the gardener but then recognized when he said her name.

There are subsequently other appearances described in the gospels. In Luke, Jesus is described as having been seen by two of his followers, one of whom was called Cleophas, the name it will be remembered of Jesus' own father or maybe stepfather and uncle. This suggests that the two may have been family, possibly James and Simon bar Cleophas, Jesus' brothers.

Two Gospels, Luke and John, have Jesus appearing before the disciples gathered in Jerusalem. Luke emphasizes that this is not an apparition. Jesus eats food and tells the disciples that he is not a spirit and that, to prove it, they should touch and handle him.

John has the story that one disciple, Thomas, was not present at the first appearance and doubted that Jesus was resurrected and alive. "Unless I see in his hands the print of the nails, and place my finger in the mark of the nails, and place my hand in his side, I will not believe."

Eight days later, Jesus appeared to the disciples at the house in Jerusalem when Thomas was with them, and this time he did believe.

John also recorded another appearance of Jesus to the disciples at Galilee when they did not at first recognize them. Matthew similarly has them unsure whether it was Jesus they encountered at a mountain in Galilee, to which Jesus had directed them.

According to the now lost Gospel of the Hebrews, in a passage quoted by the Early Church father Jerome, Jesus first appeared to his brother James:

> *But the Lord, after he had given his linen clothes to the Servant of the Priest, went to James and appeared to him. For James had sworn that he would not eat bread from that hour in which he drank the Cup of the Lord until he should see him rising again from those that sleep.*
>
> Gospel of the Hebrews quoted in *Lives of Illustrious Men* by Jerome

Very early confirmation of these appearances comes in Paul's First Letter to the Corinthians which was written around AD 53. Here he stated that Jesus appeared to Peter (Cephas), the twelve disciples together, more than five hundred brethren at one time, then to James and to all the Apostles and finally, in what appears on the surface to have been a vision, to Paul himself.

The appearance to James, immediately after Jesus had given up his linen burial clothes and thus first on the list according to the Gospel of the Hebrews, appears way down the list in Paul's account. But Paul, it will be recollected, was in conflict with the Nazoraean community in Jerusalem and was motivated to diminish the role of James.

It is noteworthy that the post-resurrection appearances of Jesus, because they are recorded by Paul, have a greater degree of confirmation than many other aspects of Jesus' life.

As a story, the narrative of the passion is full of incident and drama and makes good reading. As a historical record, it is clearly full of deficiencies. One has already been mentioned, that it was the custom of the narrator in those times to make up appropriate speeches and sayings for his characters. So nothing that anyone is reported to have said can be greatly relied upon.

The passion story would also have suffered, in the case of Mark and a possible original *Cross Gospel*, from being first written down 20 to 30 years after the events. In the case of the other gospels, their origins were later still. They are believed to have been written after the disastrous war with Rome in which as many as a million people died, including many of the possible witnesses.

The other obvious factor which comes through in this collation of the passion accounts is the clear effort to make the Jews responsible for Jesus' death and minimize the role of Pilate and the Roman authorities. Pilate is portrayed as unwilling to condemn Jesus, sympathetic even, while the chief priests, scribes and elders clamor and conspire for his death.

This is clearly not credible since Jesus was given the appropriate sentence, death by Crucifixion, for a political crime, that of denying or defying the authority of Rome by claiming to be the King of the Jews. The list of Jesus' alleged offenses given in the Gospel of Luke in particular makes that abundantly clear. Pilate, as the Roman governor, could not and would not have tolerated rebellion in any form. His brutal response to the Samaritan messianic claimant, shortly after Jesus' Crucifixion, and his treatment of protesters against the appropriation and misuse of Temple funds beforehand indicate how he would, and certainly did, respond.

The later editors of the gospels created a mythical account, Christianizing Jesus and exonerating the Romans, for a religion which would have to survive and thrive under Roman power. This is shown as much in the passion narrative as in other parts of the gospel story, earlier discussed. Josephus, the

Jewish rebel leader who became a turncoat and writer for the Romans, could have given a better account, and may even initially have done so. I will suggest that he submitted himself to a degree of self-censorship, for reasons arguably of his own security and survival.

The Christian editors of the gospels made Jesus into a semi-divine being. In accordance with this, his death and resurrection are depicted as a miracle, brought about by the providence of God.

It is all the more interesting, then, that there are very many elements in the story which provide a totally different perspective.

What immediately strikes home are the ways in which Jesus' execution was unusual.

He was, for example, not on the cross for very long. His legs were not broken to bring about death, so as to enable the body to be taken down before the Sabbath and Passover. Despite strict purity rules, his body was handled by two male sympathizers instead of the women who would normally have prepared a body for burial. He was executed not in a public place, but in a private garden.

There are also other significant factors which will be discussed. The immediate point is that, according to the narrative, Jesus could well have survived his ordeal on the cross and, indeed, there are also indications that it was intended that he should do so.

This is not of course the conventional Christian message. It is all the more significant then that the underlying pattern should have survived as a counter account to conventional doctrine, within a story presented by what became Hellenized, Christian gospels.

However, as has been pointed out, there are problems with regarding the evidence as an historical account.

Could it, apart from say the mere fact of Jesus' execution, all be complete fiction?

That is what one analysis of the passion story suggests.

CHAPTER 13

FULFILLMENT OF PROPHECY

*But of the Jews none washed their hands, neither Herod nor
any one of his judges. And as they would not wash, Pilate
arose. And then Herod the king commanded that the Lord
should be marched off, saying to them, "What I have
commanded you to do to him, do ye."*
*Now there stood there Joseph, the friend of Pilate and of the
Lord, and knowing that they were about to crucify him he
came to Pilate and begged the body of the Lord for burial. And
Pilate sent to Herod and begged his body. And Herod said,
"Brother Pilate, even if no one had begged him, we should
bury him, since the Sabbath is drawing on. For it stands written
in the law: the sun should not set on one that has been put to
death."*
*And he delivered him to the people on the day before the
unleavened bread, their Feast. So they took the Lord and
pushed him in great haste and said, "Let us hale [drag or draw
the strength from] the Son of God now that we have gotten
power over him." And they put upon him a purple robe and set
him on the judgment seat and said, "Judge righteously, O King
of Israel!" And one of them brought a crown of thorns and put
it on the Lord's head. And others who stood by spat on his
face, and others buffeted him on the cheeks, others nudged him
with a reed, and some scourged him, saying, "With such honor
let us honor the Son of God." And they brought two
malefactors and crucified the Lord in the midst between them.
But he held his peace, as if he felt no pain. And when they had
set up the cross, they wrote upon it: this is the King of Israel.
And they laid down his garments before him and divided them
among themselves and cast the lot upon them. But one of the
malefactors rebuked them, saying, "We have landed in
suffering for the deeds of wickedness which we have
committed, but this man, who has become the savior of men,*

*what wrong has he done you? And they were wroth with him
and commanded that his legs should not be broken, so that he
might die in torments. Now it was midday and a darkness
covered all Judaea. And they became anxious lest the sun had
already set, since he was still alive. [For] it stands written for
them: the sun should not set on one that has been put to death.
And one of them said, "Give him to drink gall with vinegar."
And they mixed it and gave him to drink. And they fulfilled all
things and completed the measure of their sins on their head.
And many went about with lamps, [and] as they supposed that
it was night, they went to bed. And the Lord called out and
cried, "My power, O power, thou hast forsaken me!" And
having said this he was taken up.*

Gospel of Peter 1:5–19

A lthough the Gospel of Peter is dated from the second century AD, it
may have derived from an early version of Mark or a common
source, the "*Cross Gospel*" written in the middle of the first century.
There are a number of improbabilities in this gospel, such as ordinary
people, rather than soldiers, actually carrying out the execution and the
governor of the northern province of Galilee Herod Antipas, rather than
Pilate, being in charge of an execution in Jerusalem. With neither soldiers nor
the Roman procurator taking part, Rome was distanced and exonerated
from what took place. These factors take further the pro-Roman and anti-
Jewish stance which is present to a degree in all the gospels.

The Gospel of Peter also presents some interesting variations and
confusions.

A mixture of vinegar and gall is reported as being administered to Jesus,
echoing the wine and gall which Jesus was offered at an earlier point in the
proceedings but which he refused, according to the Gospel of Matthew
account.

But the opiate to deaden pain offered in Matthew is now in the Gospel of
Peter something else, more deadly and more sinister. The motivation by
implication is to poison Jesus to ensure that he dies swiftly, because an
unusual darkness in the middle of the day is causing worry that the sun
might be about to set. Jewish Law required that the men be taken down
before sunset, the onset of the Sabbath.

This is somewhat contradicted by the decision not to break the legs of one
of the victims in order to prolong his agony. From the text it appears that this

may have been directed, by way of retribution, against the crucified robber who spoke out on Jesus' behalf. It is not entirely clear. But more likely this is an explanation for the decision not to break Jesus' legs.

But, either way, that cannot be right. There would in any case have been a need to break the legs of the men to hasten death so that they would not still be on the cross after nightfall and thus, by the way days were then calculated, on the following Sabbath.

It now has to be supposed that the legs of the other men had been broken before midday and that they were already dead. Poison was given to Jesus, according to this version, because he alone was still alive when the sun was–extraordinarily–apparently about to set.

But there would have been no reason to break the legs of the robbers at such an early stage and at midday they too would still have been alive. So why poison just one of the three convicted men?

While the essential factual ingredients of this gospel story may or may not be right, the explanations provided by the text do not really add up.

The question is whether the *Cross Gospel*, imbedded within the Gospel of Peter, is an early attempt to describe and explain the passion story which later gospels writers made more convincing and tidied up. Or, alternatively, is it simply a variant composed by someone who had access to early written material but not to anyone linked to the events who would have known enough to make sense of it?

Thus the point about the administration of gall and vinegar, for example, could have been factually right. But the assumptions made about what sort of bitter-tasting fluid the gall was and the reason for giving it may have been wrong. The author of the Gospel of Peter may have had no way of finding this out, nothing against which to check his source. Hence the confusions or mistakes which have been detailed above.

The Gospel of Mark, by contrast, is reputed to have been written by someone the early commentator Papias describes as having traveled with Peter and acted as his interpreter. Mark was needed because Peter only spoke Aramaic and needed to communicate with Greek-speaking audiences. He may either have written the earliest version of the Gospel of Mark or indeed the presumed source for all the narrative accounts, the *Cross Gospel* itself. As someone living at the time, Mark had a direct link into the passion events which the author of the Gospel of Peter apparently did not. Papias refers to Peter's interpreter as Mark and this would appear to be the same person who appears in the Acts of the Apostles as "John whose other name was Mark".

Crossan, who has produced a fascinating and scholarly account entitled *The historical Jesus*, believes that the *Cross Gospel* embodied within the Gospel of Peter was essentially an act of explanation, rather than a record of fact. In his view, the passion story derived from attempts to understand what happened to Jesus which were based on the analysis of scripture. These were exercises comparable with the Qumran interpretations, "pesherim" in Hebrew, in which single passages of scripture were interpreted piece by piece in sequence and applied to current circumstance or alternatively where different passages were brought together to provide an explanation. Both the former, defined as *sequential biblical texts*, and the latter, defined as *testimonial biblical texts*, would be interlaced with explanatory commentaries.

Crossan suggests that Jesus' followers knew nothing more about the passion than the fact of the Crucifixion, that they fled and that later they had no available witnesses to discover the details of what had happened.

The Romans afterwards dumped the body and, if any of them knew where it was, they did not care. His followers, who cared, did not know. Their concern then, Crossan maintains, was to establish whether their leader's death negated all their beliefs and so accordingly they scoured the Old Testament scriptures for texts which could justify, explain and make positive sense of what had happened. These collected prophetic pronouncements were then combined into a narrative and refined with detail to give added plausibility. The boundaries between the texts and commentaries became blurred over time and they merged. The provision of a framework in an attempt to understand came by degrees to be the understanding itself, taken as a literal description of the events that took place. But, of course, the framework was invented and so had no bearing on what may actually have happened.

In the early stages of the process, biblical prophecies were teased out and explained. Developed into a narrative, some of the prophecies and allusions would either end up seamlessly buried in the text while others, as in John's account of the passion, would be directly alluded to.

However, the prophetic references in Mark, as in the Gospel of Peter, are left beneath the surface.

Taking the account given in the Gospel of Peter, Crossan suggests that the underlying theme is that of "innocence rescued", following a long biblical tradition including the saga about Joseph in Genesis and the stories of Daniel in the Lion's den and his companions Shadrach, Meshach and Abednego in the fiery furnace.

The connecting prophetic texts or textual allusions in the Gospel of Peter are seen as follows:

Authorities at the trial: "The kings of the earth set themselves, and the rulers take counsel together, against the Lord and his anointed," from Psalm 2:2;

Abuse and torture of Jesus: "I gave my back to the smiters, and my cheeks to those who pulled out the beard; I hid not my face from shame and spitting", from Isaiah 50:6 and "when they look on him whom they have pierced, they shall mourn for him", from Zechariah 12:10;

Death among thieves: "I (that is, the Lord) will divide him (His suffering servant) a portion with the great, and he shall divide the spoil with the strong; because he poured out his soul to death, and was numbered with the transgressors", from Isaiah 53:12;

Jesus remains silent: "He was oppressed, and he was afflicted, yet he opened not his mouth; like a lamb that is led to the slaughter, and like a sheep that before its shearers is dumb, so he opened not his mouth", from Isaiah 53:7 and "therefore I have set my face like flint, and I know that I shall not be put to shame", from Isaiah 50:7;

Garments divided by lot: "they divide my garments among them, and for my raiment they cast lots", from Psalm 22:18

Darkness at noon: " 'And on that day,' says the Lord God, 'I will make the sun go down at noon and darken the earth in broad daylight'", from Amos 8:9;

Gall and vinegar drink: "They gave me poison for food, and for my thirst they gave me vinegar to drink", from Psalm 69:21;

Death cry: "My God, my God, why has thou forsaken me?", from Psalm 22:1.

What Crossan suggests is ingenious and clearly has some validity, given the known way in which scripture was used and interpreted, especially by those who called themselves "the poor", the communities at Qumran and elsewhere at that time.

This way of retrospective interpretation has nonetheless its limitations. Some biblical text could be found by diligent searching to relate to almost every element of any narrative story. The theory is that the early compilers did just that to generate a good narrative for the passion story of Jesus. Quite so. But did *they* do it then? Or are *we* really to an extent doing it now, initiating rather than treading in someone else's footsteps?

To put this another way, what is alleged is that the Gospel of Peter is a testimonial biblical text comprised of interwoven scriptural sayings, but without real substance. In analyzing it, however, it is being treated in the same way as the Hebrew scribes treated a sequential biblical text, making it fit with previous scripture. If the original process cannot be relied on, then by the same token neither can this.

To take first the offering of vinegar, it was apparently customary practice to do this to help alleviate thirst for someone executed on the cross. So it would be unsurprising to find in the Gospel of Peter narrative, as in the New Testament gospels, Jesus offered vinegar passed up to him on a sponge. But *in fact*, in the Gospel of Peter, Jesus is offered vinegar mixed with "gall" and it must be surmised what the latter was. The supposed original scriptural allusion and source for this, Psalm 69, says nothing about his being given gall to drink. Taking this as the source is to make a presumption and then select the facts to fit.

This is not at all convincing, given that vinegar on its own might in any case have been usually available and administered at a crucifixion–thus useful cover it can be argued for a sedative drug.

Jesus would have been scourged, and is very likely to have been mocked and abused, by the Roman soldiers. Josephus, for example, records a number of instances where soldiers showed their contempt for their Jewish subjects and their customs. So, again, the argument that the event came from the Isaiah 53 prophecy seems less convincing than the possibility that the prophecy was actually used to explain and comment on the event. The scourging was something that would have happened in such circumstances and was what did in fact happen.

The detail of drawing lots for the victim's clothes does appear to be too good a reflection of Psalm 22 to be true, though again it could well have been the practice at the time to take and share out the victim's immediate possessions.

The description of "darkness over the land" at midday appears to be a straight steal from Amos, so this is one element which would support Crossan's theory.

On the whole, however, these details of the Crucifixion are what might be expected to have happened. The trawl of Old Testament prophecy does not explain them all, which makes the alleged process suspect while there is, as will be seen, a better explanation which does. The theory that the narrative was created solely from interwoven prophecy begins to look a little thin.

As will be seen, outside of this central section, there are other important elements in the passion story which do not appear to have any ancient biblical source but which form part of a coherent and credible whole. The main events from the New Testament gospel accounts were described and summarized in the previous chapter. There were in fact plenty of witnesses for these, many of whom would still have been available when the source gospels were first written. This is especially likely if, as is possible, the very earliest narrative was written before the turmoil caused by the Jewish uprising in AD 66–70.

It is more useful, in my view, to see the reference back to scripture as functioning in different ways to complement a narrative that could have a relation to real events.

In Jesus' time, religious and political life were intermixed and scripture formed the background to everyday life. By the gospel accounts, Jesus was well able to quote from and defend an argument by the use of biblical texts. In his role of itinerant preacher, he would necessarily have educated himself to a higher than ordinary level. He may have spent some years studying.

He had an agenda and, though it can be argued what precisely this was, it would in some way have fitted with the views and lifestyle of his followers who had known him. These were the Nazoraeans led by James in their community at Jerusalem. They were followers of Jewish Law and they believed that Jesus, as the Messiah, would return to establish a kingdom on earth.

So it is very possible that, as the gospels stated, he saw himself or came to see himself as the Messiah, Jewish King, liberator of his people. He did not however see himself as the divine ruler and savior of all the world; that's what later "Christian" writers in the mold of Paul put into the text. His mission was, as he stated, specifically and only to the "lost sheep of the House of Israel". Note, for example, the quote from the Gospel of Matthew, given at the start of chapter two.

It is thus quite feasible and consistent that Jesus would, knowing his scripture, have deliberately chosen to ride into Jerusalem on an ass in order to fulfill Zechariah's prophecy. The implications would not have been lost on his fellow pilgrims who also knew this common and much-quoted text.

So here is an example where Jesus, as main actor in the story, may have consciously acted in accordance with prophetic scripture as a way of both highlighting and adding validity to his position. There would have been hundreds or even thousands of witnesses on the way into Jerusalem who could confirm or deny this. So it is much more likely that this is a real historical detail than an element interwoven into an account, where information is lacking and padding needed. The early writers, I suggest, would not have invented details when there were many people living who could have pointed out that it was simply fiction.

Scripture was consciously used by Jesus. He may even have quoted the first words of Psalm 22 to express his anguish on the cross, just as we might now quote the bible or Shakespeare (often without realizing it) to express reactions to different circumstances. In Mark's Gospel, he made the cry and was then given the drink which caused him to lapse into a stupor. Was it therefore a prearranged signal?

This is one way that biblical prophecy could have come into the text, through the deliberate actions of the participants in the drama or through their own words in quoting biblical passages. Remember, however, that events would have been better remembered than comments and it was also the practice of authors at this time to invent dialogue for those taking part.

Scripture came into the gospel narrative in a second way, quoted by the author as a comment or explanation for what has happened. This is more like the pesher in which a textual sequence is examined against other sources, that is sequential biblical exegesis. It is also akin to the process by which a present-day analyst, such as Crossan, might dissect a text, though here in order to show not how it may be justified but where it came from.

There are some good examples of this kind of interpolation in the passion narrative given in the Gospel of John. "The disciple whom Jesus loved", unnamed but for convenience referred to as John, claimed to have witnessed the Crucifixion in an account passed on in his old age to the author of this gospel. This second person, the actual writer of the gospel, wrote the story down and also gave the text as a whole his own particular anti-Jewish perspective.

It is related in the gospel that the Roman soldiers came to break the legs of those crucified, to speed death and so enable the bodies to be taken down before sunset which marked the beginning of the next day, the Sabbath. But, finding Jesus already or apparently dead, one soldier contented himself with plunging his spear into Jesus' side, out of which came blood and water. John comments, "For these things took place that the scripture might be fulfilled, 'Not a bone of him shall be broken.' And again another scripture says, 'They shall look on him whom they have pierced.'"

The first of the two quotes most probably derives from Psalm 34, verse 20, which described the Lord, in looking after the righteous person, as ensuring that "He keeps all his bones; not one of them is broken."

The second of the quotes comes from Zechariah 12, verse 10, when the Lord promises (on the day of reckoning) to "pour out on the house of David and the inhabitants of Jerusalem a spirit of compassion and supplication, so that, when they look on him whom they have pierced, they shall mourn for him ..."

Either the author of John invented details of the passion on the basis of existing scripture and then used the scripture as prophetic justification, or he had some information on what had happened and scoured scripture for prophetic references as confirmation. With the references left explicitly in the text, however, it does appear that he was embarked on a form of sequential biblical analysis. That is, he was using old biblical texts to explain more recent happenings on which he did have evidence.

It is, incidentally not hard to find whatever is needed to explain present circumstances among thousands of Old Testament verses. Imagine, say, the disasters of a landslide of stones, a war, a fire, a flood or fountain of water sweeping people away, a large proportion of the population killed, false prophets arising, even diseases that blind horses or make people go mad, flocks of sheep scattered, idolaters punished. References to these and other such predicted happenings could be found, as well as the reference to piercing and mourning quoted by John, in the 23 verses of Zechariah 12 and 13. John looked for and was easily able to find what he wanted.

These prophecies collected in Zechariah date from the third century BC and look forward to the Israel's eventual triumph over her enemies. But there would be a price, as with the suffering servant in the earlier Book of Isaiah, someone "pierced" and then mourned by the nation.

A third use of biblical text as prophetic explanation occurs where it is interwoven, as a form of testimonial explanation, as Crossan has outlined in his analysis of the Gospel of Peter.

Not the only type of usage, this latter type also does not, as I have argued, provide the whole of the explanation for any part of the passion narrative.

Looking at the whole of the story of events leading up to, through and then after the passion, as summarized in the previous chapter, it does appear as an interconnected, coherent account. The key elements for the most part have nothing to do with biblical prophecy.

But what the accounts do show firstly is that Jesus undertook a series of actions which would either risk or certainly result in his death, most probably by Crucifixion since he would be judged as a political offender, as a rebel, by the Roman authorities. Secondly, a number of precautions and circumstances are evident which indicate that Jesus, while he may have realized he might have to suffer on the cross, did not intend if it could be avoided to die on the cross. This is the better explanation of the passion narrative which I have suggested.

It is one which is well in accord with the concept of the suffering servant bearing the nation's grief and sorrows in Isaiah, "despised and rejected of men, "led like a lamb to the slaughter" because it was "the will of the Lord to bruise him" and "put him to grief".

But then the Lord's servant, the suffering righteous one, would receive his due reward and prosper: "when he makes himself an offering for sin, he shall see his offspring, he shall prolong his days; the will of the Lord shall prosper in his hand; he shall see the fruit of the travail of his soul and be satisfied". (Isaiah 53:10–11).

So, it will be noted, I am now doing exactly the same sort of thing as the author of the Gospel of John and for that matter John Crossan, selectively taking a biblical text to illustrate my argument. That is, I am working back from what I know or have decided is true to find the prophecy to prove it.

But my point here is that Jesus, who was clearly familiar with Zechariah, would also have known well the works of the prophet Isaiah. He would surely have taken comfort from those parts of the text indicating that the suffering righteous one would not have to die.

He might in any case die, but the testament book did not necessarily require him to. So there was nothing against the will of God which forbade him from taking measures designed to ensure, or at least increase, his chances of survival. The gospel accounts, as will be seen, indicate a very high degree of conscious planning by Jesus directed towards this end. This shows through, even though the gospel editors had no plausible reason to present the text in a way which suggested this–if anything, quite the reverse.

If Jesus did in the event survive in the teeth of death, he would have experienced a very Jewish form of individual resurrection. But it was not a Christian one. That was something written in to the account afterwards.

Even devout Christian believers are uneasy with the story of the Crucifixion as an effective execution, because of its glaring irregularities. Chief among these are the facts relating to this Roman method of execution, which will be discussed in further detail a little later. There were essentially two methods of achieving the death of the victim. The first was simply to leave him tied or nailed to the cross, when he would expire after prolonged agony through the combined effects of slow shock, pain, exposure, thirst and hunger, in two, three or more days. The second involved, after an appropriate interval, breaking the legs of the victim with a heavy wooden club. Following this, he would die in a matter of no more than an hour.

Neither method, according to the evidence, was fully carried out in Jesus' case. He was taken down from the cross after only a few hours, when he should still have been alive.

Before proceeding, I refer again to my summary in the previous chapter of the gospel accounts of the passion and also to the original gospel accounts. It is not at all a convincing story of Christian resurrection, not what might have been written from an position without any real evidence to demonstrate miraculous, divine intervention. It is, shorn of its Hellenized overlays, what a Jewish follower of Jesus might have recorded from what he knew of events.

So what were the apparent indications of intent and the measures that were taken?

These can be enumerated for convenience under a number of headings:

Declaration of kingship

While to begin with being circumspect, Jesus in several ways declared or indicated himself to be the Messiah, the expected King and therefore liberator of the Jews. This process seems to have begun in the weeks leading up to his move to Jerusalem for the Passover in AD 36.

First, he got his disciples to say or realize that he was the expected Messiah. Then, he indicated what he thought his status was in the discussion at Capernaum about the Temple tax. He allowed himself to be anointed (which is the derivation of the word "Messiah") by Mary in the manner of Jewish kings. He entered Jerusalem the way a king would, according to the prophecy of Zechariah. Finally, he admitted to the Roman Governor Pilate and/or the High Priest that he was King of the Jews and that was the charge Pilate posted on the cross.

The effect of these actions was, in combination with other circumstances, to bring about a confrontation. The sequences of steps taken bear the mark of calculation and intent.

Abandonment of discretion

At first Jesus avoided admitting his assumed status, but later made admissions at times of his own choosing. This is reflected in the admonitions given to those he healed early in his healing ministry but not later in the narrative when he was on the way to Jerusalem. There was thus no attempt to silence the blind man at Jericho calling out, "Jesus, Son of David" and no instruction given to him to remain silent about the healing he received.

According to the gospel record, Jesus was in Jerusalem preaching for several days before his final arrest on the eve of Passover. Although questioned closely by representatives of the High Priest, he did not (and it can be presumed took care not to) reveal directly that he believed that he was the Messiah. This admission, which could have led to his immediate arrest, was made later after he had apparently given himself up.

Predictions of death and resurrection

At a number of points in the story, Jesus is recorded as telling his close disciples that he would suffer, die and then rise again. This could certainly be retrojection into the story by the gospel writer, from he knew or presumed had happened. The writer's objective would have been to bolster the tale's credibility and perhaps also to add to Jesus' reputation for prescience, in the manner of the story about the woman drawing water who had had five husbands (see chapter 2). On the other hand, considering all the other elements which suggest that Jesus anticipated (or even planned) that he would suffer on the cross, this is what one might expect to have happened. He would have confided to his closest companions his expected fate and also the better news that he hoped to survive. So this element, even though it might have been spuriously added by the gospel authors, also fits with the overall picture presented of conscious intent.

At the Passover meal, Jesus arranged to meet the disciples afterwards in Galilee. This circumstantial detail is confirmed by John's account that the disciples went to the shores of the Sea of Galilee after the Crucifixion and met someone there whom they wanted to believe was Jesus. It was a very specific arrangement and it suggests that Jesus planned and expected to survive his ordeal.

Use of helpers

If Jesus was embarked on an audacious plan, one element of which was to cheat his executioners, then he would have needed help. He could not have broadcast his intentions to everyone; otherwise the authorities would have heard and simply taken counter-precautions to ensure that he did die. So those entrusted with his fate had to be few in number, discreet and trustworthy, and absolutely reliable.

It seems he told his closest disciples in general terms what to expect. But who were the people who gave him the practical support and help he needed to survive?

They are, astonishingly, still there in the text despite the centuries of alterations by editors with very different agendas.

These are the men dressed in white robes, members of a male priestly community, the self-ascribed poor and the meek. They came, if not from Qumran, from another one of a similar network of communities, one of the assemblies of the camps or the towns to which Jesus and his followers had links, or even belonged.

Jesus arranged for someone to provide a room and the means for the Passover meal in Jerusalem. His followers were instructed to follow a man carrying water in a jar. But the only men who fetched water, which was woman's work, were those living in the Essenic-style all male communities. Present at the meal, in addition to the twelve, was the "disciple whom Jesus loved" who is believed to have been a priest.

The Passover meal was not eaten on the Friday evening, the eve of Passover, according to the orthodox practice but according the tradition of the poor, the community at Qumran, of having it the Wednesday before. This adds to the evidence that it was this community, or more probably a similar offshoot in Jerusalem, that was providing practical support.

Jesus had also arranged for someone to have the ass tethered and ready at Bethany for him to ride into Jerusalem. A helper was involved again, perhaps one of "the poor", or perhaps Lazarus, to whom Jesus was very close and who I have argued was in fact his brother-in-law.

Someone was also needed who would, with absolute reliability and certainty, at the right moment administer the mixture of vinegar and "gall" that would immediately plunge Jesus into a comatose, death-like state.

When Jesus was arrested, or handed over, Mark records that a young man followed him, dressed in a linen cloth, the robe of the priest or initiand or one of "the poor". Was there something that this person had to ask Jesus, perhaps some vital detail of the arrangements that still needed to be cleared up?

When the women arrived at the tomb, according to Mark, there was a young man dressed in white robes who told them to tell the disciples to go to Galilee as arranged where Jesus would meet them. Matthew has a white clothed "angel", in the Greek literally a "messenger", while Luke has two men in dazzling clothes. John record two "angels in white" and Jesus close by, encountered by Mary.

The Gospel of Peter provides some extraordinary circumstantial detail.

While Roman soldiers stood guard, two in every watch, they witnessed the stone over the entrance rolled back, two men enter the tomb and then bring out a third, "the two of them sustaining the other".

The image could hardly be clearer: Jesus between his helpers, still in a state of weakness and shock even after more than a day of intensive assistance, an arm maybe over each shoulder, being helped away from the tomb.

It was two other men, it will be remembered, Nicodemus and Joseph of Arimathaea, who took Jesus' body into the tomb, in defiance of purity rules which required that women should do this job. The reason for this highly unusual arrangement, it may be assumed in the context of all the other evidence, was that these two were party to an undertaking to take Jesus alive from the cross. They had with them a suspiciously large sack, with 100 lbs weight supposedly of burial herbs and spices. But nothing of this was noted in a later description in John of the empty tomb's contents, just the bandages and the head napkin neatly folded. The sack could have contained clothes for Jesus, food and water, plus ointments and dressings for the wounds.

Someone would have been left in the tomb to give medical assistance. Mark records that there was such a young man found by the women in the tomb when they visited on Sunday morning, the first day of the week. Two or more assistants would have been needed to help Jesus out. These are also there in the Gospels of Luke, John and even more graphically in the Gospel of Peter.

Joseph of Arimathaea also had the task of asking for the body, and presumably somehow ensuring that the Roman soldiers did not break Jesus' legs to make doubly sure that he was dead.

Control of timing

Jesus gave himself up to face trial and execution. These events were not sudden, accidental or unforeseen and this makes it possible, and even likely, that he and his followers took steps to maximize the chances of his survival.

To appreciate how timing was of the essence it is important to understand how victims actually died from crucifixion.

Where the object was to inflict maximum suffering and make an example of the condemned person, the Romans simply nailed him through the wrists and feet to the cross and just left him there. The victim died from the cumulative effects over several days of thirst, hunger, exposure and shock.

Nailing the victim contributed eventually to his death and also reduced the chances of rescue during the long period that he would take to die. But there would have been a horn or seat supporting the body weight, or the effort taken to lift the torso every time to draw breath and exhale would have rapidly led to exhaustion and death in a much shorter time. It was a long process which, if interrupted, could result in the victim's life being spared. Josephus reports that he recognized and pleaded for three of his acquaintances who were being crucified during the Roman siege of Jerusalem. The Roman general Titus ordered that the men be taken down and given medical attention. Although it was too late for two of the victims, who died, the third survived.

Where inflicting suffering was not the prime objective, a quicker method was used. The victim now stood on a small platform and he was bound by leather thongs to the cross. When the moment came to kill him, his legs were broken by a heavy club. The effect was to cause the body to sag and induce extreme shock, with a loss of blood from the circulation to the broken and swollen legs. Unable to breathe properly, the victim then died fairly quickly from suffocation, shock and heart failure.

Given the time of Jesus' Crucifixion in all the gospels, on the eve of the Sabbath which was also the day of the Passover Feast, it is evident that the fast method of execution would have been used on Jesus and the two thieves who, it is recorded, were crucified at the same time. According to Jewish Law, which the Romans respected, it was absolutely forbidden for bodies to remain on the cross on the Sabbath, that is after sunset on the Friday evening.

John's Gospel actually describes the process. The Roman soldiers broke the legs of the two thieves, but were astonished to find that Jesus was already dead–astonished because he had been on the cross for a matter of only three hours. A man in his prime well used to feats of endurance, Jesus at this point should still have been alive. This would be the case even with the account in Mark's Gospel, suggesting that the Crucifixion lasted as much as six hours.

The conventional picture of a crucified Jesus nailed to the cross is thus probably wrong. It is relevant that none of the gospels give any details of the mechanics of Jesus' execution: they might have said that he was nailed to the cross if that had happened, but did not do so.

Only in John, among the four gospels, is there a retrospective suggestion that Jesus was nailed to the cross, in the story of "doubting Thomas".

The story given here is that Jesus appeared to the disciples, it seems in the safe house in Jerusalem where they had held their Passover, or Last Supper. He showed them his hands and his side. Thomas was absent.

The other disciples told Thomas what had happened. He replied, "Unless I see in his hands the print of the nails, and place my finger in the mark of the nails, and place my hand in his side, I will not believe."

So, eight days later, an interestingly specific time, Jesus came again to the house and Thomas was confounded and believed.

The Gospel of Peter has "the Jews" drawing out the nails from his hands, before Joseph of Arimathaea came and took the body and placed it in his own tomb.

It should be noted, however, that in John's Gospel Jesus is described as showing the disciples only his hands and his side, and not his feet. Thomas wants to see the print of the nails but he also only mentions hands, and not feet. In the Gospel of Peter, the nails are only taken from Jesus' hands.

There is an important point about this.

By the later Christian slant put on the text, it would not matter one jot whether Jesus had been nailed by the hands, feet, both or neither. He died. God miraculously restored him to life and it was but a small matter to restore his body also to what it had been. It made no difference how the body had been damaged or deformed.

But the early Jewish, Nazoraean writers were describing something else, someone who had *survived* crucifixion, still miraculous and still in their perspective a personal resurrection. To them, it certainly did matter whether or not Jesus had been nailed through the feet, rather than just his hands. The reason was that, if he had been nailed through the feet, he would have been severely injured. Assuming he did survive, he would not have been able to walk about, as he apparently did, for weeks or even months following the Crucifixion after a short respite. He might well have been crippled for life.

So which version of the story is correct? There is no certain way of knowing.

If the first gospel writers had evidence of Jesus' appearances in the days immediately following the Crucifixion, then they had to assume that Jesus wasn't nailed through the feet. But then there was a story of Thomas refusing to believe unless he saw Jesus' wounds, and the dramatic detail of nail marks in hands was added.

Given a crucifixion that had to be completed and the body taken down by sunset, it is my view that the Romans would have used the quick method. They had no reason to do otherwise and very strong reasons to stick to the appropriate procedure in the circumstances. The execution had to be got over swiftly to avoid trouble if possible during Passover and, for much the same reason, some regard had to be shown to Jewish religious prohibitions. Granted that it is only negative confirmation, but none of the gospels in describing the act of crucifixion say anything about nails or nailing. If anything, they rather curiously avoid such detail.

Where there is mention in other contexts, in the Gospels of John and Peter, nothing is said about nailing through the victim's feet. Later Christian writers would have had no reason to leave this detail out, had it happened, because they believed Jesus' resurrection was in any case miraculous. And they certainly did not put it in, because the information is not there. This tends to confirm the other evidence which suggests that the quick method of execution was used, or intended, and that Jesus would have been able to walk afterwards if he survived it.

So, why eight days? Why did it take eight days before the doubting Thomas arrived to meet the risen Messiah? Jesus it will be remembered asked the disciples to meet him in Galilee. His helper, one of "the poor", at the tomb restated the message.

But it was a vastly overoptimistic plan and, after being flogged, tied or possibly nailed by the wrists to the cross, and maybe wounded by a spear thrust, Jesus simply could not make the 90-mile journey immediately.

So someone else was sent on instead to meet the disciples. Some of them had already gone to the Sea of Galilee. Still in a state of shock at the fate of their leader, hearing about the empty tomb but finding it scarcely credible that he had survived, they then met someone who knew all about the situation. They were confused. They didn't recognize this person. Could it be a risen Jesus, in some other human guise? They went back disappointed but Thomas, I surmise, stayed behind to look after his family and the fishing boats.

When he had recovered sufficiently, Jesus met his disciples in a house in Jerusalem. But Thomas was still in Galilee. The eight days accounts for the time it would have taken to go all the way on foot to the Sea of Galilee to alert Thomas, and for him to come back.

Returning to the question of timing, it was vital for Jesus to deliver himself up in time for him to be put up on the cross, crucified by the quick method and taken down before the eve of Passover. But not too early, or he would be on the cross too long and die in any case. Nor too late, because Pilate might then have decided to postpone proceedings until after Passover week–when the outcome would have been still more certain.

What was in Jesus' favor was the fact that Pilate would not have wanted an imprisoned rebel leader (as he would have seen it) as a focus for disaffection and discontent in the charged atmosphere of Passover. Jerusalem would have been swelled to bursting point with fervent pilgrims and Pilate had at his disposal a military force inadequate to deal with any major disturbance.

So, if Jesus could control and get his timing right, then there was every chance that the Roman authorities would have responded in accordance with it.

The evidence from the gospels suggests that Jesus acted with enormous discipline, using his helpers and controlling events as far as possible. He chose when to hand himself over. He sent a messenger, Judas, to ensure that this is what would happen at the time of his choosing. Before that, he had made a deliberately messianic entry into Jerusalem. He then capped it all by turning over the money-changers' tables in the Temple (though John's Gospel describes this as having happened at a previous Passover). His already great popularity with the people, arising from his healing and preaching, would have been enormously increased by these measures. On the other hand, he had done as he had calculated—provoked the High Priest and his followers, who depended for their positions on Roman patronage, to a state of almost apoplectic fury.

There were many among the ruling council particularly the Pharisees, as I have argued, who were sympathetic to Jesus' religious position. In its principles, this did not differ markedly from theirs. Some might well have also agreed that monetary exchange at the Temple was being abused to fund an indulgent lifestyle for the few, the ruling clique, at the expense of the many poor inhabitants of Judaea.

Why they didn't simply outvote the High Priest and his cronies, as they did when Peter and some of the other Apostles were subsequently put on trial, will become clearer when the question of Jesus' motivation is considered. The question for the moment is how, rather than why, he did what he did.

What Jesus did in provoking his enemies was ensure that they acted without too much reflection and calculation. What he achieved by his superlative timing, in the whole roll up of events to the final handover at the Mount of Olives, was ensure that he would be crucified on the eve of Passover and not remain on the cross for very long. Other elements in his planning would be needed to ensure, as far as possible, that as well as suffering in accordance with scripture he would also survive.

There is some evidence that fine-tuning of timing was extended to the proceedings once Jesus was arrested. The gospels report him going back and forth between the High Priest and Pilate and even Herod Antipas, who was in Jerusalem for the Passover Feast. There are some obvious defects in these accounts, reflecting the later efforts of editors to exonerate the Roman authorities and blame the Jews as a whole for Jesus' Crucifixion.

It is improbable, especially in the context of other events as will be seen, that Pilate would have wanted to liberate the rebel leader in his hands. It is equally unlikely that "the Jews", who had only a few days previously clamorously welcomed him into Jerusalem as their Messiah, would now have demanded his crucifixion.

But the element which does ring true is that of Jesus controlling the timing of events to the last, keeping silent as witnesses contradicted themselves, engaging in obscure argument with an exasperated Pilate. Then, when he judged the moment right, he admitted that he did see himself as the Messiah, the King of the Jews, and thus guilty of the political crime of treason, denying the authority of Rome. For which offense he was sentenced with precisely that charge, posted by Pilate above the cross.

Conserving strength and life

The fact that Jesus used helpers throughout in a directed way is of itself evidence that he meant if possible to survive. His helpers provided the physical means necessary to achieve his objective, for example the use of a safe house in Jerusalem for meetings and in particular for celebrating the Passover Feast. They also provided the assistance he needed to conserve his physical resources, avoiding any injury that could be avoided, and then to recover in safety.

Jesus knew that he might be flogged and that he would be hung on a cross. But he timed it so that the quick rather than the protracted method of crucifixion would be used, so that he would not be nailed–his feet especially would not be nailed–to the cross. He arranged it so that he would simulate death and he had helpers there to demand his body and ensure that his legs were not broken.

What else would have helped? He needed to conserve his strength and to do this it would certainly have helped not to have to carry the heavy crosspiece all the way to "Golgotha", the place of execution. Simon of Cyrene in North Africa, a "passer by" according to Mark's Gospel was compelled to do that.

This may have been coincidental, an oddly compassionate act by the Roman soldiers, or it may have been something brought about by Jesus' followers and helpers. They would surely have enrolled an apparent stranger, to disarm suspicion, rather than someone the authorities knew. It could have been a fortuitous circumstance. But if the theory is right, that Jesus and his followers planned for him to survive crucifixion, then this also fits the overall pattern.

The next interesting point is that Jesus is recorded by Mark as refusing the offer of wine mingled with myrrh at the place of execution. This was apparently something customarily given to the condemned as an act of mercy to deaden their senses.

Why Jesus may have refused it subsequently becomes clear. On the cross, he cried out in a loud voice and was according to the canonical gospels given vinegar on a sponge to drink, which he did. Immediately, he uttered his final cry and slumped forward, apparently dead.

Vinegar would have been mildly stimulating and would have had, if anything, the opposite effect. The drink would have tended to revive Jesus rather than, as described, render him unconscious. It is the Gospel of Peter which provides, quite simply and powerfully, the explanation.

Jesus was given not vinegar but vinegar and gall, meaning some bitter substance. That substance immediately induced a death-like state and so it is likely to have been something like an opiate. The juice from the opium poppy was commonly available at the time and it was bitter to taste.

So what is described as having happened is what would have had to happen, if there were in action a plan to save Jesus' life, if at all possible. He would have needed to be sufficiently alert to take the drugged vinegar when it was offered at a time judged suitable. Enough time would have had to elapse for death from the effects of the ordeal, possibly from say heart failure, to have seemed plausible or feasible. But the drug had to be administered before twilight when the soldiers would have come round in any case to break the legs of the three victims.

In order to be alert for this, Jesus could not afford to take anything that would have rendered him confused or drowsy. So that is why he refused the mixture of wine and myrrh offered, as Mark describes, as an anodyne before crucifixion. Pain was not his overriding consideration: he had to remain aware and able later to take the potion passed up on a sponge.

Once Jesus' body was rendered apparently inert by the vinegar and opium, the next step was to retrieve it as swiftly as possible. Joseph of Arimathaea went to Pilate, using his status as a member of the Sanhedrin, and asked for it. Pilate asked the centurion to check that Jesus had died, and then agreed that Joseph could have the body.

According to John's Gospel, the Roman executioners came round and broke the legs of the two thieves crucified at the same time but desisted upon discovering that Jesus was (apparently) already dead.

Now this was a possibility that Jesus' presumed rescuers had to take into account. Presumably they did, because the gospels record that Jesus' legs were not broken.

But it would have been odd for all the other elements of conscious planning, so far identified, to have been present and then for this one, absolutely vital factor to have been left to chance.

The appearance of death created would make it less likely that the soldiers would then bother to break his legs. It is probable that there was also a contingency plan. Joseph could have arranged for himself, Nicodemus and a group of other prominent supporters to place themselves firmly between the Roman soldiers and the cross. And make their points:

Jesus was clearly dead. He needed to be taken down before sunset. They did not want his body broken.

The soldiers would have considered these arguments. It was Passover. Tension was running high especially because of this execution and they had been instructed not to provoke any more incidents. Moreover, they were outnumbered and there was no room around Jesus even to swing a club. Why risk trouble when the man was clearly already dead?

There may perhaps have been just room enough to thrust a spear through the human shield, at a stretch, a token gesture. That is, if what John alone recorded, was correct. "Blood and water" flowed, but the soldier missed the significance of this: there was still some circulation in the body, so Jesus was still alive.

To conserve Jesus' remaining vital strength, it would have been essential that he got help immediately–and was not carted away and thrown, as he might otherwise have been, on a garbage dump outside the city.

So he was taken to a tomb, not just any old tomb but one close to the place of Crucifixion and, according to Matthew, one belonging to Joseph of Arimathaea.

Furthermore, John's Gospel describes the place of Crucifixion and the tomb as being in a garden, presumably also belonging to Joseph. It would thus have been a private place rather than the bare public place of execution that it is often depicted as being.

This latter impression derives from the fact that the gospels "interpreted from the Hebrew" that Golgotha meant "the place of a skull" or "Gulgoleth", whereas the name would more convincingly have come from "Golgeth" meaning "stone press". Written Hebrew at that period had no vowels so these always had to be deduced from the script. So, for example, the holy name of God, only spoken by the High Priest on the Day of Atonement, might as spoken equally have been "Jehovah" or "Jahveh". There is no way of knowing, since both can be derived from the written word Jhvh.

From Glgth it is similarly possible to extrapolate Golgotha which means nothing in particular or Golgeth which means stone press–but not Gulgoleth, the place of a skull, which would have been written down as Glglth.

A stone press would have been a possible name for a garden where plants were grown and oils or juices extracted.

Just how Jesus came to be executed in a garden will be considered later. But that is what Joseph of Arimathaea had apparently prearranged, so making it easier to have the means to revive and restore Jesus after his ordeal. The bag, supposedly containing 100 lbs of burial spices (an excessive quantity), could have held all that was necessary. A medical helper could easily have been concealed within the tomb beforehand, leaving him free to work as soon as the stone was rolled across the entrance.

The narrative, I suggest, fits together in a connected whole. The theory that the story of the passion had to be invented because the disciples had fled, and no one knew what had happened, is full of weaknesses. The idea that the passion story is simply an interwoven collection of prophecy depends on a selective treatment which disregards bits that do not fit in. The theory does not deal with the many key elements contributing to the goal of survival that have nothing to do with prophecy, such as Simon of Cyrene carrying the Cross, Jesus' refusal of the wine mixed with myrrh, the subsequent administration of "gall" with the vinegar, men who were supporters of Jesus acting in an unusual role to carry out the burial duties, the Crucifixion taking place in a private garden and the timing of events to occur just before Passover.

The theory disregards evidence that Jesus and others taking part knew and consciously used scripture and that the authors of the gospels also used scripture to explain, rather than to make up, what had happened.

Even for the core passion events, there were witnesses, such as "the disciple whom Jesus loved" whose recollections were incorporated into the Gospel of John. Onlookers were present when he was taken to the place of execution, a private garden. There were "passers by" there at the cross and also close members of Jesus' family.

Beyond the core narrative of trial and Crucifixion, thousands would have seen Jesus make his entry into Jerusalem, crowds witnessed his preaching at the Temple and the disciples were with him at the Passover supper and for the Mount of Olives hand-over. After the Crucifixion, post-resurrection appearances are recorded by Paul, writing just a few years afterwards.

What emerges is a story of conscious intent, with many details combining to show that Jesus made careful provision, willed and timed events, particularly his Crucifixion, to maximize the chances of his survival. The subsequent appearances of a solid and physical Jesus, able to eat food, talk and be touched, suggest that he did survive.

Now, this was clearly not the work of the later Christian writers and editors who wanted to, and did, present the events as leading up to a miraculous resurrection. They had no reason to invent connected detail which suggested that Jesus might have planned to survive and did survive his Crucifixion. So these were details which they did not edit, which they left in simply because they were there, or because they provided color, and the significance of which it must be presumed they did not fully appreciate.

This must then be very early material which came from the original sources and writers.

This leaves one further possible explanation. Did these earlier writers make the story up in order to tell their readers that Jesus did not die, when actually he had? It should be remembered that these accounts, such as the presumed *Cross Gospel* and the Gospel of the Hebrews, are dated by Crossan and others at around AD 50, just a matter of years after the Crucifixion.

It would have been an extraordinary enterprise for the first gospel writers to have invented it all, with all the circumstantial detail, just to present a case–implicit rather than explicit–that Jesus had survived. The tale simply knits together too well, and there were still many witnesses available at the time who could have pointed out what was not true. The simpler explanation is more convincing and likely: the earliest authors used their own knowledge, the accounts of others, stories handed down to them and any written evidence available. They wrote down what they knew or believed to be true.

However, what they wrote down had of necessity to be a circumspect description of events, in order to avoid compromising those who had helped Jesus and might still be at risk. The details of what happened are there, including the execution in a private place, the potion given of vinegar and gall, the early request for the body, its removal to an unused private tomb, the "angels" or messengers left to tell family and supporters where Jesus might be found. But the explicit description of precisely who did what to help preserve and conserve Jesus' life could not be made. This lack of directness, although necessary at the time, made it easier for a miraculous interpretation of the passion story ultimately to gain sway.

It is highly probable that the first Passion accounts emanated from the Nazoraean community in Jerusalem which was initially led by James, the brother of Jesus. At the outset, there may have been just this one community of followers of Jesus. These accounts were written down at a time when possibly Simon Peter was still alive, probably James was alive and certainly when Simon or Simeon, the second brother of Jesus, was alive. Simeon was finally crucified under Trajan at a great age, around AD 100.

It is my suggestion that the planning and precautions which Jesus undertook to survive Crucifixion were known only to a few. The reason for this was that the more people knew, the more likely it was that information would come to the attention of the Jewish or Roman authorities and the scheme would be thwarted. It is possible, then, that initially some of Jesus' closest followers and even his brothers were kept in the dark.

But, once Jesus had survived, this was no longer such an imperative. According to evidence of the Gospel of the Hebrews, supported by Paul who lists a number of appearances or meetings with disciples and followers, Jesus first went to see his brother James.

At this point, Jesus' close family and supporters would have been informed of what had happened. One imperative, to keep secret the details of the plan to save Jesus, was then replaced by another, to get him away as soon as he had recovered sufficiently to a place of safety.

So, when the gospel accounts were first written, this was undertaken by people who had the basic facts available.

The alternative theory that the story was made up from prophecy is not credible. Jesus was far from being a nobody, whose execution was of little significance at the time and whose body the Romans might have dumped and forgotten. The evidence from the gospels and other sources suggests, on the contrary, that Jesus and the movement he helped initiate presented them with a very real challenge. In the context of other events at the time, what happened was of great significance. The Romans had every reason to be aware and focused even though, as I will suggest, they were not entirely in control of events.

Jesus did try to exercise some control, albeit from a position of much less strength, using his intelligence and all the resources he had at his disposal. His life of physical labor, fasting and arduous travel would have given him the stamina and powers of endurance he needed to face the ordeal of the Crucifixion.

But there was an element apparently missing from the plans and preparations he made, together with a small and trusted group of followers.

The pivotal moment would be the administration of a drug to induce in Jesus the appearance of death on the cross. How did the helpers know which drug would work best? Mandrake, for example, was a commonly grown plant which had a narcotic effect and could have been used as an alternative to opium. But would it have been powerful enough?

How did the helpers know how much of the drug to administer? Too much would simply kill Jesus, rather than render him unconscious. Too little would leave him visibly still alive.

A dress rehearsal or practice run would have provided them with the answers they needed. But, of course, this is not described in the gospels. It just didn't happen …

Or, did it?

CHAPTER 15

RAISING LAZARUS

And they come unto Bethany. And a certain woman whose brother had died was there. And, coming, she prostrated herself before Jesus and says to him, "Son of David, have mercy on me." But the disciples rebuked her. And Jesus, being angered, went off with her into the garden where the tomb was, and straightway a great cry was heard from the tomb. And going near Jesus rolled away the stone from the door of the tomb. And straightway, going in where the youth was, he stretched forth his hand and raised him, seizing his hand. But the youth, looking upon him, loved him and began to beseech him that he might be with him. And going out of the tomb they came into the house of the youth, for he was rich. And after six days Jesus told him what to do and in the evening the youth comes to him, wearing a linen cloth over his naked body. And he remained with him that night, for Jesus taught him the mystery of the Kingdom of God. And thence, arising, he returned to the other side of the Jordan.

Secret Gospel of Mark, quoted in letter from Clement of Alexandria (lived c AD 150–215)

Now a certain man was ill, Lazarus of Bethany, the village of Mary and her sister Martha. It was Mary who anointed the Lord with ointment and wiped his feet with her hair, whose brother Lazarus was ill. So the sisters sent to him, saying, "Lord, he whom you love is ill." But when Jesus heard it he said, "This illness is not unto death, it is for the glory of God, so that the Son of God may be glorified by means of it." Now Jesus loved Martha and her sister and Lazarus. So when he heard that he was ill, he stayed two days longer in the place where he was. Then after this he said to the disciples, "Let us go to Judaea again."…
Then Jesus, deeply moved again, came to the tomb; it was a

*cave, and a stone lay upon it. Jesus said, "Take away the
stone."...
So they took away the stone. And Jesus lifted up his eyes and
said, "Father, I thank thee that thou has heard me. I knew that
thou hearest me always, but I have said this on account of the
people standing by, that they may believe that thou didst send
me." When he had said this, he cried with a loud voice,
"Lazarus, come out." The dead man came out, his hands and
feet bound with bandages, and his face wrapped with a cloth.
Jesus said to them, "Unbind him, and let him go."*

John 11:1–7, 38–39, 41–44

———◦——

Successive overlays of textual addition, excision and alteration make the
analysis of gospel material very frustrating. Wouldn't it be wonderful if
an early document were to turn up in a monastery somewhere, perhaps
a copy of the earliest version of the passion narrative which had lain
forgotten and had escaped the attention of the censors? Better still, imagine
the discovery of the original collections of the sayings and an account of the
life of Jesus, hidden by the Nazoraeans during the crisis of the siege of
Jerusalem and then buried when the city was ransacked by the Romans.

Perhaps the Nazoraeans did hide copies of their texts and maybe
something will one day be discovered.

It is not that far-fetched. This is precisely what did happen with another
similar community, of "the poor" at Qumran, who the Romans correctly
identified as a group with a messianic message. The Romans interrupted
their siege of the city of Jerusalem in AD 68 just to attack and lay waste
Qumran. Most of the inhabitants were killed, apart from a few who
managed to escape to the stronghold at Masada. They had time, or the
foresight, to hide their precious writings, scrolls of parchment in pottery jars,
in caves along the hillside by the Jordan valley.

There they remained untouched, unaltered and unedited, for nineteen
centuries.

These astonishing time capsules give details of the organization of the
community, its beliefs and its interpretation of scripture. It has, by virtue of
this discovery, been possible both to confirm both the antiquity of many
existing biblical texts and see the ways in which these may have evolved.

But there were no collections of the sayings of Jesus among the Dead Sea
scrolls and no description of his life and passion. This is simply because these
people were not the early followers of Jesus led by James, even though there

were similarities in their religious beliefs, discipline, diet, baptismal rites, sharing of property, celibacy for some members and their messianic vision.

In its writings, the sect puts its founding to a point in time 390 years after the fall of Jerusalem to the Babylonians which happened in 587 BC. So this would have been towards the beginning of the second century BC. Their "Teacher of Righteousness", so far not positively identified, arose soon afterwards and found himself in opposition to the "Wicked Priest" or "Spouter of Lies" who had been "called by the way of truth" before he betrayed God for the sake of riches on becoming Israel's ruler.

Tempting though it is to make the association, the "Wicked Priest" cannot be Paul (not in any case Israel's ruler) and the "Teacher of Righteousness" cannot be James, because this fits neither the detail of the Qumran commentaries nor the possible time frame. The Wicked Priest may well have been one of the Hasmoneans, Jonathan, who took the office of High Priest even though he had no claim or qualification for this role. So there is no connection here with the Jerusalem community either.

But, as has been noted, the beliefs and way of life of "the poor" and the Nazoraeans were so similar in many respects that there was clearly some sort of association, even if only indirect.

Like the Nazoraeans, the members of the community at Qumran were messianic in their expectations: they were the faithful who would one day under their expected King or Messiah rise and defeat the Gentiles, including the "kittim" or Romans and establish an eternal kingdom on earth. The Nazoraeans already had their Messiah in Jesus and were awaiting his return.

The messianic expectations of both groups put them in danger. They were a potential or even a real threat to Roman authority and were generally treated as such. It seems the "Essenes" from Qumran had participated in the Jewish uprising in AD 66 and were punished by having their settlement destroyed.

Because of the risk involved, if the scrolls were to fall into the wrong hands, false names or pseudonyms were used in the text. "The Wicked Priest" possibly stood for Hasmonean leader, Jonathan. The "Chief of the Kings of Greece" could have been Tryphon, a general under Antiochus VI, who arrested and killed Jonathan. "The last Priests of Jerusalem" may have been a general description for the Hasmoneans, while the "kittim" were the Roman legions who exacted punishment on them.

Early texts, which must have originated from the Nazoraeans, do much the same thing in describing the life of Jesus. His helpers were not identified because, after Jesus had been "resurrected" or in other words survived crucifixion, both he and anyone who had assisted him were being sought by the High Priest and the Romans. The cult was becoming a nuisance. By claiming that Jesus was still alive, they were denying the reality and effectiveness of punishment, thumbing their noses at authority and creating a focus for resistance.

So that is why the men in white who helped at the tomb and provided the safe house at Jerusalem are not identified. It is also why, in the first of the passages quoted at the beginning of this chapter from a now-lost early version of Mark's Gospel (Secret Mark), there is an unidentified man raised by Jesus from the dead.

Comparison with the passage in John shows that the man must have been Lazarus. Both lived at Bethany, a small village close to Jerusalem, and both had at least one sister. Both apparently died and were entombed, with a stone rolled across the entrance. Then, in both cases, Jesus restored the apparently dead men were back to life.

A further point is that the young man with a sister in Secret Mark is described as being rich. This fits with the fact that Lazarus' sister Mary, who anointed Jesus with a whole pound of the precious spikenard, must also have come from a wealthy family. She was one of the women who, according to Luke, traveled with Jesus and the Apostles and "provided for them out of their means".

Still further confirmation comes from a second fragment of Secret Mark quoted by Clement of Alexandria. This adds to the commentary in canonical Mark the note that, when Jesus arrived in Jericho, "the sister of the youth whom Jesus loved and his mother and Salome were there, and Jesus did not receive them". Elsewhere in the gospels Mary Magdalene is grouped with Mary, the mother of Jesus, and her sister Salome. This Mary, as confirmed here and as earlier argued, was identical with Martha's sister Mary who had a brother named Lazarus. She was also, I have argued, married to Jesus.

Why did these three women find it necessary to present a deputation to Jesus in Jericho? The reason may be that he was on his way to Jerusalem for the Passover celebration where his life would be in danger. They may also have had more than an inkling of what he planned to do.

It can be presumed that Jesus did not receive them because his mind was set, and he did not want to be distracted by family pressure.

As John's Gospel reports, the "chief priests" planned to kill Lazarus as well as Jesus. This was because the miracle or sign given by the raising of Lazarus made many people believe in Jesus, that is in his special, messianic authority.

So the author of Secret Mark did not directly identify, in first telling the story, someone who was then probably still living and potentially in danger. Lazarus was a member of the family at Bethany to whom Jesus was very close and with whom he regularly stayed. I have argued earlier that Jesus was married to Mary and so Lazarus was also Jesus' brother-in-law.

When the author of John came to write his gospel, he based his account on the recollections of the "disciple whom Jesus loved", who had evidently lived to a great old age. By this time Lazarus had died, perishing quite probably in the Jewish uprising. So there was no longer a need for secrecy and John could name names. The exception was his own long-lived source, the disciple whom Jesus loved, who retained a pseudonym to protect his identity.

The text quoted by Clement of Alexandria from an edition of the gospel, which he described as "Secret Mark", has some very strange features. The story of raising from the dead appears to have included a baptismal rite, even though there are no indications elsewhere that Jesus himself–unlike John the Baptist, James and Paul–baptized his followers.

The text may have been used in the Christian community at Alexandria for their baptismal rites. There are also overtones of homoeroticism and this may be the reason the story was eventually deleted from the Gospel of Mark. It was part of an earlier version, called for convenience Secret Mark, older than the canonical gospel which has been preserved.

Crossan maintains that the story was actually dismembered. He argues that one part remains as the incident of the young man dressed in a linen cloth, running after Jesus on the Mount of Olives. The other part, he claims, became the story of the resurrection in the last eight verses of Mark.

With evidence as old and as altered as this, and the trail gone cold almost two millennia ago, nothing is impossible. Crossan's theory could be right.

But there are many differences between the story of the interment of Jesus and the raising of Lazarus. These details, if not true, would have had to be invented to fit the different circumstances.

The interpretation given by Crossan requires that the author of Mark deliberately apply a story to Jesus' burial, derived from some other situation and which he therefore knows to be untrue. Then, he has to invent the details necessary to make it fit.

This interpretation further requires that the source for John, the "disciple whom Jesus loved" who claimed to have been present at the Crucifixion, go along with this falsification. The author of John's Gospel has then to retain the story of Lazarus, as well as the version derived from it and fictionalized for the resurrection of Jesus.

Crossan's contention also suffers from the drawback of leaving the miracle of the raising of Lazarus up in the air, with no real explanation.

Given that there were other witnesses to the events, and given that the story fits well with other elements, demonstrating as will be seen detailed planning towards the objective of preserving Jesus' life, it is more likely that Mark and John were simply telling the story as they knew it. This goes back to one of the first principles given at the outset of my analysis: believe the source unless there is reason to do otherwise.

Like the rest of the passion narrative, the story of the burial and resurrection of Jesus was not, as I have argued, simply invented because of a lack of knowledge.

So, to return to the texts under consideration and the question posed at the end of chapter three, what kind of miracle was the raising of Lazarus?

What happened to Lazarus falls within the small category of "impossible" events, rather than the larger category of acts of faith healing which Jesus could well have carried out. There were, I suggested earlier, three types of explanation for these miracles: mistranslation, misunderstanding and mistaken association. None seemed to apply in this particular case. The miracle does not depend on any word or text that could have another meaning. It is not apparently a case of witnesses or the writers simply misunderstanding something else that Jesus was doing, and so interpreting a miracle where none was intended. There is no conjunction of events which really have another explanation.

I suggest that Jesus was in this instance doing something with a particular purpose. But, for a variety of motivations, he deliberately allowed what was happening to be misunderstood.

The raising of Lazarus was an event of some significance, described in detail in John and also in Secret Mark. It took place immediately before the approaching Passover Festival and caused many more people to believe or become Jesus' followers. This provided added reason for the pro-Roman High Priest's party to seek Jesus' downfall.

As reported in John, Jesus was informed of the severe illness of his close friend (and I suggest brother-in-law), but then waited a further two days before going to Bethany. By the time Jesus and his disciples arrived, the body of Lazarus had been placed in a tomb.

The detail of the two-day delay is not present in Secret Mark. The author of John has great difficulty in explaining why Jesus was so uncharacteristically ineffectual and did not immediately come in haste to give assistance to his mortally afflicted friend. John has rather lamely to suggest that it was for the "Glory of God". That is, Jesus was intent on performing an even bigger miracle, raising a man who had been dead for days so as to impress people and gain more converts! So, according to this version, he waited to ensure that Lazarus would be dead when he finally arrived, and dead for some time.

Since the awkward fact of the two days of apparent dithering before Jesus went to help Lazarus was not present in Secret Mark, why did the author of John include it at all? He could, for example, have made the miracle a much simpler affair with Jesus at hand to revive Lazarus shortly after being pronounced dead. Or he could have retained the element of delay by having Jesus located further away and having to make a longer journey, involving an extra two days, to get to his friend. This would still have led to the impressive miracle of a man being brought back to life, after having been dead for a number of days. Jesus would not then have been shown either as indecisive, indifferent or ready to put reputation and prestige (the Glory of God) before the welfare of his friend. The time lapse would have arisen entirely as a result of the messenger's journey to reach Jesus and tell him the news and for Jesus to return to Bethany.

When there were these other options, why did the author of John chose a version which made it difficult to put a positive gloss on Jesus' action? It is widely held that the gospel author used as his direct source "the disciple whom Jesus loved", years later relating events to which he had been a witness. The gospel author wrote down what he was told and he had no reason, other than to put Jesus in a better light, to change it. It is also possible that other written or verbal accounts were circulating at the time, and fictitious detail could have been contradicted.

The reason therefore that the author of John kept in the difficult-to-explain delay by Jesus before going to Bethany is this. He did so, I suggest, because it came from his source and he knew it to be true.

As I have argued, Jesus was a faith healer but not a performer of "impossible" miracles. So the raising of Lazarus, like the small group of other presumed miraculous events in the gospels, was either invented or has a rational explanation.

The circumstantial detail, the appearance of the story in more than one source and the lack of any motive for making it up suggest that the story was not invented.

The explanation I suggest is simple, though astonishing.

What follows is speculation, but it has the merit of fitting the facts as presented. I welcome any better explanation.

Jesus knew at this point in the chain of events that he was going to have to face or risk the ordeal of crucifixion. Just why he felt himself impelled to take action will be considered later. He had made, or was in the process of making, what provision he could to increase the chances of his survival.

Among these was the necessity to give the appearance of death on the cross, so that he could be taken down early without his legs broken. He also needed to test a potion that could do this. But he could hardly take it himself, because this might later create suspicion: the authorities would then surely take steps to avoid a second such resurrection.

So Lazarus was enlisted, or he volunteered, to undertake the risky business of trying the potion and simulating death. Who else should have responsibility but a close friend, member of the family that Jesus loved and, as I have argued, Jesus' brother-in-law?

Jesus needed to be available so that he could arrive at the right moment and "raise" Lazarus. But he had to be sufficiently far away, so that he wouldn't arrive too soon. That way, it would be possible to see whether the drug used would simulate the required effect over a long enough period. Jesus stayed about a day's walk away, while the plan was put into operation. Someone then came with the message that Lazarus was very sick.

Jesus was, however, expecting a message that his friend and brother-in-law had died. So he waited a day or so longer to make sure that Lazarus would be presumed dead and interred. Some provision must have been made to ensure that Lazarus was not suffocated by the bandages and had water, and maybe food, through a helper perhaps concealed in the tomb.

Jesus may have wanted to keep what happened fairly quiet. His main objectives were, after all, to carry out a dry run and test the drug. But there was in the event no chance of getting away with a quiet miracle. Jesus had by that time become a popular figure, with a reputation for healing and preaching. Word got around and there was a crowd waiting when he arrived to raise Lazarus from the dead.

The miracle enhanced Jesus' reputation. That could have been intended. But in any case the deception could not have been admitted for what it was. The incident, of course, further provoked the High Priest and his entourage. They were, as John describes, fearful that Jesus was gaining followers and that the Romans might ultimately intervene. Their rising irritation was not necessarily a problem, if it meant they would subsequently act with less calculation and perception.

But, when it came to the point, would they remember what had happened to Lazarus and suspect that Jesus might try something to bring about his own apparent resurrection?

If his enemies even thought about this, they didn't take the action necessary to thwart the plan.

Lazarus was close to Jesus and may have helped in other ways, such as in administering the "gall" to Jesus on the cross or in reviving his stricken friend on the Saturday in the tomb. The gospels say where the women were on the eve of Passover, near to the cross, but they do not mention where Lazarus was.

It is not so unlikely that Jesus, though he did not usually baptize, repaid Lazarus by baptizing him himself. That would explain why a baptism ritual appears to be mixed up in the story of the raising of Lazarus in Secret Mark.

If the explanation of events which I have offered is false, then there are questions which remain unanswered: what was the miracle of Lazarus about, was it invented and if so why was it invented, and where did the story originate?

What I have suggested has the merit of fitting the evidence as presented without any additional elaboration. It shows why, for example, Jesus waited for two days before going to see Lazarus–something that the source for

John's Gospel knew but the author of this gospel could not explain. It also fits with the story as a whole, and fills a gap among the precautions and preparations that are described, and would have had to be undertaken.

The evidence of the passion narrative, discussed in the previous chapters, indicates a sequence of conscious planning directed towards avoiding Jesus' death on the cross. If this is true, then the question which needs to be answered is this: what would have otherwise been done to test the safety and effectiveness of the potion of gall? If not the raising of Lazarus, then what else?

It was risky, as was indeed was the whole enterprise. The issue as to what was safe or sensible in the circumstances, however, begs an even greater question. Jesus was at risk because he preached a message directed to the poor and the oppressed, and against the rich, because he performed or was believed to perform miracles and because he was believed by many to be the Messiah.

But, providing he did not do anything overtly rebellious, he may not have been in any immediate danger.

So why did he go to Jerusalem, act in a way indicating that he believed he was the Messiah, the King of the Jewish people, overturn the money-changers' tables in the Temple and challenge the authorities? Why did he then meekly wait, when he was quite safe and could easily have escaped into the desert, and instead have himself handed over?

This is something which has never been satisfactorily explained.

It is the story, that of meek and inexplicable surrender, now presented in the gospels. But it may not be what originally happened.

CHAPTER 15

GLIMPSES

After this he [Pilate] stirred up further trouble by expending the sacred treasure known as Corban on an aqueduct 50 miles long. This roused the populace to fury, and when Pilate visited Jerusalem they surrounded the tribunal and shouted him down. But he had foreseen this disturbance, and had made soldiers mix with the mob, wearing civilian clothes over their armor, and with orders not to draw their swords but to use clubs on the obstreperous. He now gave the signal from the tribunal and the Jews were cudgeled, so that many died from the blows, and many were trampled to death by their friends as they fled.

    The Jewish War, Josephus

There were some present at that very time who told him [Jesus] of the Galileans whose blood Pilate had mingled with their sacrifices.

    Luke 13:1

And among the rebels in prison, who had committed murder in the insurrection, there was a man called Barabbas.

    Mark 15:7

So the chief priests and the Pharisees gathered the council, and said, "What are we to do? For this man performs many signs. If we let him go on thus, every one will believe in him, and the Romans will come and destroy both our holy place and our nation. But one of them, Caiaphas, who was High Priest that year, said to them, "You know nothing at all; you do not understand that it is expedient for you that one man should die for the people, and that the whole nation should not perish."

    John 11:47– 50

Again he asked them, "Whom do you seek?" And they said, "Jesus of Nazareth." Jesus answered, "I told you that I am he; so, if you seek me, let these men go." This was to fulfill the word which he had spoken, "Of those whom thou gavest me I lost not one."

John 18:7–9

———◦——

When the layers of reinterpretation and alteration are stripped away, the gospels reveal that Jesus was preaching not the Christian religion but the Jewish religion. His message was indeed radical, disavowing possessions and aimed at humble people, outcasts, the disfigured and diseased, the downtrodden, sad and lonely. He taught the hardest lesson of all, to put the needs of others on a par with one's own. He preached a Kingdom of God in the here-and-now which people could plug into by altering their lives.

So he was at least a spiritual liberator. He was seen by many, and ultimately appeared to see himself, as the Jewish Messiah, that is the king promised by scripture who would liberate Israel. It was for that crime, treason against Rome, that he was ostensibly condemned and punished.

But the movement of which Jesus was a part had many faces. Jesus was not an outright political revolutionary. There was no major bloody battle with lots of casualties. Had there been, there is no doubt that Josephus, for all his evasions and equivocations, would have recorded it.

Had there been, there is also no doubt that the position of James and the Nazoraean followers of Jesus would then immediately have become untenable.

But James and the other Apostles in Jerusalem were initially left alone, as recorded in Acts, while Saul and other officers of the High Priest went after a more radical group of Jesus' followers. It seems that there were, following the Crucifixion, two factions, one preaching a spiritual message and awaiting their king's return and the other following a course of more overt resistance.

James did in fact remain as head of a thriving and growing community of followers for 25 more years.

The dividing lines between the two groups may not have been that clear, especially as the Roman authorities came to recognize the messianic overtones of the Jesus movement. Jesus' brothers and their descendants were sought out, investigated and in most cases executed. It was a purge that went on for many years, intensifying after the eventual failure of the Jewish uprising which began in AD 66.

James the Righteous, abstemious, devoted to the Jewish Law, his knees worn hard by constant praying, was eventually killed by the Sadducee High

Priest and his followers in AD 62. It can be presumed, from early sources, that this was because his popularity as a religious leader had become a threat to them. He may also have challenged the religious compromises they had to make with the Roman authorities.

But, if the beliefs and practices of James and Jesus were similar, notwithstanding efforts to make it appear as if Jesus had broken with Judaism, why did Jesus suffer the fate of a political revolutionary? He was after all, like James, preaching what was primarily a spiritual message.

The gospels depict Jesus as engaging in an arduous preaching and healing ministry before suddenly going to Jerusalem, making some symbolic gestures and then inexplicably turning himself in. There was no fight, no real resistance that would have led to his brother James and his other immediate followers also being hunted down.

But there are glimpses, beneath the surface, of something else going on, something running counter to the main story line presented in the gospels.

There are throwaway references, strewn almost accidentally in the text, which give hints of a serious conflict in which there were casualties: Galilean blood mingled with sacrifices, "murder" committed in an insurrection, rebels languishing in prison.

Pilate was the Roman procurator or governor of Judaea at this time, holding the office from AD 26 until AD 36 when he was relieved of his post, shortly after Jesus was crucified. The gospel accounts provide a record of his jurisdiction, giving on the surface the impression that all was fairly calm. But there is other historical evidence, particularly from the writer Josephus, of friction and conflict.

The dynamics by which the Romans created and maintained an empire were not so different from others before them or since. They were centrally organized, efficient and made better use of their resources, or had better technology, than their enemies. They had economic power. When they gained territory they used overwhelming force, but to maintain their dependencies or vassal states they used much less force. Otherwise, they would have been permanently overstretched in every direction.

What kept conquered territories compliant was as much the threat from forces that the centralized power could muster, as the number of occupying troops actually present. If there had also been insurrections brutally suppressed, memories of these would reinforce the point. The situation for the Jews, under Roman occupation in the early first century, provides a clear demonstration. When the tyrant Herod died, rebellions broke out in several different parts of Palestine. But legions were posted in, the uprisings were crushed and several thousand captured rebels were crucified, including perhaps many who were simply sympathizers. The action was exemplary and for a while it worked.

Fear may not however be the best means, especially if it is the only means, to secure the cooperation of an occupied people.

An occupying force generates economic needs and creates opportunities for traders and suppliers, and also political collaborators needed for the purposes of justice and day-to-day administration. The development of a class of beneficiaries provides the cement that can weld an empire together.

There was certainly such a class in Israel, and prominent among them were the High Priest and his immediate followers, owing their position to the favor of Rome. The Romans added legal and judicial functions to the ceremonial role of High Priest, and took over for themselves the power of appointment. Although the Jewish council of elders, the Sanhedrin, was still left with considerable powers of internal administration, this interference was deeply resented by many Jews. Even without their failings being pointed up by activists like Jesus, the High Priest and his faction among the Sadducees were distinctly unpopular.

So there were limitations as to what could be gained by shaping a Romano-Jewish middle class, by dividing society and diminishing resistance as some people gained from participation in the fruits of empire. It would seem that, on the contrary, the vast majority of ordinary Jewish people lost through the imposition of extortionate taxes.

The Romans had a particular kind of difficulty in dealing with the Jews, as compared with other subject peoples. The Jews had a religion which they had defended through centuries of occupation by different powers and it was associated with their very idea of nationhood. Religious and political life were inextricably intertwined. So it was never really feasible to get a significant part of the population onside, as willing collaborators.

The occupying powers that fared best were those that allowed the people to carry on with their religious practices, as opposed to imposing upon them an alien religion and way of life. For this reason, the Persian kings ruled over Israel with far less trouble than the hated Seleucid ruler Antiochus IV.

The Romans in theory allowed the Jews freedom to worship in their own way, but did not always follow this through into the details of administration or appreciate the offense that particular actions might cause. A lot depended on the sensitivity and understanding of individual rulers.

For much of the time, however, these qualities were manifestly lacking. The Emperor Caligula, for example, ordered Petronius, his legate in Syria, to place a statue of himself as Zeus incarnate in the Temple at Jerusalem. There were at once massive popular demonstrations involving large-scale passive resistance. Petronius stalled, a tactic that saved the situation and himself because it gained time. While Petronius delayed, Caligula was assassinated and the statue became an irrelevance.

This episode happened in AD 41, not long after Pilate's term as procurator in Judaea.

Pilate's record was itself patchy. He was, by surviving accounts, irascible and impulsive and inclined to taking action without thinking through the consequences. He was, however, sufficiently aware and prone to reason to realize when he had gone too far. He could, if circumstances demanded, back down.

The writer Josephus records some major disturbances, though not necessarily all of the incidents, which occurred while Pilate was in charge in Judaea. The first happened not long after Pilate was appointed; he certainly did not get off to a very good start.

While previous procurators had apparently used plain standards for troops stationed in Jerusalem, Pilate decided to deploy troops which had standards with attached, embossed busts of the Roman Emperor. While this might seem a trivial consideration, the Jews considered such images idolatrous, especially when they related to someone the Romans considered had a god-like status. It was the reason that the Jews required Roman coins to be changed into Temple coinage for the purchase of the doves used for religious sacrifices.

The outraged population of the city gathered themselves up and went to Caesarea, attracting other protesters along the way, and proceeded to mount a picket outside Pilate's residence. Here they remained for five days and nights, immovable in a sit-down strike.

Pilate decided to break the deadlock by inviting the demonstrators for an audience in the stadium where he had soldiers hidden. Once they were inside, he threatened them with execution unless they abandoned their action.

The demonstrators responded by offering en masse to accept death, rather than give up their protest.

Faced with the invidious prospect of having to massacre so many, and for so little apparent reason, Pilate was himself forced to back down. He thus agreed to remove the military standards with their offending images from Jerusalem. Since legions and their standards were inseparable, he must have done this by redeploying other troops.

Another subsequent incident, also described by Josephus, was the sequestration of sacred Temple funds for the mundane purpose of building an aqueduct to bring water into Jerusalem. A very large crowd gathered and began to hurl abuse at the Romans. Pilate hid some of his soldiers in the crowd, disguised as civilians, with clubs concealed under their clothes.

They had orders to bring these out and beat protesters, rather than use their swords. The object presumably was to beat the rioters into submission without causing any loss of life. This was another ill-conceived scheme which not surprisingly failed to turn out as Pilate planned.

The intervention caused panic, as the protesters hit back at attackers they may not even have identified. A number of bystanders were killed or injured, amid the general confusion.

The events leading to Jesus' Crucifixion are believed to have taken place at the end of Pilate's term of office, judging from a number of details in the gospels including associations with the life of John the Baptist. These events were only mentioned by Josephus in passing, possibly for reasons which will be discussed in the next chapter.

Following the Crucifixion of Jesus, presumably immediately afterwards since there was not much left of Pilate's rule, came a very serious incident in which a number of Samaritans were massacred.

It will be recalled that the Samaritans had separated from allegiance to the Temple at Jerusalem and had established a cult of their own. They were expecting a messianic figure, the Taheb, who would reveal where on Mount Gerizim Moses had buried the sacred vessels of the tabernacle, the portable sanctuary used by the Israelites during their time in the wilderness.

A man appeared, claiming to be the Taheb, and led a crowd of followers to Mount Gerizim.

Pilate sent a detachment of cavalry and heavily armed infantry to block the way up the mountain. There was according to Josephus a pitched battle, though it was probably more like simple slaughter. The Taheb's followers had not been going to a place where they would be confronting anyone. So most would not have been armed.

Some were killed and others were taken prisoner. Pilate executed all the leaders.

The Samaritans appealed to Pilate's immediate superior, the Syrian legate Vitellius, claiming that they were not rebels but refugees from Pilate's persecution. Vitellius ruled in their favor and Pilate was sent to Rome to explain his actions. He was found wanting and replaced.

This action happened just after the incidents involving Jesus. But what about the clubbing of demonstrators in the protest over misuse of sacred Temple funds for an aqueduct?

Luke gives a description of Jesus being informed of an incident in which Pilate had mingled the blood of Galileans with their sacrifices. This is placed either just before or at the beginning of Jesus' travels through towns and villages on the way to the Passover festival at Jerusalem.

This was clearly not a minor disturbance and it must either relate to an incident described by Josephus or there must be a reason why the historian did not record it.

If it was recorded by Josephus, then it is most likely that Luke was alluding to the Temple funds demonstration.

The attack on demonstrators which also injured bystanders would fit: the innocent bystanders could easily have included Galileans present at the Temple to make their sacrifices. Doubtless, some Galileans were also there to protest because they also contributed to the Jerusalem Temple funds.

If this suggested timing is correct, then the misappropriation of Temple funds would have happened at about the time of the census, held every fourteen years to provide a base for collecting tax. In this context, it would have appeared even more as a gratuitous imposition and affront to Jewish religious rights.

The sequence of three incidents which were either mishandled or had awkward repercussions provides a plausible culmination to a climax in which Pilate was sacked, not just for one mistake, but for a whole series of misjudgments over a period.

So I will suggest that it was the aqueduct/Temple funds protest incident that was reported to Jesus, in which some of his supporters were injured. It is something that helps to explain how Jesus acted, making what seemed inexplicable now totally rational.

A number of people had been killed, including someone on the side of the authorities, possibly a Roman soldier or official. Some of the Temple fund protesters had been arrested, among them Barabbas.

It was a very tricky situation, since the Jewish leaders of all factions had made bitter complaints about the misappropriation of Temple funds and now were making equally strong representations over the provocative act of using soldiers in disguise to club the protesters. Pilate needed to be right, and he needed a culprit.

But clearly, as he himself might have conceded, he had not acted wisely. The leaders of the Sanhedrin were warning him that if he executed any of the protesters, there would be a riot with possibly a huge loss of life. The timing could not be worse, from the point of view of the Roman authorities, before the approaching Passover–a celebration of Jewish national liberation–when the population was swelled by many thousands of pilgrims, and feelings would be running high.

So this was one trajectory, Pilate feeling provoked and possibly being provoked, acting without deliberation and building up to an explosion of anger and frustration.

The other trajectory is provided by Jesus and the two intersected just before the Feast of the Passover.

A recapitulation can be made of Jesus' life up to this point. All the significant points have been argued through in previous chapters. There are gaps in the story, especially relating to his early years, but these do not affect the main thrust of the argument. So, some intelligent surmises will be made.

Jesus was born in a family which had some priestly connections. This may not have been all that significant, since many could claim to be "Sons of

David"; after many centuries and after years of exile, the exact genealogical connections had been lost. But it did provide a basis, for anyone who felt so inclined, to offer himself up as a candidate for the Jewish kingship, as the people's "anointed one" or "Messiah".

He was the eldest of a family in which there were four or five brothers and two or more sisters. Their social father was called Clophas or Cleophas, although Jesus may have had a biological father called Joseph who was Cleophas' brother.

As potential messianic claimants Jesus and a cousin, who became John the Baptist, may have been in danger from the tyrant King Herod who was prone to exterminate potential rival claimants.

Jesus was bright and showed early promise. As a young boy, his knowledge and understanding caught the attention of religious teachers, while on a visit with his parents to Jerusalem.

Jesus then disappeared for some time, at least from the record as given, and reappeared as an adult ready to embark on a teaching and preaching ministry. The lapse of time, as well as his gain in stature and confidence made the people who once knew him a little uncertain: "Is not this the carpenter's son?" they asked according to Matthew and Mark, with slight variation. Jesus was a boy when he went away and now he was a grown man; they weren't sure that the young person they once knew could be capable of such learning and forceful eloquence.

Jesus championed the marginalized and oppressed and taught a way of life in accordance with Pharisaic thought. He spoke of a kingdom of heaven on earth, in the here and now, approached and achieved by following a good way of life. His followers, the Nazoraeans under his brother James, had a way of life and practices similar to those of the Essenes, the self-styled "poor" who had initially retreated to the wilderness, believing themselves to be the true upholders of Jewish Law. The Essenes had communities in other places besides Qumran, their "assemblies of the camps" also in the desert and their "assemblies of the towns".

One of these was in Jerusalem, where there was a "gate of the Essenes" in the old city wall, and there was probably one also in Galilee.

In Jesus' crucial, planned confrontation in the period leading up to Passover in AD 36, he had helpers. A safe house was provided. The man who led the disciples to it carried a jar to fetch water, which was almost invariably women's work. This man must have belonged to a largely celibate community: the "poor" or Essenes in Jerusalem. The men described in the gospels as being dressed in white at the tomb were also helpers, and probably from the same community.

Jesus clearly had spent some time developing his knowledge of Judaism. I would suggest, because of all the evidence, including the convergence of

Nazoraean and Essenic practices, that at least some of this time was spent with one of the communities of "the poor".

This could possibly have been at Capernaum, but it was more likely to have been at Jerusalem where his intelligence and knowledge of scripture first came to the attention of religious elders. This would account for the comments in the gospels of Matthew and Mark which indicate that, when he eventually returned to Galilee, people were not even quite sure who he was. A youth had gone away. But here was a man, confident and knowledgeable. Was it really the carpenter or builder's son?

For several years, while he was growing up to be a man, Jesus studied and participated in the life of the community, I surmise at Jerusalem. He became part of the background, dedicated and able, but otherwise unnoticed. He made friends who would help him later on. He may have been initiated into the community. He may well have had one or more of his brothers with him.

He helped cultivate in the community gardens and vineyards and he developed a knowledge of medicine, healing and herbs.

He read the prophets and he applied what he learned to his own background. He or one of his immediate family could be the promised Messiah, the expected king, who might suffer but ultimately deliver his people.

Jesus left the community, perhaps for several reasons. He wanted to take his understanding and the message of the kingdom to a wider audience beyond the closed circle of the community. He had met Mary Magdalene/Mary of Bethany, who came from a relatively wealthy family. He no longer wanted a celibate life; he sought and married Mary at Capernaum which was at or near his family home.

The wedding was a large one bringing together two families, one at least with wealth and the other with a respectable, and it may be presumed Davidic, priestly lineage.

Jesus encountered his cousin John, known as John the Baptist, and son of the priest Zechariah. He must earlier have been aware of John's existence, but it seems they had gone their separate ways perhaps both into separate seclusion to escape the attentions of Herod or other powerful Herodians.

John had begun to baptize followers in the river Jordan, preaching the coming of the Last Days and demanding repentance. There may have been some confusion as to who should take precedence, but Jesus allowed himself to be baptized by John.

The ruler of Galilee, the tetrarch Herod Antipas who was one of the sons of the former King Herod, understandably saw John as a threat. He was on the brink of war with the Nabataean King Aretas, whose daughter he had married and then discarded in favor of his brother's widow.

As a pre-emptive measure, to prevent trouble on one front while fighting on another, Herod Antipas had John arrested, imprisoned and then executed.

This left Jesus, baptized by John and the eldest son of Mary and Joseph or Cleophas, as the prime messianic contender.

He embarked on a peripatetic preaching ministry to take his message to the people, and possibly also to keep one step ahead of Herod Antipas who, as the gospels indicate, also saw Jesus as a potential threat. Jesus moved in and out of Galilee, traveling west to the coast, east to the desert and south to Judaea. As he went along, he attracted increasingly large crowds. He healed the sick and delivered a message of salvation.

His ministry of healing, he made it clear, was directed to the Jews and not to any wider audience.

He had an inner core of helpers and disciples chiefly from his own family, his brothers, half brothers and cousins, as well as a few trusted friends like Simon Peter.

Jesus also had contacts with leading Pharisees and among "the poor" or Essenes, from his time spent within one of the communities, most probably in Jerusalem. He had an idea of confronting the corrupt Sadducean inner circle of the Roman-appointed High Priest and his followers. He was aware of the risks. Like others before him with messianic claims, he was likely to be treated as a political rebel and killed.

Some of his criticism of the ruling elite was presented in the form of parables. He could not afford to be direct since the Herodian network of spies was still everywhere.

"He who has ears to hear, let him hear," he said. The increasingly large crowds heard the message, and they loved it.

Jesus knew his scriptures. He had come to see himself as the Lord's servant, the suffering righteous one, in terms of the prophecies of Isaiah. But the scripture suggested that the Lord's servant, having suffered on his behalf, might then thrive and prosper. He might have to suffer, but there was no biblical imperative that he had to die.

He could confront and also make provisions if possible for his survival and safety.

Jesus was well aware, through his contacts and also visits to Jerusalem, of the difficulties of the increasingly frustrated and embattled governor Pilate.

News reached him of Pilate's botched plan to break up a demonstration against his misuse of Temple funds for an aqueduct. Soldiers with hidden clubs caused mayhem; there were a lot of injuries and some deaths among the protesters and others present in the Temple to make their sacrifices. A number of protesters had been arrested, including some of Jesus' Galilean followers who had gone down to Jerusalem for the demonstration. Someone on the other side, a soldier or an official, had also been killed.

Jewish religious leaders made vigorous protests. Pilate hesitated to punish the arrested protesters for fear of a violent uprising. But releasing them might be taken as a sign of weakness. The Feast of the Passover was fast approaching, when many thousands of pilgrims would be in Jerusalem.

Pilate decided to temporize and took the unusual course of leaving the protesters in prison, though without trial or sentence. This was even though their continuing captivity might itself become a focus of unrest. He would, he considered, possibly have them tried and executed after the Passover.

Told of the misfortune affecting his fellow Galileans caught up in the Temple funds protest, as reported in Luke, Jesus avoided an unspoken question.

His comment was to the effect that death can catch up with anyone at any time. The bystanders who suffered in Jerusalem were not more sinful than anyone else, but their fate reinforced the necessity for everyone to repent in time.

It must be borne in mind that this could simply be a piece of editorial sermonizing on the part of Luke; it was a common practice at this time to insert speeches considered appropriate in writing up events. However, there is a similar structure between this incident and the one concerning the Feast of the Tabernacles, in the Gospel of John. Jesus' brothers urged him to go to Jerusalem. Jesus said he wouldn't but then later secretly did.

In Luke, the unspoken question was, "What are you going to do about it?"

"What are you going to do about the protesters, including your fellow Galileans, now arrested and in jail?"

Jesus avoided answering this directly, but he had a plan of action which he decided to extend to cover this eventuality. He did secretly decide to do something about the situation.

Jesus' strategy for a confrontation and his contingency plans for surviving it were already, and indeed had to be given the timescale, in an advanced state of preparation.

So he may well with the cooperation of Lazarus have already tested the drug which, when added to vinegar, would simulate his death on the cross.

The new circumstances, the imprisonment of the protesters, could be made to work to his advantage.

Lazarus knew of his plans in detail and liaised with members of the "poor" in Jerusalem whose efforts would be crucial in ministering to a beaten and badly injured Jesus and getting him safely out of the burial tomb. One or two leading Pharisees, Nicodemus who spoke to Jesus at length and at night and Joseph of Arimathaea, also knew in outline what was proposed. Their help was also going to be absolutely vital.

But Jesus could not afford to confide in too many people, or the authorities might find out. In which case, all his efforts would be in vain and he would almost certainly die a degrading and painful death. So Jesus probably did not tell his brothers or other close disciples of his plans. He may have told them in general terms that he was going to suffer and "rise again". They were uncertain what to expect.

Jesus abandoned his former caution, allowing himself to be described as "Son of David" and, as a final act of piety by his devoted wife Mary, was anointed with spikenard, the oil of kings. He approached Jerusalem, riding on an ass, in fulfillment of the prophecy of Zechariah that the expected Messiah would approach the city in this way.

He had joined with a band of pilgrims going to Jerusalem for the Passover and so managed to enter without being challenged or detected.

He had a large band of followers, some of whom were armed, surrounding him so that he could move about freely and fairly safely in daylight. Jesus spent a few days in Jerusalem, returning to the comparative safety of Bethany each night. He symbolically cleansed the Temple, turning over the tables of the money-changers. He preached on the Temple steps.

With the Passover fast approaching, and the Temple fund protesters still in prison, feelings were running high. The city was crowded. It just needed a spark to cause a riot and, following that, massive Roman retribution.

The High Priest and his followers were outraged and incensed at Jesus' intervention. Others, among the Pharisees, who knew that the system of exchange at the Temple was onerous and corrupt, secretly or openly admired what Jesus had done.

Meanwhile, Pilate was still in a highly anxious state over the Temple funds affair. It was his job to keep order. If there were a riot and the Syrian legate Vitellius had to bring legions in to quell it, he would be seen as having ignominiously failed. He had already made too many mistakes. It would cost him his job, maybe his liberty or life.

The activities of the Galilean preacher Jesus had been reported to him. It appeared to him to be an internal religious matter which was for the Jews to sort out. Jesus, though a nuisance in an already inflamed situation, did not necessarily pose a threat to Rome.

This prophet had moreover a large band of followers and Pilate's resources were limited. He was reluctant to intervene, cause more unrest and possibly make matters worse.

Jesus celebrated Passover with his brothers and other disciples on the Wednesday night, following the custom of the "poor" and in a safe house to which members of the community had led them, if not provided. Then he sent Judas with a message to the High Priest and Pilate and went with his followers, some at least of them armed, to the Mount of Olives and waited.

Now the structure of this incident, as described, is not consistent with the explanation that Jesus was simply handing himself over. He could have done that in Jerusalem at any time of his choosing. Why go through the cumbersome procedure of sending a messenger and then having to wait, causing a possible delay which could destroy all the planning and preparation?

Jesus was embracing a fate, but planning to survive it. To do so, it was crucial that everything should go exactly to plan. If events happened too swiftly, he would endure many hours on the cross and die as a result. If too slowly, then his execution would be postponed until after Passover and the same would happen, only with even greater certainty.

The scenario does not make sense for a simple handover. But it all makes perfect sense, and the conditions are absolutely classic, if what was happening was *an exchange*.

The Romans occupied and controlled towns and cities while the wilderness was the province of the pious and the poor. In between was the Mount of Olives, in effect neutral territory providing a high vantage point, a safe place for an armed group to position itself for an exchange of prisoners or hostages. If there was any hint of treachery or trouble, they could retreat, disappearing back into the desert.

This then was what Jesus had offered, his life for the release of the prisoners taken during the riot over the appropriation of Temple funds. It was the message taken by Judas and received with astonishment and not a little incredulity by the High Priest Caiaphas. It was the message then conveyed to a slightly bemused Pilate, woken from his sleep because he had to authorize the exchange.

But this was not before a meeting had been hastily convened of the Sanhedrin, or at least those members who could easily be reached. Some argued against the exchange. But feelings were running high among the people over Pilate's misappropriation of Temple funds, his provocative action against the demonstrators and his action in imprisoning some of them. It would not take much to start a riot, causing the full might of Rome to fall upon them. Jesus himself might cause a rebellion. The consensus, expressed by the High Priest Caiaphas, was that it was better that one man should die than the whole nation perish.

The Pharisees on the whole went along with the plan. Key figures like Nicodemus and Joseph of Arimathaea, who might have argued against it, did not do so because they knew exactly what was behind the deal. They had inside knowledge.

Had it been a betrayal and handover, the Pharisees as a whole might have used their votes on the Council to veto it, as they later voted to have Peter and other disciples released. The reason they did not was that it was not that type of situation. It was not a handover; it was an exchange.

Pilate may have suspected some possible double-dealing but at the same time he saw an opportunity. The prisoners were an encumbrance, the situation was in deadlock and there was a real possibility of more conflict. Pilate saw the offer as a means of getting out of a difficult position without losing face. Yes, he would authorize the exchange. But he ordered that a detachment of soldiers should go up with the prisoners and Jewish police to ensure that there was no trickery. He could not allow the prisoners simply to be abducted.

So, after a long interval, the group of soldiers, prisoners and officers of the High Priest made their way up to the Mount of Olives. They were seen by the light of their torches by Jesus and his followers, waiting on the mountain.

So the exchange was effected. It was a tense situation which Jesus did his best to calm. One of his followers swung a sword, cutting the ear of one of the High Priest's servants. But there was otherwise no serious bloodshed.

Jesus could be content that not one of the followers entrusted to him had been lost. He may, as this is quoted in John's Gospel (see above), have simply meant his followers waiting with him on the mountain. But he could also have been referring to the prisoners. All of them, including Jesus Barabbas, had been handed over. Not one of these had been lost.

Jesus was taken away to be examined and tried the next day. Once this happened, Joseph and Nicodemus began to make their preparations.

Pilate, greeting a new day, was not sure what he wanted to do with his prisoner, a religious prophet and healer of some kind who had gathered crowds and caused a minor disturbance in the Temple. The exchange had been made and so this man's life was in theory forfeit. But was he a threat? He didn't appear to be. He should be executed in place of Barabbas, but only if proper charges could be laid.

Pilate was in two minds: he needed a life for the life taken by the protesters and he needed an example to be made. But, above all, he needed the Passover celebrations to take place without any major incident.

He was perplexed by Jesus' attitudes and values, that he should have offered himself up for a few paltry troublemakers. He noted how the man maintained his calm, in spite of being mocked and buffeted, and in the face of an horrific fate. Pilate reminded Jesus that he had the power of life and death over him, that he either could release him or order him to be crucified. He found himself entangled in verbal sophistries.

Jesus was keeping control of himself; he temporized.

Pilate went back to the High Priest. He could not see anything seriously threatening about Jesus. He had been promised a dangerous rebel in exchange for the prisoners and had got instead a mild-mannered religious eccentric.

Caiaphas and his faction were adamant. The protesters or rebels had committed murder; Jesus was they claimed the leader of all these troublemakers and he had to die. If, they insinuated, Pilate did not punish

Jesus, he would not be seen as Caesar's friend, his loyal and effective servant.

The High Priest and his faction wanted Jesus out of the way for a number of reasons. He had mocked and undermined their authority, he was too popular and he threatened to disturb the balance and their profitable relationship with the Roman authorities, on whose patronage they depended.

You are not asking the right questions, they told Pilate. Ask him if he claims to be a rival to Caesar, the King of the Jews.

So Pilate did just that and Jesus calmly and politely agreed that he was the Messiah, the expected King of his people. The Roman governor was astonished. Jesus had condemned himself out of his own mouth; he had only himself to blame.

It was by now late afternoon, merging into early evening. Pilate found Jesus guilty of treason and sentenced him to death by crucifixion.

There might, however, still be a problem: Jesus could possibly be just as great a focus of discontent as the prisoners, now released. There was a difference, though. Pilate had been put under pressure by all the Jewish leaders over the Temple funds affair. Now all of them seemed to want Jesus executed.

The High Priest and other leading Sadducees wanted Jesus killed immediately; they feared trouble, possibly even a possible rescue attempt if Jesus were to be kept in prison over the festival. Leading Pharisees, Joseph of Arimathaea and Nicodemus, argued the same, though for their own very different reasons. They were privy to a plan which could lead to Jesus' survival, providing he was put on the cross on the eve of Passover.

So Pilate set the next day, Friday the eve of Sabbath and the Passover, as the day of execution.

Now Joseph of Arimathaea came to Pilate with an even more delicate mission. He pointed out that Jesus had many followers and, if he were to be executed in a public place, it might lead to demonstrations. Joseph had a garden, used for cultivation, in which there was an as yet unused family tomb. If this place were used for the Crucifixion, the public could be kept out and there would be less chance of trouble. Moreover, Jesus came from a respected priestly lineage and deserved to be given a proper burial.

Pilate could see the logic of this and even the faintest hint of a threat: if the execution were undertaken in a public place, there *would* be trouble.

But he had got out of a hole and he had had more than enough of Jesus. What did it matter what happened to the body? He agreed to Joseph's suggestion.

However, as he retired to bed again, he may have sensed obscurely that he was being led by the nose, manipulated for a purpose he could not quite comprehend.

Events then proceeded, as they have been described.

The formalities were completed on the Friday morning, the eve of Passover. Jesus was flogged and sent up to the place of execution, outside the city. It seems that two criminals convicted of robbery were to be crucified with him.

Jesus, even though in a weakened state, would have been made to carry the heavy bar of the cross to which he would be tied or nailed. Probably through the efforts of his helpers, a sympathizer, though someone unknown to the authorities, was enlisted to do this for him.

Before being crucified, Jesus was offered a mixture of wine and myrrh to help deaden the effects of pain. But he refused because he needed to remain alert and aware, in order to be ready to take the drugged vinegar when it was offered.

Another helper, possibly Lazarus, was there to perform this task when Jesus cried out and gave the signal. Someone, possibly Lazarus again, had secured men from the community of the poor in Jerusalem who had knowledge of first aid and healing. At least one man was ready, hidden in the tomb. Joseph and Nicodemus got together all the supplies and equipment that would be needed in a large sack, to be taken on the back of a mule to the tomb.

As soon as Jesus had fallen into a stupor, Joseph approached Pilate and asked for the body. Pilate sent a soldier or soldiers to investigate. The legs of the other condemned men were broken, as sunset was approaching and with it the Sabbath, the day of the Passover. Jesus appeared to be dead already. Joseph, Nicodemus and others positioned themselves in front of the cross, demanding that the body be left whole. It was unnecessary and disrespectful, they argued, to break the man's legs since he was already dead. One soldier may have thrust his spear through the throng just to make sure.

Jesus was taken down and into the tomb. For two nights and one whole day, his helpers worked to revive him. Eventually, he was helped out, supported on either side by two helpers.

He appeared first to his brother James and then to other family members and disciples. But, because of the severity of his injuries, he failed to make it to the original meeting place he had arranged with his disciples beside the Sea of Galilee. A messenger was sent on to meet any of the disciples who turned up there.

Within days, rumors began to fly that Jesus had miraculously "risen from the dead" after his Crucifixion. The High Priest's faction suspected and alleged that Jesus' followers had taken the body.

But if there proved to be any truth in the rumor, that Jesus had survived, they would have made sure a second time that he really died. That is, they would have done so had they caught up with him.

The same went for the Roman authorities. Although, in the event, the Passover Festival was concluded peacefully, Pilate was annoyed by the rumors circulating that Jesus had "risen" from the dead. The rumors could not be true, of course. But he felt he may have been too ready to agree to all the suggestions of the Jewish leaders. He had admittedly been in an awkward position.

The rumors grew in intensity; it seemed there was even a growing cult of a "risen Messiah". Pilate felt that somehow a mockery was being made of the judicial process and his authority.

Then, without warning, a new front opened. Perhaps encouraged by the example of Jesus, a Samaritan had come forward claiming to be their version of the Messiah, the Taheb, their King in competition with Caesar. This man had gathered his followers to go up Mount Gerizim and find the sacred vessels of the tabernacle hidden there by Moses.

It was all too much: one rebel king that he had executed but could not keep down and now weeks later another one in Samaria. Pilate vowed this time to make sure it was stopped. He sent in the cavalry and his heavily armed infantry. He broke up the procession, killed a number of the Samaritans and then had all the leading figures executed.

By the time he drew breath and calmed down, Pilate had vented his pent-up frustration and, in one sense, he may even have felt better. But this time he knew that he had gone too far. The Samaritan authorities were already complaining to Vitellius. Pilate was recalled to face the music in Rome. He escaped lightly; he simply lost his job.

Pilate was the Roman procurator and would certainly not have connived in any scheme to save Jesus. But, through his interrogations, he possibly developed a degree of respect for the Galilean preacher.

Despite objections, Pilate had Jesus crucified as "King of the Jews". According to the author of John's Gospel, the chief priests wanted the inscription on the cross to read "This man said, 'I am King of the Jews.'" Which, of course, is not at all the same.

Pilate could have intended his inscription as an ironic comment or alternatively as a flat statement, based on his knowledge of Jewish history, one calculated to annoy the collaborating Sadducees.

Jesus had admitted that he was or that he claimed to be the King of the Jews. But it was apparently not quite what he was formally charged.

The author of Luke researched his gospel based on the existing Gospel of Mark, the available sayings of Jesus (the *Sayings Gospel Q*) and whatever other material he could find to hand. This could well have included the official records of charges kept by the Romans.

Luke records the charges thus: "We found this man perverting our nation, and forbidding us to give tribute to Caesar, and saying that he himself is

Christ [the Messiah] a king."

This is curious, given that even in Luke's version of events, Jesus is shown as careful not to deny the lawfulness of the payment of the Roman tax.

He did however do so in a way that put such considerations in their place. Mere material things may be due to Caesar, but spiritual things were due to God. That made a point, especially as the Roman Emperor claimed to be semi-divine.

If, however, Jesus was operating as this story suggests on a spiritual plane, and if he took care not to appear to suggest that people should not pay their tax, where could this allegation have come from? Was this simply one of the false accusations brought against Jesus, as alluded to in the Gospels of Mark and Matthew?

The author of Luke could hardly have "borrowed" a charge leveled thirty years beforehand at Judas the Galilean, tax protester at the time of the census by Qurinius. But he might well have included a contemporary charge made against one or more of Jesus' followers, who took a more militant line.

As I have suggested, the movement of which Jesus was a part had many faces. This is what offers a possible explanation.

CHAPTER 16

SONS OF DAVID

A certain impostor named Theudas persuaded the majority of the masses to take their possessions and to follow him to the Jordan River. He stated that he was a prophet and that at his command the river would be parted and would provide them an easy passage. With this talk he deceived many. Fadus [Roman governor of Judaea AD 44–46], however, did not permit them to reap the fruit of their folly, but sent against them a squadron of cavalry. They fell upon them unexpectedly, slew many of them and took many prisoners. Theudas himself was captured, whereupon they cut off his head and brought it to Jerusalem.

Jewish Antiquities, Josephus

For before these days Theudas arose, giving himself out to be somebody, and a number of men, about four hundred, joined him; but he was slain and all who followed him were dispersed and came to nothing. After him Judas the Galilean arose in the days of the census and drew away some of the people after him; he also perished, and all who followed him were scattered.

Acts 5:36–37 [part of speech attributed to Gamaliel]

Besides this James and Simon, the sons of Judas the Galilean, were brought for trial and, at the order of Alexander [Roman governor of Judaea, AD 46–48], were crucified. This was the Judas who, as I have explained above, had aroused the people to revolt against the Romans while Quirinius was taking the census of Judaea [AD 6].

Jewish Antiquities, Josephus

There are connections between The Nazoraean movement of James in Jerusalem, following the Crucifixion, and the practices of communities of "the poor" as they described themselves, or Essenes, at Qumran, Jerusalem and elsewhere. Despite the editorial glosses in the gospels, the teaching of Jesus was not at all antagonistic to Pharisaic thought. It is likely also that there would have been little disjunction between the founder and followers, between Jesus and his brother James and the Nazoraeans.

People who can be identified as Essenes helped Jesus; he even appears to have celebrated an Essenic Passover. If Jesus had spent time in one of the "assemblies of the towns", most probably in Jerusalem, this would explain these associations, as well as how he had gained his detailed knowledge of scripture. It would also fill in what had happened in the years of his young adulthood, which are not described in the gospels.

This explanation does not require that Jesus was "really" a member of the Essenes. The term itself, as I have argued, often used simply a label. The "poor" at Qumran were it seems a discrete monastic group, perhaps the spiritual center for a scattering throughout Israel of assemblies with fluid membership and bound by less rigid rules. There were at the time many sects within Judaism and there is insufficient evidence to decide precisely how they related to each other. Further confusion is caused by writers like Josephus who used terms interchangeably and sometimes indiscriminately. From a distance of 2,000 years, it may never be possible to tease out what were distinct groups and how they were organized.

It may not matter that much. What seems more important is what held many of these groups or tendencies together: devotion to Jewish Law, opposition to collusion with their country's occupiers, rejection of corruption and support for nationhood.

Jesus was popular and James, by all accounts, even more so. Within a few years of the Crucifixion, there were thousands or even tens of thousands of James' Nazoraean followers among Jews in Jerusalem. It should be remembered that these were Jews, not Christians, a term later used to apply to followers of Paul in the Church at Antioch in Syria.

The Nazoraeans differed from devout fellow Pharisee Jews only in one essential respect: their belief that one of their number was the awaited Messiah who, having been executed, had "risen" from death and would one day return.

It may be that James came to have majority support among ordinary Jews in the city, for whom he was their extremely pious leader, spokesman and even unofficial (because not appointed by the Romans) High Priest. With such a huge popular following, and without an agenda advocating violent opposition, James would have been a source of annoyance to leading

Sadducees and Herodians. He was a source of opposition. But, because he was not openly advocating rebellion, it was hard to find a reason for arresting him. Because he was so popular it was difficult to counteract his influence.

Members of the "assembly" of the "poor" in Jerusalem, which had leant support to Jesus, may have been attracted to James' teaching and joined with the Nazoraeans. In which case the two movements, if they ever had been separate, eventually became one.

After Jesus' Crucifixion, which can be placed in the year AD 36, the High Priest sent his police officers out to round up Jesus' followers while, according to Acts, leaving the Apostles alone. It seems that there was a division among the ranks of Jesus' followers, between those who advocated open resistance to the Romans and others, like his brother James, who preached piety and awaited their crucified king's eventual return.

One of the High Priest's police officers was Saul who later became known as the Apostle Paul. Having participated in the stoning of Stephen, Saul pursued other followers of Jesus to Damascus, now part of the territory of the Idumaean King Aretas, where they had fled to safety.

On the road to Damascus, Saul had a vision of Jesus which so traumatized him that he became temporarily blinded. He then converted to become a follower himself.

The details of the Crucifixion story suggest, as I have earlier argued in depth, that Jesus planned to survive and did survive his ordeal on the cross. Then afterwards, he went into hiding to recover and met members of his family and other disciples.

Jesus was however still in danger from the High Priest and his faction who had wanted him killed and the Romans who would, given the chance, have finished off their botched execution. So, after a time, Jesus too would have sought safety in exile, most probably via the immediate safe haven of Damascus.

Saul as Paul does not mention his vision on the road to Damascus in his letters, which are earlier and therefore possibly more authentic than the version in Acts. In the latter, a light flashes about Saul and he hears Jesus saying, "Saul, Saul, why do you persecute me?"

It is tempting to suggest that Jesus, hearing that the persecutor of his followers was in the vicinity, could not resist the temptation to come out and confront him.

The shock could have caused Saul's temporary blindness.

In his new persona, however, Paul presents himself as having had revelations of Jesus' intentions in dreams. It seems that more likely from this, and his treatment of the Nazoraeans, that Paul never met Jesus. Saul as Paul was prone to boast about his achievements, real or fictitious. So, if he had really met Jesus as a physical person on the road to Damascus, then he would surely have said so in his letters.

Tradition has it that Jesus went into exile in Kashmir. It would certainly not have been safe for him to stay in Palestine.

As far as the immediate followers of Jesus, led by James, were concerned, there was no real problem with this. Jesus was alive and they knew this, in many cases from personal experience, having encountered him after the Crucifixion. He was alive, resurrected, having survived the ordeal of crucifixion. His return in the relatively near future was not in doubt, not an issue.

When this did not happen, his followers needed some kind of explanation. The Nazoraeans were, however, not there to provide it since they had been dispersed and displaced after the death of James and the disastrous Jewish revolt.

The Christian movement substituted a divine savior for a Jewish Messiah, or warrior king, and a miraculous resurrection for Jesus' survival on the cross. The question of what happened to Jesus then was resolved by the doctrine of the ascension in which Jesus, like Elijah, was called by God directly into heaven.

There was, in the early years after the Crucifixion, a struggle between different factions, each seeking to gain acceptance for their own particular vision of Jesus. Paul clashed with the followers of James. The Nazoraeans were in turn divided between those following a spiritual course and others advocating active resistance.

Though fiercely important to those taking part, this was not a debate which preoccupied or impinged very much on the Roman authorities.

The Romans made no real distinction between messianic Jews preaching a future revolution and those among their subjects following a king they purported had already come. Either way, this was a challenge to the authority of Rome and its cult in which the Emperor was not only the ultimate civil authority, but also a deity. So, the followers of Paul were also at risk. The writer Suetonius reports that the Emperor Claudius ordered the expulsion of Jews from Rome for agitating on behalf of a person named "Chrestus".

Unrest continued in Palestine, not helped by the actions of Roman Emperors and governors. In AD 41, Caligula ordered that his statue be placed in the Temple at Jerusalem and this nearly led to outright revolt. Ten years later, the governor Cumanus dealt so inadequately with a clash between Jews in Galilee and Samaritans that it turned into a serious rebellion. Finally Nero, blaming Jewish "Christians" for a fire in Rome, sent a governor named Florus to Judaea with the specific brief to clamp down on Jewish dissidence. This Florus did so enthusiastically that it seemed, according to Josephus, that his intention was to goad the Jewish population into revolt.

The revolt, as recorded by Josephus, eventually began in AD 66 with a rebellion in Jerusalem by some priests against the offering of daily sacrifices for foreigners, which included Romans. There was then reportedly a standoff between forces on the side of the High Priest Ananias and those supporting his son and deputy Eleazar. This Ananias should not be confused with the High Priest Ananus who was instrumental in the death of James, the brother of Jesus, a few years before and who was as a result deposed.

A messianic contender called Menahem intervened on behalf of Eleazar, having first stormed the steep hilltop sanctuary of Masada and raided the armory there. Menahem entered Jerusalem with his forces like a king. He succeeded in killing Ananias, but was then in turn swiftly assassinated by Eleazar. As will be seen, there are some contradictory elements, which need explaining in this account given by Josephus.

Menahem's forces, a mixture of urban sicarii and peasants, then returned to Masada, where they remained until the end of the war.

The conflict lasted for four years, until the fall of Jerusalem, although some strongholds, especially Masada, held out for much longer.

There was one stunning initial success for the combined Jewish forces. The Syrian governor Cestius Gallus marched south from Antioch, with an army of 30,000 men, only to be trapped and heavily defeated in a pass called Beth-horon, a few miles north of the city. It seems, from Josephus' account, that at least some of the Essenes participated in this action.

Josephus was sent to Galilee to organize resistance, but was hampered by the fact that some towns were partly or, in the case of Sepphoris, the capital of the region, wholly pro-Roman. He lacked sufficient troops and in any case had no influence over northern Galilee, the territory of John of Gischala.

In Jerusalem, the Roman troops stationed there were treacherously killed, after being told they could go free if they surrendered. The Romans then sent one of their best generals, Vespasian, to quell the rebellion. He swept through Galilee, where Jewish forces prudently avoided pitched battles with the far superior Roman troops.

Josephus himself was captured in the desperate battle for Jotapata and John of Gischala was forced to retreat to Jerusalem, along with a collection of what Josephus describes as "zealot" forces. The zealots took control by degrees and massacred members of the aristocratic priesthood and the Herodian royal family. Eventually, they were ousted by Simon son of Gioras, another figure with aspirations to kingship who was invited in by the High Priest Matthias.

But the Romans took Jerusalem in the end, the Temple was destroyed and much of the city was razed to the ground. Simon bar Gioras was captured.

He was taken to Rome to feature in a victory parade, and then beheaded.

While Simon's claim to kingship did not appear to be based on descent, Menahem was described by Josephus as a son of Judas the Galilean who had led the protest at the time of the census by Quirinius.

For reasons which will be explained, the messianism behind much of the unrest–albeit inflamed by Roman provocation or incompetence–is disguised or suppressed in Josephus' accounts. But it was there as a strong force behind at least one part of the Jesus movement.

The pious, more pacifist tendency was represented first of all by James the Righteous, brother of Jesus, whose knees were hardened by constant praying. He became the leader of the community of Nazoraeans in Jerusalem which grew rapidly in numbers and strength. These were Jews, strict upholders of the Law and in the case of leaders like James also vegetarian and celibate. They attended the Temple with their fellow Jews and differed in just one respect, their belief that the Messiah had already come in the person of Jesus.

James became a figurehead for a large section of the Jewish community, to the extent that he was regarded almost as a High Priest, at least their High Priest even if not appointed by the Romans. He was killed, stoned to death for alleged blasphemy by members of the High Priest Ananus' faction, taking advantage of a temporary power vacuum following the death of the Roman governor of Judaea, Festus.

There are several testimonies of James' death, of which that provided by Josephus is the most detailed. Josephus records that a deputation of citizens went out to complain to the new governor Albinus, who was on his way from Alexandria. Another group petitioned the Herodian King Herod Agrippa II of Galilee, who had by favor of the Romans been given the power to appoint High Priests.

They certainly had grounds for complaint. The High Priest Ananus and his followers had executed James without the consent of the Roman governor. The Roman authorities, it will be recalled, reserved for themselves the power to authorize a sentence of death. King Agrippa responded by simply replacing Ananus as High Priest, a fairly mild punishment which suggests that Agrippa might also have been glad to see the end of James.

Following James, another of Jesus' brothers, Simon or Simeon, was elected head of the Jewish Nazoraean community at Jerusalem. There is no definite record of any offspring from Simon and he survived until his old age, according to Eusebius, when he was killed during the rule of the Roman Emperor Trajan. So it is possible that Simon was in the same mold as James, celibate, a pious upholder of the Law but not an active revolutionary. Saul and other police officers of the High Priest, it will be remembered, went after some of the followers of Jesus, such as Stephen, in the aftermath of the

Crucifixion. But the Apostles, like James and Peter who also followed Jesus, were left alone.

This accords with the picture developed here of Jesus, that he did confront what he saw as the corruption of Jewish religious authority and only incidentally clashed with Roman political authority. Moreover, as I have suggested, this clash may have been contrived, partly as a means of fulfilling scripture and possibly partly to secure the release of Jewish protesters held by Pilate. Jesus was himself, though not a celibate, similar to James and Simon in his religious beliefs.

But there was clearly a nationalist and messianic element in many of the disturbances at this time, often stirred up and even provoked by Roman insensitivity and incompetence.

The account given by Josephus of the Jewish uprising between AD 66 and 70, described briefly above, is confusing and difficult to follow. All sorts of different individuals and groups, or rather differently labeled groups, keep appearing on the scene, "sicarii", "zealots" and "brigands". The impression is of a country in utter chaos and disunity. Yet the Jews held off the efficient and formidable Roman army for four years, in a contest that they were probably always fated to lose. At the outset, they conducted a brilliant campaign which almost led to the complete destruction of the forces of Cestius Gallus. This could only have happened as a result of close cohesion and coordination.

Within months, however, a picture of rivalry, division and the settling of old scores emerged while their enemies, the Romans, were at the gates of Jerusalem.

What went wrong? Or, to put the question another way, what went right at the beginning that did not continue? The revolt was probably doomed to failure because the Romans had the resources to call on and were determined to keep this piece of their empire. It was also weakened by the rebels' failure to resolve quickly and decisively their initial struggle with the pro-Roman Sadducee elite. But the death of Menahem was, I believe, what dealt a very severe blow to the Jewish rebellion.

Josephus is unfortunately not at all forthcoming. At the very end of his first work, *The Jewish War*, published about AD 79, he reveals something he had previously neglected to mention: that "the thing that most moved the people to revolt against Rome was an ambiguous prophecy from their scriptures that one from their country should rule the entire world". This was the prophecy that there would be a King, an anointed one or Messiah, who would liberate the Jewish people.

So, who among the various characters in *The Jewish War* and the later work by Josephus, *Jewish Antiquities*, were the messianic leaders? Even more to the point, where does this fit in with the Jesus movement which was definitely messianic?

Jesus was crucified, if the gospels are right, for claiming to be the King of the Jews. Yet he did not start a political revolution, either because he was more interested in a kingdom on earth of spiritual values or because the time was not right.

But the time must surely have seemed right once the die was cast in Jerusalem, the Roman sacrifices suspended and priestly order challenged, at first from within. So where was the successor to Jesus and John the Baptist, in the Davidic priestly line? Was there no "Son of David" prepared to step forward and take charge?

The reason that Josephus was not more forthcoming was the very delicate and dangerous, although privileged, position in which he found himself.

Josephus was born in AD 37, a year after Jesus was crucified. He came from an aristocratic priestly family and was he claimed a Pharisee priest. Josephus maintained that there were four main traditions of Jewish philosophy: Sadducee, Pharisee, Essene and "zealot". He also claimed that at one time or another he had experienced them all. As well as suggesting that either the labels or the groups to which they applied were rather more fluid or ephemeral than might have been expected, this also says a lot about Josephus' character. An establishment figure, with a privileged background, he wrote disparagingly about the lower orders in society. But he also had a chameleon nature, adapted well to changing situations and was perhaps more radical in his youth. His adaptability helped to save his life, but at the same time this makes it difficult to trust all that he wrote.

When the revolt began in Jerusalem in AD 66, Josephus was chosen as a commander, possibly because of his priestly and aristocratic background and because of his zealot credentials. He was given charge of organizing resistance in Galilee. He had insufficient men and resources, many of the towns were wholly or partly pro-Roman and some of the territory was held by John of Gischala, out of his control. It did not help that Josephus and John of Gischala were personal rivals and not on friendly terms.

Josephus got the propertied classes to pay off the armed brigands roaming the countryside, fortified some of the towns and avoided as far as possible any pitched battles in the open with Vespasian's far superior troops. He failed to hold Galilee but succeeded in limiting the damage there, particularly to the aristocratic priestly establishment. In Jerusalem, by contrast, the Jewish establishment was massacred by zealots during the revolt.

In the summer of AD 67, Josephus took shelter with his troops in the fortified town of Jotapata. After a siege lasting many weeks and, at the last, some desperate hand-to-hand fighting, the town was overrun and many of its defenders slaughtered. Josephus and several companions took shelter in a cave within the boundaries of the now occupied town. In true zealot fashion, they entered into a suicide pact rather than surrender to the Romans. But, as Josephus shamelessly recounts, having tricked the others into being killed first, he betrayed the pact with one other survivor and gave himself up.

Interviewed by the general Vespasian, Josephus would have come across as an intelligent and educated man. He had been to Rome on a previous occasion to defend some Jewish priests and he had established contacts there.

With his life at stake, Josephus was assuredly both obsequious and sycophantic. He informed Vespasian that it was foretold in Jewish scripture that someone was going to come out of Palestine and rule the world. Furthermore, Josephus told the Roman general, that "someone" was going to be Vespasian himself! This was an extraordinary application of biblical messianic prophecy and it had an outcome that must have surpassed Josephus' wildest hopes.

Vespasian decided to spare Josephus' life and use him first of all as an interpreter. So Josephus was held as a prisoner.

The following year, in AD 68, the Emperor Nero died. Vespasian, who had by now taken most of the territory up to Jerusalem, paused in his campaign to await developments in Rome. A messy, bloody struggle ensued to gain the imperial throne.

Galba succeeded but was soon murdered, leaving Otho in control. However, German legions proclaimed a rival, Vitellius, governor of Lower Germania (not the same person who was earlier the Syrian legate), as the new Emperor. Otho committed suicide and Vitellius marched into Rome.

Legions stationed in the east, in Egypt, Syria and Palestine, however, now came out in favor of Vespasian and there was also support for him in Rome. Vitellius was murdered, leaving the way clear for Vespasian.

Just a year and a half following the death of Nero, and three more Emperors later, Vespasian had gained the position of supreme power, as ruler of the known world, just as Josephus had predicted.

Vespasian went to Rome, leaving his son Titus in control to finish off resistance in Jerusalem.

The turncoat Jewish general Josephus, in the meantime, had become something of a favorite in the new Emperor's household, though he was hardly popular with his fellow countrymen. Because of his successful prediction adapting messianic prophecy, and helped not a little by Roman superstition, his status among the Romans improved. Because he could speak Hebrew and Aramaic, he was given the tasks of interviewing Jewish prisoners and attempting to persuade the defenders of Jerusalem to surrender. On one such occasion, as related by Josephus, he was struck on the head and knocked to the ground by a missile thrown from the city's ramparts. This caused onlookers on the city wall to erupt into a spontaneous cheer.

Following the successful (from the Roman point of view) conclusion to the war, Josephus was given Roman citizenship and adopted into the imperial household.

One of the services he rendered was to write an account of the Jewish War, which understandably in the circumstances shows both Vespasian and his son Titus in a favorable light. It also justified the actions of Rome, especially in the final battle for Jerusalem, in burning the holy Temple and razing much of the city to the ground.

Josephus continued with his theme of the Romans fulfilling destiny with God, albeit a Jewish God, on their side. He wrote that "without God's aid, so vast an empire could never have been built up".

Josephus blamed the misfortunes of the Jews on their own actions. In original versions of his writings now lost, other early writers report that he argued that the killing of James, the brother of Jesus, was the prime cause of Jewish calamities.

As an historian, Josephus was fairly accurate and provided considerable detail about events with which he was familiar, and in which he had participated, such as the defense of Galilee between AD 66 and 67. He also had good sources for earlier periods, such as the period of the Maccabean kings. But, for the period of the early first century, immediately preceding his own lifetime, he had no personal experience and almost certainly no written sources. So he had to rely on what he could gather from people who were witnesses, or who had known people who were witnesses, to events. It would be rather like trying at the beginning of the 21st century to reconstruct the course, say, of the second World War 60 years previously without any film or television archives, books or newspaper reports, using a handful of very elderly witnesses and a few others whose parents had taken part. The outcome from such an exercise would be hazy, full of gaps and short on detail in many parts, if not at times downright misleading.

But, with Josephus, there is an additional problem. Having secured his position, if not his life, on the basis that Vespasian would fulfill biblical prophecy by becoming Emperor, he might not have wished to underline continuing Jewish messianic activities and claims. While he was certainly recounting and recording history, he was also doing a public relations job for Vespasian and the Romans. Writing about rival claims, which might on examination look more like the genuine article, would have had no part in this. In addition, Josephus on his own admission had a radical past which he might well have wanted to forget. This included considerable time spent with one "Banus", a baptizer maybe in the mold of John or James, someone associated with the Essenes or Nazoraeans.

The unrest in Palestine by no means ended with the taking of Jerusalem. It would continue to ferment and surface into other acts of revolt. There were still people about who had a claim to power, or were zealous and nationalistic enough to take on the might of Rome. Josephus was reasonably secure, having provided useful service and been adopted into the Flavian family household. But he was not completely secure. So he either ignored or modified what might by association have drawn attention to his own past and thereby constituted a personal threat.

Apart from one throwaway comment at the end of *The Jewish War*, there is no indication that the real driving force of the whole rebellion was nationalistic and messianic. It was portrayed rather as the result of provocation by Nero and the Roman governor Florus, combined with the foolishness of the Jews in being led astray by "impostors" and "deceivers".

But Vespasian himself was in little doubt. According to Eusebius, quoting Hegesippus, after the capture of Jerusalem Vespasian ordered a purge in which all the descendants of David would be ferreted out and eliminated. This was a purge visited not on Christians, of the Hellenized kind generated by Paul, but on messianic Jews including the followers of Jesus.

Vespasian was succeeded briefly by his son Titus, and then for a longer period by another son Domitian, who maintained the same policy, rounding up those who were considered to be descendants of David. Among them were grandchildren of Jesus' third brother Judas, called according to some versions Zoker and James. Again the source is Eusebius, quoting Hegesippus.

Domitian is reported to have let them go because they were simple laborers, professing a spiritual kingdom which was not considered to be a threat to Rome. But, according to Eusebius, the next Emperor Trajan instituted another purge against the descendants of David in which he crucified Simeon bar Cleophas, Jesus' second brother, who would by then have been very old. Zoker and James are likely to have perished at this time too.

So, according to sources independent of Josephus, the Romans by their actions made it clear what they thought was the source of disaffection behind the Jewish revolt. They saw themselves as dealing with Jewish nationalism, centered on a kingship based on actual descent, and they dealt with it by attempting to eliminate all those "Sons of David" who had a claim based on descent. They were dealing essentially with the relatives of Jesus and their descendants, not apparently with several strands of messianism, but just one.

It was a fairly concerted persecution, over a period of some 25 years, following the Jewish uprising. The purge is reminiscent of the treatment which Herod had earlier meted out to the Maccabees.

The question then arises: if these Sons of David, relatives of Jesus, were implicated, why don't they show up in Josephus' description of the Jewish rebellion?

Josephus was of course not motivated to point up the Jewish messianic implications. But all the same, the characters should have been there. Where were they?

If we take Jesus and his brothers, there were references in the gospels to five in all. But one brother, Joseph or Joses, only appears briefly in an aside in the gospels and is not referred to again. Unlike James and Simon, there are no records of his actions in other sources.

In a very early note attributed to Papias, however, four sons of Mary are listed: James, Simon, Joseph and Thaddeus. The last of these four names, Thaddeus, has been established by comparison as an alternative name for Judas. But Jesus' name is missing.

One possibility is that Joseph was one of the brothers but died at an early age, and for this reason was not part of the story later on. Another is that the character Joses or Joseph really has no independent existence, but is identical with Jesus himself. As has been noted, written Hebrew at that time had no vowels, so that the written name "Jss" could equally have been Joses or Jesus. Papias' list then includes Jesus and covers all of Mary's male children.

Either way, there are only four significant actors: Jesus, James, Simon/Simeon and Judas/Thaddeus.

Jesus was crucified and, I have argued, survived the Crucifixion and then probably went with his family into exile. James was killed by the High Priest Ananus and his supporters in AD 62 just a few years before the uprising. Simon succeeded him as leader of the Nazoraean community and appears to have been the same kind of character, one who managed to avoid presenting any immediate threat to Rome. So he survived until the dispensation to deal with the descendants of David was widened under the Emperor Trajan.

That leaves just Judas, otherwise known as Thaddeus. He must have had children, because he is recorded as having grandchildren. These children could possibly have been female, in which case they would not have counted, since women in this period of Jewish history did not lead revolutions or become Kings of Israel. Since the Romans investigated two of his grandchildren, Zoker and James, as possible messianic contenders, it does seem likely that they were related to their grandfather Judas in the male line. Judas in other words had at least one son.

But where was Judas at the time, described in one list of the Apostles as "Judas Zelotes" or "Judas the Zealot". Where were his sons, if any, during the uprising?

One tradition recorded in the *Apostolic Constitutions*, a second or third-century document of Syriac origin, notes that "Thaddeus, also called Lebbaeus and surnamed Judas the Zealot, preached the truth to the Edessenes and the people of Mesopotamia when Agbarus ruled over Edessa and was buried in Berytus [Beirut] in Phoenicia".

There is also another significant character named "Theudas" who was described by Josephus and also mentioned in Acts. Josephus disparagingly refers to him as an "impostor", a term which he usually reserves for millennial or messianic prophets.

In the story which Josephus tells in *Jewish Antiquities*, Theudas persuades the people to go down to the river Jordan *with their possessions* where he promises that the river will part, just as the Red Sea had done for Moses on the way back from Egypt. The events, at the time that Josephus was writing, had happened more than forty years previously, so there might have been some myth added to a core of facts. Theudas is portrayed as making a promise he could not deliver, to part the waters of the Jordan. If this was all that was at stake, all the Romans had to do was wait for nothing to happen and for Theudas to get his come-uppance. They need not have killed him.

The waters did not part, of course, and it seems unlikely that Theudas made such a promise or prediction. That part of the story must be an embellishment.

The clue to what actually happened lies in the fact that Theudas and his followers took their possessions with them. They were, in the light of this, most probably migrating or fleeing from Roman persecution, perhaps aiming for safe territory under control of the Nabataean King. They were then massacred by the Romans, just like the Samaritan followers of the Taheb on Mount Gerizim a few years beforehand. Josephus inserted, or invented, the myth of the promised parting of the Jordan to draw attention away from what was probably another Roman atrocity. Like the Taheb, Theudas may have been seen as a threat because he preached some form of prophetic fulfillment, either spiritual or political, for the Jewish people.

The other mention of Theudas comes in the Acts of the Apostles, when the Pharisee leader Gamaliel was advocating the release of Peter and other Apostles brought before the Sanhedrin for preaching about Jesus. The relevant quote from Gamaliel's speech in Acts is given above, at the start of this chapter. This is an early episode in Acts, before the stoning of Stephen and the conversion of Saul, so it must have taken place not long after the Crucifixion, most probably before AD 40.

But the beheading of Theudas took place, according to Josephus, during the rule of the Roman governor Fadus around AD 45 or 46. Gamaliel could not have mentioned an event which at the time had not yet taken place. So it would seem that Luke, the author of Acts writing in the late 90s or early part of the second century, made a mistake. Unless there were coincidentally two characters named Theudas involved in separate but very similar revolts, both accounts cannot be right.

It is possible that Luke mistakenly put in the wrong name, or the wrong name was transposed by a later editor in copying the gospel.

Luke may very well have had a copy of *Jewish Antiquities* before him in compiling the Acts. The way that Theudas and Judas the Galilean were introduced into Gamaliel's speech (see the quote above) suggests that Josephus' evidence for one or both of these characters did not make sense to Luke, in accordance with the time frame that Luke had from other sources.

The evidence of writers such as Eusebius, following Hegesippus, suggests that the Romans made a concerted effort to eliminate all the messianic contenders, "Sons of David" that they could find. This started under Vespasian's orders immediately following the end of the Jewish uprising in AD 70. Other persecutions may well have preceded it. There were certainly some instigated by the High Priest in which Saul took part.

As a result of all of this, many of the male members of Jesus' family were killed, including some of his brothers and even their grandchildren.

Yet Josephus, writing his histories of the Jews and the Jewish wars, gives barely any indication of what was happening. Where he should, in his *Jewish Antiquities*, have been writing about Pilate's rule as procurator or governor and giving details about Jesus, he instead includes two rather odd stories. One relates to a woman of high rank seduced by someone impersonating a god and the other to fund-raising on the false pretense of securing money for the Temple in Jerusalem.

These may well have been subtle parodies, first of the Jesus Nativity stories and second of the fundraising by Paul to placate James and the Nazoraeans. Josephus wrote here to please his audience. He cut out the dangerous story of the crucified and risen Son of David, whose relatives were rivals to Flavian Emperors–and whose cause Josephus may once have espoused and promoted.

But evidence about the messianic origins of the unrest is not entirely suppressed, as attested by Josephus' laconic note in *The Jewish War* about the "ambiguous prophecy" that "moved people to revolt against Rome".

Some aspiring messianic figures are indeed included. One was Simon bar Gioras who entered the fray towards the end of the uprising and was invited into Jerusalem to end what had become the despotic rule of zealot forces. But here the taking of political control appears to have been opportunistic, in much the same way as popular leaders arose in different parts of Israel to fill the power vacuum when Herod died. There is no indication that this Simon had a claim based on descent.

However, Menahem, on Josephus' testimony, certainly did. A prime mover in the early part of the revolt, Menahem led a daring attack to take the towering fortress of Masada, arming his soldiers with weapons from Herod's armory. He then returned to Jerusalem in the words of Josephus "like a king" and "decked with kingly robes". He became the leader of the revolution, taking the part of the rebel priest Eleazar who, according to Josephus, led the faction which objected to the daily Temple sacrifices on behalf of Rome.

Josephus described Menahem as a "son" of Judas the Galilean, the person who had objected to the census initiated by the Syrian legate Quirinius in AD 6 in order to facilitate the collection of taxes. Judas had run a campaign under the slogan "No Lord but God" and, since Jewish religion and politics were intertwined, this was nationalistic and possibly messianic.

So, as well as pretensions to royalty, Menahem also a direct link with a previous rebel leader.

Two other sons of Judas the Galilean are also mentioned by Josephus: James and Simon. They were apparently crucified by the Roman governor Tiberias Alexander, around AD 46 or 47.

Now this whole account has some peculiar aspects and poses some real problems.

In the first place, there is a very long gap of 40 years between the activities of the census and tax objector Judas the Galilean and the later execution of his two sons, James and Simon, as recorded by Josephus. This suggests that James and Simon were quite old, in their 50s or 60s, when they were taken. In those days, such an age made one a revered elder citizen, entitled to leave activities like scaling sheer rock fortresses to younger and more active brethren. What had they done then to deserve their fate and why had they presumably been so inactive for so long beforehand?

Menahem, of course, could hardly have been a son of Judas the Galilean since he did lead a force up the sheer rock face to take the fortress of Masada–and that was another twenty years later.

Some commentators resolve this difficulty by assuming that Josephus really meant that Menahem was a *grandson* of Judas the Galilean.

Which of course is a pivotal point: simply to make sense of the commentary, words have had to be put into Josephus' mouth. This is a hazardous way of interpreting, in which one theory can be as good as any other.

Luke, as the author of Acts, didn't appear to recognize the events described by Josephus. He used two previous rebellions described by Josephus, by Judas the Galilean and Theudas, as examples quoted in a speech attributed to the Pharisee leader Gamaliel. But Luke couldn't relate them to anything he knew and so he put them, apparently, in the wrong order.

As the quote from Acts at the start of this chapter shows, Luke put the events surrounding Theudas into the distant past, well before the tax disturbances initiated by Judas the Galilean around the year AD 6. Whereas Josephus is clear that the rebellion by Theudas happened some 40 years afterwards. So the events are in the wrong order. But not only that, Gamaliel could not have referred to the rising by Theudas because he was speaking in defense of Peter and other Apostles in AD 40, five years before Theudas was killed.

The next problem is that the sons of Judas the Galilean, James and Simon, would have been living as adults in Galilee, as part of a messianic line of contenders, at *exactly* the same time as Jesus and his brothers, also "Sons of David" and also contenders for the royal throne of David. It was certainly a messianic line, as witness the actions of Menahem who, having taken Masada and overthrown the High Priest Ananias in Jerusalem, entered the Temple in pomp "decked with kingly robes" to worship. Menahem was a rebel leader and so too were his brothers James and Simon and his father Judas, who must also have aspired to the kingship.

How confusing. Indeed, how improbable that there should have been two messianic movements operating in the same small territory, without bumping into each other, without leaving any record of contact in the gospels or anywhere. It simply could not have happened in this way. There would have been coalescence or conflict, some level of interaction.

But what did exist, as described in the gospels and the Acts of the Apostles, was one movement based initially on Jesus. The Romans reacted by trying to round up and eliminate all known "Sons of David" which effectively seemed to mean, according to available records, male relatives of Jesus.

So, where do James and Simon and Menahem, sons of Judas the Galilean, fit in?

This brings the argument to the next very odd point. There was a strong tradition to keep names in families. When, as Luke described, Zechariah's wife Elizabeth wanted to call her son by the name of John, others objected on the grounds that none of her kindred was called by this name. The point at issue was decided by getting Zechariah, having been struck dumb by the angel Gabriel, to write down the name he wanted on a writing tablet. Zechariah stuck by the decision to choose the name John in defiance of family tradition.

As well as the fact that names ran in families, there were not so many names to choose from compared with nowadays and people then were fairly conservative. So certain names, such as Judas and Jesus and Eleazar or Lazarus, were very common.

But it is a strange coincidence that the names ascribed to the "No Lord but God" campaigner and his first-mentioned sons are also precisely the names of Jesus' three brothers: Judas, James and Simon. The question is worth consideration: where, if they were family names, did the names of Judas the Galilean's sons come from?

The best fit that I can provide for all of this evidence, which resolves virtually all of the discrepancies described, is based on the presumption that there were not two movements but one messianic movement during the first century in Israel. The Romans persecuted messianic Jews, Nazoraean followers and relatives of Jesus. The gospels and Acts describe Jesus' movement, muted and altered to make it Hellenistic, anti-Jewish and almost pro-Roman. It is all seen through a distorting mirror but, whichever way it is looked at, there is really no other movement.

Josephus describes as little of the messianic movement as he can, but what he does describe presents a puzzle, unrelated to what is known from other sources.

The problem can be resolved, I suggest, by accepting that Menahem may well have been the son of a man named Judas as stated by Josephus and that James and Simon were also the progeny of Judas, also as recorded by Josephus.

Let's accept also Josephus' version that there was a Judas the Galilean who campaigned against registering for the census which Quirinius instigated to provide a basis for collecting tax. Josephus was often evasive when it came to names. He appeared to use pseudonyms, as in the case of "Banus", a religious and possibly revolutionary figure under whose influence he came for a time. He appeared sometimes deliberately to leave out names, as in the case of the Jewish teacher who secured money under false pretenses and who may have been Paul or Saul. Judas was also the name of the revolutionary who broke into the armory at Sepphoris, on the death of Herod, just a few years before the census of Quirinius–another interesting, apparent coincidence.

But, all right, there were clearly a lot of people named Judas around. There would have been discontent at the time of the census under Quirinius and someone would have been at the head of it. Judas is as good a name as any for the person who was at the head of the tax rebellion.

What cannot be true, because it just does not make sense, is that this person was the father of the two brothers James and Simon, crucified forty years later under the governorship of Tiberias Alexander.

Their father was, I believe, none other than Judas Zelotes, or Judas the zealot, known in another form of the name as Thaddeus, the third brother of Jesus.

Now, the whole picture, which was so obscure and distorted, suddenly clicks into place and into focus.

Theudas was a real character and he did lead an unsuccessful revolt. But the name was just another variation of Thaddeus and this of course was the name used for Judas, brother of Jesus in the Apostle's lists.

Theudas was defeated, captured and beheaded around AD 45. His sons James and Simon, if my interpretation is right, were tracked down, captured and then crucified by the Romans about a year or so later. He had another descendant named Menahem, who led a revolt some years later and who is correctly identified as a son, and not a grandson, by Josephus.

A further confirmation of this identification of persons and names is provided by another historical source. In a codex book from the third or fourth century entitled the *Second Apocalypse of James*, the main disciple of James the Just one, and "a relative" is described not as Judas or Thaddeus but as "Theuda".

So why was Luke, the author of Acts, confused over dates? It will be recalled that the identification of Judas with Thaddeus is confirmed by comparison of the lists of Apostles in the gospels and other sources such as the Papias fragment and the *Apostolic Constitutions*. The latter source directly links both names. But, while Matthew and Mark refer to Thaddeus, Luke in his gospel and the Acts refers to Judas, brother of James and thus of Jesus.

Luke did not appear to identify the name Thaddeus with Judas and so the revolt by Theudas described by Josephus might very well have meant nothing to him. He assumed that Josephus had made a mistake in dating it to AD 45 (when Judas was up in arms) and so placed it on the lips of Gamaliel as referring to a period much further back in time.

There was then just one messianic movement at the time of Jesus. Judas was part of it, and so were his sons when they later came of age. No longer is there a problem of two very similar movements apparently existing in Galilee at the same time, but without coming into contact with each other.

The messianic rebels, the Sons of David, the Romans sought to eliminate and who Josephus could not be open about–for the good reason that he had previously in one way or another supported them–are found to have been there in the story all along.

James and Simon, executed as young men some years before the Jewish uprising, had been given the family names which were those of two of their uncles. Their remaining brother Menahem took up the cause, and the mantle of messianic liberator, but was then killed by a faction of the chief priests and Sadducees. He was stoned to death, suffering the same fate as James and at the hands of the same people who had killed James, who was the brother of Jesus and by this interpretation also the uncle of Menahem. History has a rather grim tendency to repeat itself, and appears to have done so in this case. It was a major tragedy for the Jewish uprising which had until that point been going well.

With the death of Menahem, the sicarii or zealot forces as Josephus variously described them were left leaderless, without their claimant to the throne of Israel, and they retreated back to their hilltop stronghold at Masada. Here they remained, perhaps harrying the Romans but without committing themselves to the defense of Jerusalem, a lost cause once

Vespasian arrived. They finally committed mass suicide, rather than surrender, after a siege at Masada which continued for three years after the war had ended elsewhere.

The reasons for their actions may not after all have been so inexplicable. Masada was such a good natural stronghold that they were able to remain there for a very long time, coming and going as they pleased and doubtless carrying out acts of disruption or sabotage until the Romans finally encircled it. While they remained, there was still a small piece of territory which was free and not in Roman hands, a surviving piece of the liberated Kingdom of Israel. Their fate on surrender would either have been death or slavery. So they preferred to sit tight, where they were.

Their behavior in stubbornly holding out for so long in an apparently hopeless situation also suggests another possible motivation. The will is strengthened by hope, by the hope or expectation of relief.

The defenders at Masada may have expected some sort of divine rescue, if they held out long enough. Or they may been expecting some real human assistance, though where it could have come from is not immediately apparent.

The commander of the besieged forces at Masada was Eleazar, one of a number of characters of this name in the pages of Josephus. Given the lack of vowels in written Hebrew, this name written as Lzr was identical with its Romanized version Lazarus.

So Eleazar was just another form of Lazarus and vice versa. It was a fairly common name applied to a number of characters described by Josephus. So, could the commander of the sicarii forces under Menahem also have been the Lazarus in John's account?

Lazarus, I have argued, played a crucial role as Jesus' brother-in-law. He may have tested the drug that saved Jesus on the cross and helped in other ways. He appears in John's Gospel which would have been written after he had died, by which time it was safe to name him. But he does not appear in the other canonical gospels which were probably first written while he was still alive. In Secret Mark, however, there is a story of Jesus raising an unnamed young man from the dead, with circumstantial detail which strongly indicates that this was Lazarus.

The reason for all this circumspection was that Lazarus was a wanted man whose life was at risk. This much is explicitly stated in John's Gospel.

So what happened to Lazarus after the passion events? Those who had helped Jesus were at risk from the Roman authorities and from the High Priest's faction, both anxious to quell the resurrection story. Some traditions suggest that Jesus, Thomas and possibly Mary went into exile, possibly ending up in Kashmir. But there is no mention in these accounts of Lazarus.

As John's Gospel reports, the "chief priests" had sought to kill Lazarus as well as Jesus, even before the Crucifixion. This was ostensibly on the grounds that the raising of Lazarus had enhanced Jesus' messianic credentials. But Lazarus was also marked out by virtue of having been closely involved with Jesus, as I have argued as a close relative. He would not have been safe and he would have had to go underground or into hiding. The obvious place for him to be was with the active faction in the Nazoraean movement which Saul and others among the High Priest's police actively pursued.

Josephus was anxious to play down the messianic aspect of the Jewish revolt in AD 66. As a consequence, many of the major gospel characters either do not appear or have to be teased out of the text.

Jesus gets only a passing reference. In the version of his *Jewish Antiquities* which has survived, the troubled period under the governorship of Pilate is entirely missing. Where it should be, there appears a bawdy tale which parodies the story of the birth of Jesus and another story which may well relate to Paul's possible misuse of Nazoraean funds.

Someone called Saul does appear as a powerful man, with Herodian family connections, part of a delegation sent to seek help from King Agrippa II during the first stages of the insurrection. I have argued that there are grounds for regarding this person as the same as the character Saul, who became Paul on conversion, in the Acts of the Apostles.

Other characters such as Silas and Philip, named in connection with Paul in Acts, coincidentally or otherwise appear in Josephus as being linked with Saul.

There's also a character named Simon "with a reputation for religious scrupulousness" who is able to convene an assembly or Church (using the Greek word "ecclesia" as the Church is also described in Acts). Through the assembly, he seeks to bar the Herodian King Agrippa 1 from the Temple, on the grounds that he is "unclean". This king, grandson of the infamous Herod, was progressively granted territory until he was ruler under the Romans of the whole of Israel from AD 41–44. Since this was the period immediately following the Crucifixion of Jesus, it seems quite likely that this Simon was the Apostle Simon Peter of the gospels.

It is not at all surprising that characters with political as well as religious significance should appear both in the writings of Josephus and in the gospels.

As a possibility, I suggest that Lazarus as a young man may have joined with Theudas/Judas, who was part of the active opposition. He survived the defeats in AD 46 and 47 in which Judas, James and Simon were captured and killed and then joined Judas' other son Menaham, as a commander with the zealot forces participating in the revolt against Rome. By which time, he would have been in his late forties..

This of course is largely speculation, but there is another curious detail. The Eleazar who committed suicide along with fellow fighters at Masada is described by Josephus as Eleazar ben Jair. Eleazar, son of *Jairus*.

It will be recalled that Jairus, in the gospel accounts, had an unnamed daughter whom Jesus miraculously brought back to life. The other miracle of that kind was Jesus raising Lazarus, which seems an extraordinary coincidence. It is possible that two tales were passed down and became convoluted in different ways, though in actuality they may both relate to the same event. If this is right, then the raising of Jairus' daughter was not simply an act of healing, the reviving of someone unconscious and close to death, as described in chapter three. But this would only be because the story is a corruption of the tale of the raising of Lazarus.

Another indication is provided by the fact that Josephus identifies the zealot commander Eleazar as "related" to Menahem. This unspecific description is what might be expected, if my identification is correct. Eleazar/Lazarus would have been the brother-in-law of Menahem's uncle, Jesus.

If Eleazar at Masada was the same person as Lazarus, who had been "raised" in the gospel stories in Secret Mark and John, then this provides a further explanation for the stubbornness of the remaining zealot defenders. They were hoping for a message to get through to supporters of the one remaining active messianic contender who could help them. They did not know whether he was still alive or had sons who were alive. They were waiting for Jesus or one of his sons to return.

This was not a forlorn hope at all, had Jesus still been alive, because Lazarus had been one of his closest friends. Lazarus provided crucial help in Jesus' hour of greatest need.

When Trajan later decided to eliminate all the remaining "Sons of David", whether or not they appeared inoffensive, he rounded them up, including probably the grandsons of Judas, the third brother of Jesus.

Judas' own sons by the time of the siege of Masada were already dead. James and Simon, the sons of Theudas or Judas, were crucified by the Roman governor Tiberias Alexander in AD 46 or 47. Menahem was killed during the struggle for Jerusalem.

Judas himself had also been executed, or by some accounts had died a natural death, after preaching to the Edessenes (that is, people living at Edessa and not to be confused with Essenes), and been buried at Beirut.

So it may be that Judas was the one face of the Jesus movement that was uncompromising in its revolutionary zeal, promoting not just a spiritual but a political kingdom in the here-and-now. True to his zealot upbringing and aspirations, which earned him the nickname "Judas Zelotes", he may have carried the war to the Romans unsuccessfully and then perished by the sword. If Judas or Thaddeus was also Theudas in the story told by Josephus, then he was cut down with his followers in retreat, as they were about to cross the river Jordan. His two sons escaped, only to be captured, though under a different Roman governor, just a matter of months later.

This makes more sense than the disconnected events, stretching genealogical credibility, as they appear in Josephus.

It may be that it was the activities of Jesus' younger brother Judas, the real rebel in the family, which put everyone else by association at risk.

The other character with the same name, Judas Iscariot, did not "betray" Jesus, as the story in the gospels is now interpreted. Jesus had himself handed over or, I have suggested, exchanged himself for others. The idea of betrayal came from the use of a Greek word which also means "to hand over".

Some commentators have suggested that there was really only one character called Judas (Judas Zelotes), a brother of Jesus who was associated with the sicarii. He could also have had the nickname, Judas Sicarius, which easily became corrupted into Judas Iscariot.

In which case, Judas' guilt came not from handing over Jesus but from his impetuous actions which jeopardized the cause. Did these include participating in the demonstration over the Temple funds affair, leading to the arrest of some of Jesus' Galilean followers?

Jesus, I have suggested, went into exile. Communications in those days were difficult and often infrequent: no post, no telephone, no swift means of transport. Months or years could go by without any certainty that a relative or friend in another place was alive and well, or dead.

Jesus may have intended to return, as he is reported in the gospels to have promised the disciples. Why he did not will probably never be known. But it may be that he did not because he could not, having succumbed to the mortality that affects us all.

Strangers in a foreign land, without extended kin or community support, Jesus and his band of family and followers may have fallen victim to disease. Or they may have been set upon and wiped out by robbers.

Meanwhile atop Masada, Eleazar or Lazarus, watched the sun go down over the plains each day and waited, and waited, for the help that would never come.

CHAPTER 17

CENSORED REBELLION

Florus [the Roman procurator], however, as if he had contracted to fan the war into flame, sent to the Temple treasury and removed seventeen talents on the pretext that Caesar required it. Uproar followed at once and the people rushed in a body into the Temple, where with piercing yells they called on the name of Caesar, imploring him to free them from Florus' misrule.

    The Jewish War, Josephus

Meanwhile some of those most anxious for war [Menahem and his sicarii forces] made a united attack on a fort called Masada, captured it by stealth, and exterminated the Roman garrison, putting one of their own in its place. At the same time in the Temple courts Eleazar, son of Ananias the High Priest and a very confident young man, who was Temple Captain, persuaded the ministers of the Temple to accept no gift or offering from a foreigner. This it was that made war with Rome inevitable; for they abolished the sacrifices offered for Rome and Caesar himself ...

    The Jewish War, Josephus

This same Josephus records the tradition that this James was of so great holiness and reputation among the people that the destruction of Jerusalem was believed to have occurred on account of his death.

    Lives of Illustrious Men, Jerome

Reinstating Jesus in his proper social, cultural, and historical context is hard for a number of reasons. The early inventors of Christianity, most notably Paul and a following of gospel writers and editors, did their best to distance the Jesus they recorded from his Jewish origins and family background. They bestowed on him a semi divine status which he never claimed, and would have found quite alien, and which had moreover no foundation in the real business of Jewish nationalism and its expectation of salvation by a "Messiah" or warrior king.

Careful reading of the gospels reveals the flaws, inconsistencies and falsehoods in this portrayal of Jesus. In combination with reference to other sources, such scrutiny begins to show something more convincing and consistent. That something was a messianic movement centered around a group of four or five brothers, not entirely unlike the early Hasmoneans who had claimed and created a Jewish kingship a century earlier.

They were Jews, they were in their thinking and beliefs similar to Pharisees, they had common cause with other distinct or fluid groups such as the assemblies of the towns, otherwise known as "the poor" or described by others as Essenes.

Jesus, the eldest of the brothers, and the others were known as Nazoraeans, because they were "keepers" of the covenant. They opposed, in one way or another, either the Roman occupation or the imposition of its culture and pagan ways on their religion.

Small wonder, then, that the gospel editors had to remold the text in generating a religion acceptable to the Romans and, more ambitiously, eventually the empire's official religion. For many reasons, there was no wholesale rewriting and enough clues and original facts were left in to provide us with a fair understanding of what was the original situation.

A further obstacle in understanding lies in the way that Christianity has generated a mythology and life of its own, independent of its origins and permeating over the centuries through Western culture. It is hard to step outside of this and be objective, especially if inculcated in this imagery and thinking. It is worth the effort because the Jesus of history proves every bit as worthwhile as the Jesus of our imaginings.

But this person Jesus and his brothers and his movement were not only censored by the gospel writers; the process for the most part began before ever a word was set down. The Jewish historian Josephus, who wrote before Matthew, Luke and John, censored Jesus and the other Nazoraeans by omission. There remain scarcely any references to this messianic movement in either of his major works, *The Jewish War* or *Jewish Antiquities*.

It may be that there were early versions of Josephus, including one he mentions that was written in Aramaic but now no longer survives, which were more explicit. However, to the extent that Josephus left out facts that were inconvenient, this could not have helped the later gospel writers casting about for material to amplify their sources. It may also be there was a degree of congruence of motivation between Josephus and these other writers in diminishing the Jewish messianic role of Jesus and his followers.

If Josephus left Jesus out, apart from one brief aside, could this have simply been because in his eyes Jesus was not that important? It is true that Josephus, as a former Jewish general, liked to concentrate on military battles and other dramatic events. The gospel accounts agree that Jesus did not lead anything that amounted to an uprising.

On the other hand, he would have appeared then, as he does now, to be a highly significant figure. He conducted a healing ministry over a period of years, attracting large crowds which, with his own followers, were numbered in hundreds or even thousands.

He claimed ultimately to be the "Messiah" and in Jewish eyes this was the warrior king who would lead them from subjection. He confronted the High Priest's faction among the Sadducees and the Romans and was crucified. His followers, the Nazoraeans, claimed that he was "risen", that is had escaped or overcome death and would return to lead them.

In addition to this, his younger brother James became a priest of such stature and with such popularity among ordinary people, that he was a focus of opposition to the Rome-appointed official High Priest. His Nazoraean followers, according to Acts, were numbered in "tens of thousands". James was succeeded by his brother Simon, and Judas was initially there too as Apostle, helper and possibly one of the movement's activists.

In the aftermath of the Jewish rebellion, the Romans sought out and persecuted the messianic "Sons of David". Simon was eventually crucified and two grandsons of Judas were picked up and interrogated, probably in the end suffering a similar fate.

Taken as a whole, the evidence suggests that Jesus was far from being insignificant. He was in fact a prime figure in a messianic movement which had a major impact over time.

So why did Josephus apparently skate over some facts or leave them out? The reason was twofold. In the first place, having been captured he owed his life and subsequent welfare among the Romans to his prediction that the Roman General Vespasian was really the messianic figure expected by the Jews and would become Emperor. When that prediction, based on a breathtaking and outrageous adaptation of Jewish prophecy, was fulfilled, Josephus was taken on as a sort of court favorite and adopted into the royal household. He had the task of writing history to please the Romans.

Given that Josephus had, by his own admission, tried out all of the main Jewish persuasions including that of the most forcefully messianic zealots, the exercise of writing his history of the Jewish War and the events leading up to it was a delicate matter.

He would not have wanted to draw attention to his own allegiances surrendered, however it may have come to be seen, only through defeat and in threat to his life. Describing in detail the messianic credentials of characters such as Menahem and Simon bar Gorias or more generally the role of the Nazoraeans in the war might well have led to questions as to where he himself, as Jewish commander of the forces in Galilee, had stood in all this. A description of other messianic claims could moreover have diminished the credibility of the prophecy he had applied to Vespasian, which it may well be saved his life.

It was more expedient therefore to downplay the messianic element and emphasize more immediate causes such as the procurator Florus' brutal treatment of the Jews or the stopping of Roman sacrifices in the Temple, without going into details as to the reasons for this either. A flavor of this is given by the first two quotes at the start of this chapter. In contrast, the messianic roots of the uprising were accorded just one passing reference in the whole of Josephus' history the Jewish uprising. Towards the end of his book, *The Jewish War*, Josephus notes that the Jew's "chief inducement to go to war was an equivocal oracle also found in their sacred writings that a man from their country would become monarch of the whole world". Josephus then hastens to point out that the prophecy really applied to Vespasian!

Josephus could however have had a second, more creditable reason for the omission of details about messianic credentials and that was a real concern for the safety of survivors of the movement. Emphasizing the place of Jesus could have imperiled his brother Simon. Telling too much about the activities of Judas, or sons of Judas, might well have threatened the safety of Judas' surviving grandchildren. That this was not a groundless fear is shown by the ultimate of fate of Simon and maybe also James and Zoker, crucified by the Romans, merely it would appear by reason of their genealogical connection as "Sons of David" to other activists. Josephus, for all that he was hated as a Roman turncoat, had not entirely abandoned his Jewish loyalties.

In terms of numbers of people, in terms of continuity of beliefs and in terms of an identifiable succession through the Nazoraean community in Jerusalem under James, there was certainly what can only be described as a messianic movement. It was also, as I have argued, one movement.

Jesus himself attracted large crowds and had bands of followers who were there to protect him, as for example in the days he spent preaching in Jerusalem leading up to the Passover Feast and the Crucifixion. While it seems clear that he did not lead an army as such, there are references which show that some at least of his followers were armed. In Luke's Gospel, for example, Jesus is reported at the Last Supper as telling his followers to buy swords. All four gospels describe the incident in which a follower, described as Simon Peter in John, drew his sword and cut off the ear of the High Priest's slave.

While there may then have been a degree of tension and ambiguity in the political intentions of the messianic movement at the time of Jesus, the religious position was clear. In their teachings and observances, Jesus and his immediate followers, who included his brothers, were Pharisaic Jews. They went to the Temple and prayed like others and they observed the Law, if anything say in respect to adultery more strictly so. They were "keepers" of the covenant, which is the base meaning of the term "Nazoraean".

Just as the Hellenizing gospel writers and later editors depicted Jesus as being apart from his family and against his fellow Jews, so they also sought to portray Jesus as being in opposition to Jewish Law and so thereby weaken his message. Though there are in the gospels several references to Jesus as a Nazarene or Nazoraean, it is suggested simultaneously that this really means that Jesus came from Nazareth, a settlement that cannot be identified as even existing at the time. But the roots and spellings of the words Nazareth and Nazoraean are different.

The reality is that the movement continued under James, after the Crucifixion, when its followers were certainly called Nazoraeans. The fourth century writer Epiphanius notes that all Christians were first called Nazoraeans and, interestingly, also observes that they were once also called Jessaeans or Essenes. This tends to confirm the idea that Jesus and his followers had a link early on with one of the communities of "the poor", most probably in Jerusalem.

Even as the movement continued, it remained firmly within the bounds of Judaism. The followers of James were observers of the Law, differing only from their fellow Pharisees in that they believed that the Messiah had already arrived, had "risen" from death and would soon be returning. It should be noted that the "zealots" as described by Josephus, also differed from the Pharisees in one respect only, that is their willingness to suffer and die for their beliefs.

Rather than strictly defined sects with closed memberships, it would appear that these were for the most part fluid groups without well-defined boundaries. As a Jew, one could probably have become a Nazoraean simply by espousing the core belief that Jesus had "risen" and by associating with others so like-minded. That would be without compromising one's general way of life or position within the Jewish community. Likewise being a zealot might likewise have meant no more than a proclaimed readiness to take on the Romans in the cause of restoring a Jewish kingship. Until, that is, the time really came for action.

The Essenes, at what was probably the mother church at Qumran, were a defined group, not easy to get into or possibly even out of. New recruits went through a three-year period of initiation and training as apprentices, before being allowed to become full members. But the rules for the assemblies of the town were more relaxed and members there were freer to marry and associate with their fellow Jews.

The evidence suggests that Jesus had help from one such group in Jerusalem and may have derived his learning from time spent with them. However, the dynamics of the messianic movement generated by Jesus and his brothers was such that it would soon have outstripped in numbers and probably absorbed the original assembly of the "poor" in Jerusalem. Whether the original movement was derived from, or just associated with, the Jerusalem assembly, the ultimate effect was the same.

By the time that Saul, as the self-proclaimed Apostle Paul, was writing his letters, James was a formidable figure and could number his followers in thousands or tens of thousands. James was immensely popular, celibate, a vegetarian and a very strict religious observer.

The argument with Paul, it will be recalled, was over how strictly Gentile converts should follow Jewish custom and practice. James' ruling involved a restatement of the old Noahide rules for "god fearers" among the Gentiles, including abstention from food which had been "sacrificed to idols" and observing dietary restrictions, including draining blood from meat before eating it. Paul in the meantime not only continued to flout these rules but was also advocating that Jews abandon the Law, including the practice of circumcision.

As James became more popular, a sort of icon for ordinary Jews dispossessed even of their freedom to practice freely their religion, so he came up against the Sadducee establishment of the High Priest and his followers, appointed by and under the patronage of Rome.

Some early writers record that James had taken on the trappings of the High Priest, and had entered the inner sanctuary on the Day of Atonement to supplicate on behalf of the people. In which case, he had made a very direct challenge and had, at least in the eyes of the official High Priest, committed an act of blasphemy.

Taking advantage of a temporary power vacuum, with the old Roman governor Festus dead and the new one Albinus on his way, the High Priest Ananus convened an assembly and had James charged and then stoned to death in AD 62. But surviving records do not say what the charge was, and it does seem improbable that there could have existed for even a short time two parallel High Priests in Jerusalem, one official and one unofficial.

What James was is clear, leader of the Nazoraeans within the Pharisees, a grouping which had grown so much that it could well by then have accounted for the bulk of ordinary Jews and many in the priesthood. He was also a strict upholder of the Law, as can be seen from his dialogue with Saul or Paul, and he would doubtless have been contemptuous of at least some of the compromises made by the High Priest's faction.

Among these would have been the daily sacrifices allowed in the Temple to the Roman Emperor and Roman gods. His admonition to the "god fearers" among the Gentiles to "abstain from the pollutions of idols" would have been something he felt applied even more keenly to himself and his fellow Jews. He was probably, like the Simon described by Josephus who can be identified as the Apostle Simon Peter, against allowing Herodian kings into the Temple. He would have disapproved of their delegated power to appoint High Priests.

It was the question of the Temple sacrifices made to pagan gods and related matters which brought James into conflict with the pro-Roman Sadducee establishment. The death of James did not resolve the issue, even though Albinus gave a new High Priest license, according to Josephus, to persecute "the leaders of the multitudes" in Jerusalem. As this reference indicates, James' Nazoraean followers were still there and in some numbers. Just as significant, there were still people available to lead them.

Josephus describes the existence of numerous "brigands" or "sicarii" at about this time, attacking and plundering villages and also using the cover of crowds to assassinate opponents using short daggers or sicae. Hence the derivation of the term, "sicarii".

It is evident that some at least of these attacks were politically motivated, rather than merely criminal acts carried out for gain.

The stoning of James was a judicial murder, since the High Priest required but did not secure Roman authorization. This would have tended to politicize the many thousands of followers of James as one of the leaders, if not the leader, of the more passive tendency within the messianic movement. This was the side that focused on efforts to maintain religious integrity and purity in the expectation of eventual divine deliverance, rather than military action. With the killing of James, the dynamic tension between these active and passive elements was disturbed, and the balance tipped in the direction of direct action.

Josephus was therefore right in a sense in attributing the destruction of Jerusalem to the death of James. This was part of the causal chain. Had James been spared, there might of course ultimately have been a war though not the war that actually took place and at the time that it happened. The observation which Josephus made, in an early copy of *The Jewish War* or *Jewish Antiquities* known to the Early Church historians and theologians Origen, Eusebius and Jerome, was eliminated by later editors.

The active elements, labeled sicarii by Josephus, were emboldened because they knew they now had greater support within the general population. They carried out selective killings and kidnappings, even taking members of the

High Priest's staff as hostages for exchange with their members who had been taken prisoner.

The conflict rumbled on, and became more acute as the latest procurator Gessius Florus appeared to seek to provoke the population.

It finally came to a head when a number of events happened at about the same time, probably with a degree of coordination. One faction within Jerusalem acted to prevent the daily sacrifices to the Romans. This was opposed by the Rome-appointed High Priest and his followers among the Sadducees. The High Priest's party sent delegates to the governor Florus and to the Herodian King Agrippa II, ruler of a province to the north of Palestine, requesting intervention.

Agrippa responded by sending in support a large detachment of cavalry, numbering as many as two thousand according to Josephus.

A bloody battle then ensued over a period of several days in which the insurgents were opposed by the High Priest and his supporters backed by Agrippa's troops and the Roman garrison.

It was more than an even match. The rebels, who must also have constituted a substantial force, drove back the Romans and King Agrippa's forces and took control of the upper city.

Meanwhile, Menahem (son of a certain Judas from Galilee) led a successful assault on the fortress of Masada, armed his followers with weapons from the armory and then went on to Jerusalem to put himself in charge of the forces besieging the beleaguered Roman and Herodian troops. The situation of the remaining defenders trapped in three towers along the old city wall was by now hopeless. They petitioned for an armistice, but only King Agrippa's troops and Jewish nationals among the fighters were allowed out.

The Roman defenders were then left even more isolated. The chief priest Ananias and his brother Hezekiah were found among those who had vacated the towers and they were killed.

In outline, this account by Josephus makes sense. But there are some points that are very curious. The most significant is that Josephus names Eleazar, son of the High Priest Ananias, as the leader of the faction opposing Temple sacrifices to the Romans and initial leader of the revolt. He is described as being the Temple captain and thus, in the priestly hierarchy, second-in-command.

As a leader of the revolt, he would have been taking up arms against his own father. There are of course plenty of examples from the bible of families set against each other, father against son or brother against brother. But it does seem strange that a person so compromised by his close association with the Sadducee power elite should have become leader of a popular revolt. This Eleazar had plenty to gain from retaining his loyalties:

preferment from the Roman authorities and possibly in time the office of High Priest itself. He had a lot to lose by changing sides.

But then, having adopted the position of a rebel leader, Eleazar is described by Josephus as suddenly turning against Menahem when the latter entered the Temple "in pomp to worship, decked with kingly robes". The "rest of the people" are then described as also taking up arms against Menahem, in the hope that his overthrow will end the revolt. Menahem is caught, tortured and killed. Implausibly, "the people" continue to implore the rest of the insurgents led by Eleazar to abandon the siege. But their imprecations only inspire Eleazar to continue the assault more vigorously!

Thus, at one point, "the people" are the instrument by which Eleazar manages to defeat and kill Menahem, formerly his ally. Then, only moments later, he is able to ignore them all completely and press on with an attack against the popular will.

It is clear from the detail and flow of Josephus' description that it was a popular uprising, which indeed could not otherwise have succeeded against a well-armed Roman garrison augmented by King Agrippa's troops. Just why he had, at this point in the narrative, to make it appear that it was an aberrant minority acting out of accord with popular will becomes clear from the next, dramatic episode. This was a betrayal which would have still rankled with the Romans, when Josephus was writing several years after the war.

The commander of the Roman garrison Metilius again sued for peace, offering to surrender the soldiers' weapons if their lives were spared. They were then promised their safety on oath, if they laid down their arms.

Metilius, who had by this time few options left, led his men out without hindrance. They laid down their swords and shields. But as they were marching away, they were surrounded and killed by Eleazar and his men. Only Metilius survived, apparently by offering to become a Jew and be circumcised. To add to the horror, the massacre happened, according to Josephus, on the Sabbath day.

As carefully described by Josephus, this was not an act committed by "the people", and so therefore it was not something that should incur or instigate further Roman ill feeling or vengeance. The action was the responsibility of insurgents led by the High Priest's son, someone safe to blame.

Eleazar, deputy High Priest and son of Ananias, at this point conveniently disappears from the story; presumably he too was killed in the fighting.

Confusingly, there are no less than four characters called Eleazar who appear, within a short space of time in the story, as leaders of the insurgent zealot or sicarii forces. Apart from Eleazar, the son of the High Priest Ananias, there was another Eleazar, son of Jairus, who fell back to command the forces at Masada on the death of his "relative" Menahem. A third

Eleazar, son of Simon, featured in the subsequent rout of a Roman army led by the Syrian legate Cestius Gallus and took charge of the zealot forces in Jerusalem. Finally, there was an Eleazar, who was the son of the chief priest Neus. He was chosen to be a general to take command of part of Israel in the coming battle with Vespasian.

Eleazar was a common name at that time, so that these occurrences must for the most part be coincidental. But there is an overlap in the action which may not simply be a coincidence, one which links with the unconvincing performance attributed to Eleazar, son of the High Priest. First of all, this Eleazar is portrayed as abandoning his allegiances and opposing his father. Then, he kills his supposed ally, Menahem. Finally, he is shown as committing one of the most ferocious and infamous acts in the war–against his former Roman benefactors.

At the very end of Josephus' other major work, *Jewish Antiquities*, sicarii forces are described assassinating opponents and taking hostages, just following the death of James and immediately prior to the general uprising. These were the active messianists, described again as sicarii, who next appear at the beginning of *The Jewish War* under Menahem, taking and holding Masada. Among the hostages they took was the secretary of the Temple Captain's son and Deputy High Priest, Eleazar. At this point at least, Eleazar was on the side of the establishment and therefore a target for the militant messianic nationalists or sicarii. So, what made him change? More pertinent still, did he really swap his allegiances?

If Josephus' possible motivations are taken into account, in first protecting himself and then his former comrades, another explanation becomes more plausible.

The basic facts, as related, are still the same. A group of insurgents, probably with substantial popular support, are objecting to the Roman sacrifices. Menahem, fresh from his success at Masada, joins them and is instrumental in the death of the High Priest, Ananias. The battle ebbs and flows, and then Menahem is killed by forces led by the son of Ananias, his second-in-command Eleazar.

In this scenario all the essential facts are the same, *except that the High Priest's son is not in charge of the insurgents and does not change sides*, but instead remains with the pro-Roman faction all the time. Now, it all does make sense. The actions of the various participants are understandable and so is the death of Menahem.

But who then was the Eleazar who betrayed his oath and had the surrendered and defenseless Roman garrison put to the sword? Quite possibly, it was the zealot leader Eleazar, son of Simon, who is in any case portrayed a little later on as taking command of the Jewish forces in Jerusalem.

And, if not the son of the High Priest, who were the real first leaders of the insurgents, objecting to the Roman Temple sacrifices?

The answer is that we do not know for certain. But some of them may have still been alive at the time that *The Jewish War* was written, and Josephus may well have wanted to protect them.

This explanation, which I have deduced, makes sense and avoids the unlikely and contrary acts attributed to one of the protagonists, the Temple Captain Eleazar.

Josephus could afford to place the blame, and then even privately enjoy the irony of opprobrium heaped on the High Priest's son. This Eleazar had almost certainly perished in the struggle, like most of the pro-Roman Sadducees, and was therefore in no position to contradict him. Nor was he in a position to be punished for actions incorrectly attributed to him. By cleverly shifting the blame, Josephus was I believe protecting people who were at the time of his writing still alive.

Surviving leaders of the revolt in Jerusalem still faced the prospect of summary execution, if identified. So they would have had no motivation contradict the official record and claim their rightful place in history. Did they but realize it, they might also have had cause to be grateful to the hated Jewish turncoat and traitor, Josephus. He wrote a version of history which all but covered their tracks.

If anyone with knowledge did come forward to correct him, Josephus was well covered. He had not misrepresented the essentials. Menahem had been killed by forces led by Eleazar. He could, if he had to, concede that maybe Eleazar son of Ananias had all along been on the loyalist Roman side. If it was not this Eleazar but another one who had subsequently slaughtered the Roman troops, then he could contend that this was an easy error to have made, a simple mix-up of people with identical names.

This was certainly, if I am right, a very clever elision, a subtle blending of the plot to suit the circumstances.

Josephus carried out the same sort of obfuscation in dealing with the genealogy of the Messianic contender, Menahem. This was someone who had a father named Judas, a Galilean. However, as Josephus almost rushes to relate, this was not any old Galilean, but "Judas the Galilean, the very clever rabbi who in the time of Quirinius had once reproached the Jews for submitting to the Romans after serving God alone".

The problem is that the census, organized by the Syrian legate Quirinius to facilitate tax collection, had taken place about sixty years before in AD 6. Menahem could hardly have been the son of the contemporaneous figure, Judas the Galilean, who led the tax revolt under the slogan "No Lord but God." He would by this reckoning have been around eighty years old, when leading his rebels up sheer cliffs to capture the Roman stronghold at

Masada!

This same Judas is likewise described by Josephus, in his *Jewish Antiquities*, as having two other sons, James and Simon, who were put on trial by the Roman governor of Judaea, Alexander, and crucified around AD 46 or 47. Again, this is also stretching credibility. Judas the Galilean must have at least been of mature age when he led his revolt. So his grown-up sons 40 years later would have been about 60, old by the standards of the times and probably too old to be the active leaders of a revolt.

Moreover, there is now the peculiarity of *two* messianic movements acting side by side, but without interacting, from about AD 30 onwards in the small territory of Galilee. One is the movement (described in the gospels) was led by Jesus and the other (alluded to by Josephus) was active under James and Simon, the sons of Judas the Galilean. It is a striking coincidence, or maybe not a coincidence at all, that the names of the putative tax revolt protagonists–Judas, James and Simon–are the also precisely the names of Jesus' three brothers.

There is an explanation, as I argued in the previous chapter, which makes the discrepancies and unlikely coincidences disappear. This is that the Galilean Judas–father of James, Simon and Menaham–might also have been the Galilean Judas who was Jesus' brother. If this is the case, then it is no longer surprising that two of his sons have what can now be recognized as family names. There would also no longer be any problem with their ages. Judas would have been born a few years after Jesus and his sons would have been mature adults, though not improbably old, when they came into conflict with the Roman authorities. Instead of two messianic movements, improbably coexisting in Galilee, this theory provides for just one, led by Jesus and his brothers.

If this is correct, then Josephus has again been extremely clever. All he might have been accused of, had there been anyone left able or willing to do it, is mixing up characters with identical names. But what he succeeded in doing was shift the blame for the struggle with the Roman authorities away from the real messianic Judas (the brother of Jesus), Judas' sons and their descendants. There were certainly grandchildren of Judas still living at the time Josephus wrote *The Jewish War*, first in Aramaic and then in a Greek translation in AD 75, and also a few years later when he wrote *Jewish Antiquities* around AD 93.

If he intended to deflect attention from the descendants of Judas, as seems probable, then he succeeded partially or only for a time. Judas' grandsons, identified by name in some sources as Zoker and James, were rounded up under the Emperor Domitian around AD 90 as part of a group of possible subversives, who claimed to be or were considered to be of the genealogy of David. Eusebius, following Hegesippus' account, describes the grandsons as simple country laborers who, in response to questioning, said that they believed not in an earthly kingdom but in a heavenly kingdom. This, they are reported to have claimed, would come about miraculously when the Christ or Messiah (their ancestor) would return to judge both the living and the dead. Thus, not claiming to be part of a movement to free Israel, they were not at this time perceived as a threat to Rome.

Messianic unrest continued however and a decade or so later the Emperor Trajan ordered a round up of "descendants of David" including Jesus' brother Simeon bar Cleophas, who was tortured and crucified. Eusebius claims that Simeon was then 120 years old. Though almost certainly an exaggeration, Simon/Simeon, as one of the younger brothers in Jesus' family, would have been an old man by then, possibly in his 80s or 90s. The Romans, when seeking to make an example of someone, were no respecters of persons. It seems likely, in view of Simon or Simeon's fate, that Zoker and James were also among those who died in this wave of persecution.

By cleverly mixing up names, I maintain, by confusing the rebel leader Eleazar with the son of the High Priest Eleazar and also the Galilean Judas, brother of Jesus with an earlier tax rebel "Judas the Galilean", Josephus sought to protect messianic survivors of the rebellion against Rome. Josephus was certainly a survivor. He put himself first; he appears to have been conceited and self-opinionated. He was undoubtedly a traitor. So he would not have taken too great a personal risk and, indeed, there was probably not a very great risk from this minor deception. The Romans probably did not bother to learn too much about the culture of Israel, just a small, subject people. They did not for the most part understand Hebrew; Greek and Latin were the languages of empire. There were also few survivors of the rebellion who might be able to correct what Josephus could have represented as a simple mixing up of names, an easy error to make.

But Josephus was, I believe, to an extent acting as a literary fifth column, writing certainly to please the Romans but also to protect his former comrades.

Josephus was clearly only human; he exaggerated, he was credulous and he made mistakes. So the accounts of the same incidents given in *The Jewish War* and *Jewish Antiquities* do not, for example, always agree.

He would, however, have known precisely who the main characters in the drama of the uprising were. Jerusalem, though a city, had a population of around 100,000, about the size of a small town today. There would have been a few score people at most with real religious, political and economic influence. Josephus grew up with them and was one of them. He had a priestly background, possibly revolutionary credentials as well, and was considered sufficiently able and important to be made commander of the forces defending Galilee. When he is vague in his accounts of what happened, it is because he wants to be or because he is lazy, not because he doesn't know.

He was certainly devious enough to make the transpositions I have identified and there may also be others. Here, after all was the man, who memorized the numbered lots in the suicide pact of survivors at Jotapata so that he could choose to be last or next to last in line. Then, after the throats of his comrades had successively been cut, he surrendered to the Romans.

He was never able to return from Rome to Judaea because of the threat to his life. The Jews never forgave him. Yet Josephus did the best that he could, certainly no harm and possibly some good to Simeon, Zoker and James and possibly still others unnamed who survived many years up until the reign of the Emperor Trajan. When he surrendered, to become an interpreter and writer of history for the Romans, the cause was already lost.

It will be remembered that there were two alternative strands in Jewish messianism. In one, it was expected that deliverance would come through an act of miraculous, divine deliverance as described in the Book of Daniel (chapter 6, above). This was the sort of Messiah that the grandsons of Judas claimed to be looking for, or at least this is what they said when interviewed under threat of their lives. The other sort of messianism was the more practical kind. A warrior king would arise and lead the people to drive out foreign occupiers. This was the message in psalm 17 of the Songs of Solomon (chapter 7 above). It was what the many unsuccessful revolts against the Romans were about, including three after the death of Herod and the uprisings by Menaham and Simon bar Gioras.

Those Jews looking for the former sort of deliverance were generally left alone.

However, once some sort of line of inheritance became established, along the lines of the succession enjoyed for a while under the old Kings of Judah, then all possible claimants by descent were treated with utmost suspicion, whatever they purported to believe.

King Herod pursued and exterminated Maccabean descendants. The Romans in the first century persecuted and eliminated other "Sons of David", at least some of whom from the evidence were relatives and descendants of the historical Jesus. In both cases, what was involved was a group of brothers with tenuous claims to be linked to the royal House of David. The Maccabees came from a minor priestly lineage. Jesus, and therefore also his brothers, may have had similar priestly origins. The claim that Jesus was the Jewish Messiah is supported in the Gospels of Luke and Matthew by genealogies going back to King David. But these genealogies bear no relation to each other; they are utterly different!

This is not at all surprising, given that the lines of descent were lost after the mass deportations into exile which happened when Israel fell to the

Babylonians in 587 BC, many centuries before. Biblical prophecy required a warrior king, a Messiah, who was a "Son of David" and a pedigree, which could not in any case be reliably established, would be manufactured if necessary.

The Maccabees were clearly warriors along the lines of the Songs of Solomon, zealous of the Law, taking up arms against an unpopular foreign ruler, Antiochus IV, who was seeking to suppress and replace their religion.

But the situation with Jesus and his brothers is lot more unclear. As has been noted, Jesus did not according to the gospels lead an overt rebellion. No such conflict is recorded by Josephus who, for all his faults, did not miss out on major battles.

Had Jesus led a serious armed uprising, as a proclaimed "Messiah", then his brothers and particularly the first in line, James, would subsequently have been at serious risk, picked up and dealt with. But James was left largely unmolested, building up the Nazoraean following in Jerusalem for a further 25 years. It is reported in Acts that, following the Crucifixion of Jesus, a purge of the active followers of Jesus was initiated, leading to the death of Stephen and others but leaving James and the other Apostles alone.

So, at least ostensibly, there was one faction within the Jesus movement preaching a pacifist kingdom on earth, involving religious purity and spiritual values. This was at least initially the largest component.

The other faction was prepared to take up arms. It included, I have deduced, Judas the brother of Jesus and his sons who were called Simon, James and lastly Menahem.

But, even among the core of the Nazoraean followers of Jesus, there was a degree of tension between the two modes of messianism. This is shown in the warlike names of some of the Apostles including Judas Zelotes, Simon the zealot and Judas Iscariot which seems a corruption of Judas Sicarius, from the sicae daggers that the so-called urban "sicarii" assassins used. Jesus is reported in Mark to have named his cousins, James and John, the sons of Zebedee, "Boanerges" or "sons of thunder". He also called Simon, the brother of Andrew, Simon "the rock" which became Simon Peter, from the Greek "petros". There are also occasional references to followers of Jesus carrying arms.

There is actually no surprise in finding that a movement, that was both political and religious, should have been carried on to the next generation. The Maccabees operated as a band of brothers before the mantle was passed on to Simon's son, John Hyrcanus. The evidence for what happened to any offspring of Jesus and his brothers is elusive and would appear to have been suppressed, though I have identified three possible sons of Judas who continued to be active in the struggle. There are other possible identifications which can be found in the pages of Acts and Josephus.

I have suggested, from the evidence in the gospels, that Jesus knew his bible well, saw himself in a messianic role, as a possible suffering servant of God who might, following Isaiah, have to suffer though not necessarily die. I have shown that the evidence points overwhelmingly to the fact that he took every available precaution to ensure that, having surrendered himself up to the Romans, he would not die. I have offered a credible reason, based on the evidence, for such an otherwise inexplicable surrender. This is that he gave himself up in exchange for fellow Jews, possibly including some of his supporters, arrested after a demonstration in Jerusalem that had resulted in deaths on both sides. As the writer of John's Gospel has Jesus observe, what greater love can a man have than to lay down his life for his friends?

It is interesting that the evidence of intent to avoid death is fairly firm, but the evidence of motivation has to be imputed. The theory of an exchange fits the facts, makes sense of what happened and puts the action in context.

I have suggested that Jesus may also have seen himself as a "suffering servant", making a sacrifice for his God and his people. But he may simply have tacked on his messianic claim to an audacious plan to free some of his wayward compatriots and followers and, at the same time, himself survive.

It is even possible that the messianic claim was not strongly made at the time, when the basis plot was to make the exchange in order to save the Jerusalem protesters. But it came to be asserted more strongly retrospectively, as the militant wing of the movement took action, and then again as Paul and the gospel writers and editors successfully turned Jesus into the Savior of mankind.

There was an inevitable coalescence of the two wings of the messianic movement and that occurred when there was a general uprising against Rome. At which point, it was really no longer tenable to look forward to some of miraculous divine intervention. The hour really had come, and people had to decide just where they stood.

The point which Josephus disingenuously disguises is that there was really no framework of "insurgents" separated from, and misleading, "the people" who from time to time sought to talk the rebels down. There was certainly a strong faction around the Sadducee chief priests who owed their position to, benefited from and were critically compromised by allegiance to Rome. The bulk of the Jewish population was however, almost to a man or woman, against being occupied. The only issue was what to do about it.

After the initial stages of the rebellion in which Ananias and his brother Hezekiah were killed, there developed an internal struggle for control. Rather than an outbreak of disunity, or even a failure to unite, it seems that this was really unfinished business, a continuation of the struggle between the pro-Roman Sadducee establishment and the messianic, nationalist forces.

The rage of the population was at first directed against the Romans and the then High Priest Ananias. Under an armistice, the troops of King Agrippa and Jewish nationals were allowed to surrender without harm, leaving the Roman forces isolated and exposed. The Herodians Saul and Costobar managed to escape from the city and join up with the Roman commander Cestius Gallus.

The Sadducees regrouped around Ananus, who was a member of a family in which there had been several High Priests and who was himself a former High Priest. The zealots under Eleazar ben Simon later elected their own High Priest by drawing lots. So, there were then two separate sources of power in the city, Ananus who was according to Josephus appointed by popular vote and Eleazar who came fresh from a battle in which Cestius had been defeated.

A number of factors made more internal conflict inevitable. As town after town subsequently fell to Vespasian's advancing forces, refugees and fighters flooded into Jerusalem. To those who had practiced accommodation with Roman occupation, this was further indication that the cause was ultimately lost and that they would have to come to terms. The zealots by contrast wanted to push resistance to the very end. Furthermore, Ananus was a member of an establishment Sadducee family which had been prominently involved in the persecution of the Nazoraeans. His brother-in-law Caiaphas had been the High Priest when Jesus was tried and crucified. His brother Jonathan was High Priest when Stephen was stoned, while another brother Matthias was High Priest when King Agrippa had the disciple James, the brother of John and cousin of Jesus, put to the sword. Ananus himself was the man who had presided over the trial and illegal execution of James, the brother of Jesus, for which he was then deposed. There were plenty of people with reason to hate Ananus, and there was no chance Eleazar ben Simon and his zealot forces would ever have accepted his authority.

The struggle had become one in which the active element in the messianic movement now predominated and was expressed in conflict with the Roman occupiers. It also seems to have been, on another level, almost a personal struggle between two extended Jewish families: one which provided many of the collaborating High Priests and one with messianic aspirations which opposed compromise over issues of religious purity and integrity.

The decision by some priests not to allow the Roman sacrifices in the holy Temple was what ignited the conflict. This was a pivotal point, when everyone in Jerusalem had to make up their minds which side to support.

The majority of the Jews in the city were Pharisees. It seems that a large number of them had become followers of James when he became, after Jesus, leader of the Nazoraean community in Jerusalem. They were all still, including James, simply practicing Pharisees, but they held the additional belief that the Messiah in the form of Jesus had come, survived death and would one day return. This was not the mystical resurrection as it was Christianized by the gospel editors and Paul. Jesus, as I have argued, probably survived. After the Crucifixion, Jesus is recorded as meeting a number of people, including his brother James, before going off to a safe haven and then into exile.

James subsequently made no claim to be King of the Jews, for the very good reason that his elder brother Jesus was still alive. But he was an immensely popular religious leader and his supporters in Jerusalem, according to Acts, were numbered in tens of thousands.

When James was stoned to death by the High Priest's faction, these followers did not simply go away. They remained as Pharisees and as zealous supporters of the Jewish Law, as James had been, watchful against the pollutions of idols, critical as James must have been of the sacrifices in the Temple to pagan gods and the Roman Emperor.

So, when the revolt began, I suggest that it was these people who started it and not the Sadducee Temple Captain Eleazar, who was second-in-command and son of the High Priest. They were also, along with other Pharisee Jews, supporters of the zealots in the subsequent continuing struggle with the Sadducee establishment. As described by Josephus, this was a messy and complicated struggle, a war within a war, conducted even while the Romans were advancing on Jerusalem. While the zealots lost in the war with Rome, they did nevertheless succeed in their objective of wiping out the collaborating Sadducee leadership.

With James dead, it remains an open question who the Nazoraean and Pharisee leaders were who successfully objected to the Temple sacrifices on behalf of the Romans, and so started the rebellion. Josephus does not mention their names, because his objective was if possible to protect them.

Instead, he implicated the High Priest's son, a Sadducee collaborator, who could not object because he almost certainly perished in the revolt. How Josephus must have privately enjoyed this joke! At the same time, he deflected criticism from another Eleazar, a zealot leader and son of someone called Simon, who became leader of the Jewish zealot forces in Jerusalem and was possibly responsible for the massacre of the Roman garrison after it had surrendered.

Since Josephus does not say, we are left to wonder who this Simon, father of Eleazar, might have been.

Simon was a fairly common name, so it may be that this was someone who does not otherwise appear in the text. On the other hand, Josephus has demonstrated a facility to leave out or disguise inconvenient links. On the grounds that zealot fathers, whether active or passive, would have tended to have zealot sons, there are several possible candidates.

One possibility is Simon or Simeon bar Clophas, second brother of Jesus, who succeeded James as leader of the Nazoraeans. This Simon did survive until great old age when he was crucified under the Roman Emperor Trajan.

The Nazoraeans were essentially ordinary Pharisee Jews, opposed to the High Priest's Sadducee clique, and it must be this faction which revolted against the Roman sacrifices in the Temple. So Simon/Simeon was implicated even if he was, in the mold of the prophet Daniel, pacifist in his approach.

Some traditions suggest that, on the outbreak of war, the Nazoraeans fled across the Jordan to Pella, one of the ten self-governing cities of the Decapolis. But there were, by all accounts, too many of them for that. The majority would have fought and died along with their fellow Jews in Jerusalem.

It is possible that some of the leading figures, including Simon/Simeon, might have been spirited away to safety in the early stages. If Simon, described in the gospels as "Simon the zealot", had strong and active sons, then these might well have stayed behind to fight and die.

Trajan apparently killed Simon on the grounds of his genealogical connection, and as part of a wider purge of Jews who could claim to be "Sons of David". But had the Roman Emperor really discovered something else? Had he finally deciphered Josephus and realized that Simon/Simeon and his Nazoraean followers had taken an active part early on in the uprising?

That is certainly plausible. But what is not so very likely is that the prominent rebel leader Eleazar (ben Simon), who took charge of the zealot forces in Jerusalem, was Simon or Simeon's son. This would have been a fact hard to disguise, and one pointing to his father's possible role in the uprising. That Simon survived for many years afterwards, until his death under Trajan around AD 100, indicates that he probably was not compromised by the activities of a revolutionary son. He must instead have successfully presented himself in the Pharisee/Nazoraean mold as a religious teacher rather than a fighter, a zealous upholder of the Jewish Law like James.

One tenuous possibility is that this rebel leader Eleazar was also the Lazarus of the gospels. Since his father is named as Simon, this conveniently links with the identification made earlier of Simon the Leper as a possible father of Mary, Martha and Lazarus.

There is unfortunately no direct information as to what Lazarus did in the years after the Crucifixion. In the account given by Josephus, the rebel leader Eleazar ben Simon comes into the story much later on in Jerusalem. But, if he was also the gospel character Lazarus, then he must have spent the previous thirty years somewhere else.

According to John's Gospel, the chief priests sought to put Lazarus to death. He was a wanted man partly because he was the focus of an extraordinary event, a presumed miracle which led more people to believe in

Jesus. He was also wanted because he was close to Jesus and had provided him with practical help and support.

So, on balance, I find the suggestions put forward in the previous chapter more credible. These were that Lazarus went to ground. He then joined with the only group available to help him, which in any case he identified with, the militant wing of the messianic movement. He eventually came to be with Menahem, the leader of this movement, resurfacing in the pages of Josephus as Eleazar, commander of the sicarii forces at Masada.

Josephus states that this Eleazar was a relative of Menahem. He was, as I have argued, related to Menahem because both of them were related to Jesus: Eleazar or Lazarus as brother-in-law and Menahem as nephew, the son of Judas/Thaddeus.

My conclusion therefore is that Eleazar ben Simon was not the gospel Lazarus. The Eleazar at Masada provides a more convincing candidate.

Although it would not have been beyond Josephus to split one character into two, perhaps to confuse further his Roman readers, the simplest explanation is that there were, as described, two important characters called Eleazar. One of these, Eleazar son of Jairus (the gospel Lazarus), led the forces at Masada. The other, Eleazar son of Simon, played a prominent part in the rout of the forces of Cestius Gallus.

A more credible identification of the character Simon, father of the zealot leader Eleazar, is with the disciple Simon Peter of the gospels. By the gospel accounts, this Simon was fierce and hotheaded, and one of the few Apostles playing a substantive part in the story who was not actually related to Jesus. Assigning him "the keys of the kingdom of heaven" (Matthew 16:15–19), Jesus in effect appointed him the leader of his followers. According to Acts, Simon Peter continued to play an active role in the development of the Nazoraean movement.

Simon appears in the pages of Josephus as a man with a religious reputation, able to convene an "ecclesia", a religious assembly or Church. He had the temerity to denounce the Herodian and Rome-appointed King Agrippa I and sought to bar him from the Temple as unclean.

Simon went to Caesarea to confront the king. Josephus puts a gloss on the outcome; far from punishing Simon, the king is portrayed as having such a forgiving nature that he instead gave him a present! It would seem that this Simon, able to rebuke King Agrippa with a degree of impunity, had a substantial following that could not lightly be ignored. In the Acts of the Apostles, however, it is recorded that Agrippa arrested Simon Peter who then managed to escape from prison.

There is a Church tradition that Simon Peter was later arrested in Rome and crucified, upside down at his own request, towards the end of the reign of the Emperor Nero. The bizarre manner of Simon Peter's death might well have persisted over the years as a folk memory, until it was eventually written down. But no convincing explanation is given as to why the Apostle might have wished to die like this, or had his request granted.

A more likely scenario is provided by the last, desperate stages of the siege of Jerusalem when the starved defenders tried by the hundred to break through enemy lines. Many were caught and crucified before the city walls as a grim warning to the rest to surrender, or suffer a similar fate. Josephus records that the bored Roman soldiers amused themselves by nailing up the victims on their crosses in a variety of poses. It seems to me in character that Simon Peter would have joined his fellow Nazoraean Jews during the uprising. In which case, he might well have ended his life like this, crucified upside down outside the walls of Jerusalem.

Simon/Simon Peter was certainly a religiously zealous man, proactive in his approach, and he could well have had a zealot leader for a son. That son may well therefore have been the Eleazar ben Simon who shared in the triumph over the Roman general Cestius Gallus and brought back the Roman army's money and supplies. I have also argued that it was this Eleazar who initiated the massacre of the Roman garrison.

The messianic movement, I have suggested, had two faces with Jesus as the most problematic, contradictory character. The glosses added by the gospel writers and editors have not helped in understanding his real nature.

Writers of this period followed a tradition of putting speeches into the mouths of protagonists, suggesting what they might have said in the circumstances–often without any evidence as to what they really did say. Josephus, for example, has his characters embarking on impossibly long speeches in the very heat of battle.

It was a device to add dramatic emphasis and provide explanation. Some of what is alleged to have been said in the gospels may well fall into this category: pure invention of the author rather than collected oral or written recollections. But there appears also to have been an early, circulated collection of the sayings of Jesus. By analyzing what is common to many sources, it has been possible to get an idea of the philosophy that Jesus preached.

As for actions these, especially if surprising or dramatic, may be easier to remember than words. The passion account has much circumstantial detail and records events to which there would have been many witnesses. Even though some of this evidence was later changed or augmented, there remains an underlying pattern, telling a different story from the one presented by the gospel writers.

Jesus turned over the tables of the money-changers who had corrupted the sanctity of the Temple with their greed and exploitation. James, his brother, preached against the "pollutions of idols" and became a focus of opposition to the High Priest and his faction in the Temple. The revolt began not long afterwards, with a refusal by some Jews to allow sacrifices on behalf of Roman gods and the Emperor, as pagan influences polluting the Temple.

These people, I suggest, were among the many thousands of Pharisee followers of James who had not gone away, and were as ever still fierce upholders and keepers of the Law.

These were also the people, the "Sons of David" and their followers, that the Romans persecuted in the aftermath of the uprising and for many years following.

These "Sons of David" were, the evidence suggests, for the most part genealogically linked, related to or descended from Jesus.

There was a continuity in this religious protest, from Jesus through to James and his followers and those who began the uprising. It was all the way through this period a messianic movement of upholders of the Law, with Pharisees becoming Nazoraeans by their belief that they had among them the Messiah, a man persecuted yet "resurrected" and surviving. It was simply one messianic movement.

It was this movement which was at the root of the Jewish uprising, just as messianism was also a factor in many previous rebellions. Jewish nationalism was based on the concept of a King, or Messiah, arising to deliver the nation from oppression, as foretold by prophets and according to the wishes of their one God, Jehovah. Religious and political ambitions were thus inextricably intertwined. Active political opposition and the assertion of religious belief coexisted in dynamic tension, with one to an extent always implying the other. In coming to terms with occupation, Jews were faced with a choice between complicity with the oppressor, hope in divine intervention and direct action.

Looked at in terms of what actually happened, in its historical context and in the circumstances of subsequent figures such as James, the movement led by Jesus was not something of minor consequence at the time. It was a censored rebellion. The gospel makers wanted to sever Jesus' Jewish roots to generate a wider, Gentile religion which would appeal to the Romans and could be promulgated through empire. Josephus, tame pro-Roman historian, tried to protect himself and some of the messianic figures who had survived. The first gospel writers likewise sought to protect characters like Lazarus and the John-the-priest, who were then still alive.

What is fascinating is that Jesus and other characters in the gospels are still present, even though erased from the pages of Josephus. The imprint is there in gossipy folk tales substituted in place of the description there should have been of Pilate's tenure of office and the activities of Jesus and his brothers and other followers. It is there in characters whose identities have been subtly changed or exchanged. It is there in the characters who do apparently feature, such as Saul, but whose significance is not fully unexplained.

I am not suggesting that the Nazoraeans were the only group active in the early stages of the Jewish uprising. But I do maintain that they were there and of central significance; the same body of Pharisee Jews still had the same beliefs, they were organized and they had another leader in the form of the second brother of Jesus, called Simon or Simeon. Their concerns in keeping the Law of the Torah, retaining the purity of their religion and resisting the impurities of sacrifices to pagan gods and idols provided the starting point. The accommodations of the Rome-appointed Sadducee High Priest and his faction were rejected and this put the Jewish nation on a collision course with Rome. And Rome in the person of Nero and his provocative procurator Florus appeared to be only too ready, according to Josephus, for conflict.

Though I believe I have shown a continuity of the messianic movement from Jesus and his brothers up to and through the Jewish uprising, this does not imply that Christians were involved in the revolt against Rome.

The group at Antioch, fostered by Saul and for the first time described as "Christians", was at this point still a small, aberrant faction with beliefs at variance with the main body of the Nazoraean followers of Jesus. They ultimately thrived because the Nazoraeans were crushed along with their fellow Jews in the revolt and because the surviving "Sons of David" were, as the genuine article, successfully purged and persecuted by the Romans in subsequent years.

The "poor", surviving as Ebionites and similar scattered groups, were left marginalized both physically and philosophically. They had no foothold in the religion of Christianity, with its semi-divine savior, tailor-made for the Roman world and shorn of his Jewish roots, and with its rituals of sacrifice adapted from Jewish practice. Nor could they easily survive separately from mainstream Judaism. The years passed and the predicted imminent return of their Messiah came to be seen more and more as a remote and unlikely prospect, an empty promise. Some may have gone back to mainstream Judaism but, just as likely, the movement withered because it failed to replace itself.

In making their new religion, the self-proclaimed Apostle Paul and the gospel writers and editors censored the challenge presented and the rebellion undertaken by the messianic movement. Josephus did much the same, though for different reasons.

So something else came about, with very mixed benefits over the course of succeeding centuries. The religion which evolved has some of the values, some of the original teachings. But Christianity was not the intended outcome of the mission that the historical Jesus directed to the Jewish religion and the Jewish people.

Something of what happened can be rediscovered. Something of the power of events and of personalities two thousand years ago can be reclaimed.

Put back in context, as best as can be, Jesus the man is not diminished and he grows in stature.

CONCLUSION

Greater love has no man than this, that a man lay down his life for his friends.

John 15:13

I have come to the end of a journey which started with a question. Are the beliefs about Jesus of present-day Christians, justified by and reflected in their own evidence in the gospel stories?

The conclusion which I came to, in examining this evidence, is that many of the key propositions about Jesus are simply wrong. It is neither an issue of faith, nor of opinion. It is a question of fact.

The evidence in the gospels does not, for example, support the contention that Jesus was born from a woman who was a virgin and impregnated by God.

It is not merely that the evidence of the gospels fails to support this. The mechanisms by which this fantasy was developed are clearly identifiable. The reasons the Early Church promoted it are all too evident.

Having discovered, or rather rediscovered, a person who was a character with a place in history, I went on to look at the historical context.

The gospels, which had been edited to sever Jesus from his Jewish roots and generate a semi-divine figure with wider appeal for a worldwide religion, began to yield more of their secrets.

It very soon became clear that even posing the question, whether Jesus "really" rose from the dead, was to ignore both the cultural and historical context for the story and all the evidence staring us in the face in the gospels.

The real question which had to be answered first was whether or not it was simply all made up. One argument was that early writers, who did not know what had really happened, were merely filling in the gaps with their own inventions. Their motivation might have been to take comfort and make sense of loss, to create a sort of victory out of defeat.

My conclusion was that the evidence, though far from perfect, did relate to real events and did have some validity. It was not all invented.

The next question was certainly very perplexing and troubling. What did the sequence of events described in the gospels mean? What was going on?

There appeared to be an underlying story, supported by a mass of circumstantial detail, pointing in quite a different direction from the tale told on the surface. The evidence overwhelmingly showed that, far from embracing death, Jesus took every possible precaution to avoid it. It also indicated that he may indeed, as intended, have survived the Crucifixion.

But there was still one real oddity in the narrative. Why did Jesus meekly give himself up, when he had every opportunity to escape and when survival, and not death, was apparently the objective?

Christians have really had no answer to this. It is one of the very weakest points in the gospel fable.

The idea of some sort of cosmic suicide undertaken to save mankind is implausible, at odds with the context and with the facts as presented. Here was a Jewish Messiah, on a mission to help the Jewish people which specifically excluded Gentiles.

It is at this point that putting Jesus back into his historical context offers a solution and helps to resolve some of the problems.

At the time that Jesus lived, the land of Israel was wracked with conflict. There had been three separate uprisings on the death of King Herod, all brutally put down by the Romans. There had been mass executions. People still harbored grief at the loss of loved ones.

Even more recently, a movement had developed opposed to the extortionate system of taxes. This too had been suppressed.

In Galilee, the Rome-appointed tetrarch Herod Antipas, son of the infamous King Herod, was cracking down on dissidents. He executed John the Baptist. He pursued Jesus and his followers, whose peripatetic preaching may have had something to do with the need to keep on the move, one step ahead of Herod's soldiers.

The short-tempered and impulsive Roman procurator of Judaea, Pilate, had to deal with a number of difficult incidents and managed, with great insensitivity, to provoke the Jewish population.

One of these incidents, involving bloodshed and loss of life, was reported to Jesus. People had been arrested and were held, pending trial and possible execution. It was, I have suggested, in response to this that Jesus handed himself over. With such an exchange, rather than a simple surrender, the gospel action and the dialogue begins to make sense. Jesus did, indeed, lay down his life for his friends.

In a way, anyone could become a "Messiah", literally an anointed one, taking on for himself the mantle of either kingly or religious authority as liberator of the Jewish people. It was a concept well imbedded in Jewish holy scripture. Although, in theory the expected liberator of Israel was going to be a descendant of King David and thus a "Son of David", the actual line of descent had been lost many centuries before following the expulsions instigated by Babylon.

Some revolts were principally opportunist, like the ones which took place after the death of King Herod. But there had been, under the Maccabees, a brief restoration of the monarchy and the principle of descent. Mattathias, who struck down the representative of the hated Seleucid, or Persian Greek, ruler Antiochus IV, and his sons were an embodiment of the active messianic principle. They were warrior liberators who in a short time became warrior kings. It took 38 years of constant conflict to create a sovereign and independent Judah, after which there followed a period of consolidation and expansion through wars with neighboring kingdoms. This was then followed by protracted internal power struggles over the question of succession, leading to decay, decline and finally conquest by the Romans under Pompey in 63 BC.

It took just 100 years for all of this to happen. The flowering of Jewish nationalism and independence was squeezed in between the might of a decaying empire and the rise of another one. The timescale was compressed: all the battles that had to take place to achieve liberation were there but what were largely squeezed out were the years of peace. The Jewish people had little time to savor and enjoy the independence they gained.

For people living at the time of Jesus, this was far from being distant history. When Jesus was born, there were many people who had been alive at the time of last of the Maccabees or Hasmoneans: Antigonus and John Hyrcanus II. Sovereign independence was something that people had experienced and could look forward to when the next Messiah or liberator arose.

So parallels between the Maccabees and what took place at the time of Jesus are not entirely misplaced. The difference was that, by this time, the jaws of the closing vice had squeezed shut. There was no time or space left for an independent Israel to flourish between the fall of one powerful empire and the rise of another.

But what is clearly apparent is the rise of another messianic movement, based on the principle of descent and with a claimed link, however tenuous, to the Old Testament kingship of King David.

According to the gospels, Jesus claimed or admitted to be the Messiah (and remember this was an entirely Jewish Messiah) and was crucified for it. His brother James was stoned to death by the Sadducee High Priest, Ananus, possibly with the connivance of the Herodian ruler King Agrippa II. His second brother Simon/Simeon, who like James became the leader of the Nazoraean community, was crucified under Trajan, on account of his genealogical connection as a "Son of David". The grandsons of Judas, third brother of Jesus, were investigated and set free, and then probably also picked up later and executed in the purge under Trajan.

The messianic movement was dealt with as ruthlessly as Herod the Great had earlier persecuted and eliminated his rivals, who were the descendants of Maccabean kings. It was always there, bubbling beneath the surface, but there was never any space for it to flourish. Jewish messianic nationalism was simply suppressed by Roman rule.

There were two aspects to the movement that had evolved over a very long period, during which the Jews of Israel were dominated by a succession of great powers.

One response was introspective, causing people to turn to religion for solace and for the hope one day of divine deliverance. This was essentially the message of the prophet Daniel, that the enemy would be defeated directly by the hand of God. The other way was indicated in the Psalms of Solomon. A warrior king, a Son of David, would arise and rescue Israel. This king, the anointed one or Messiah, would lead his people to victory.

Under Jesus, James and then Simeon, until there was an actual rebellion, the chosen route to salvation was by means of spiritual improvement. At the same time, there was the hope or expectation that the enemy would confound themselves or come to grief by an act of God.

The gospels, incorporating remembered and written down sayings of Jesus, show that he taught and adapted Pharisaic values. The Kingdom of God he preached was innate and all around people, and could be attained by choosing a better path in life.

This choice of approach, the way forward outlined by Daniel, would have reflected a particular religious perspective. But it might also have been adopted for more practical reasons. Relying on eventual divine intervention was a means of avoiding confrontation for the time being, necessary in view of the overwhelming power of Rome.

Jews like Josephus and Saul, who had been to Rome, saw the ultimate futility of resistance and so adapted their approach to the Roman occupiers. Josephus, even while charged with defending Galilee and then its last stronghold of Jotapata, advocated coming to terms with the Romans. His fellow Jews refused but, at the last gasp, he had a chance of making his own personal terms and he took it.

Saul allied himself with the High Priest and the Sadducee elite, persecuted the early followers of Jesus and was, it seems, part of a delegation which sought to invite the Romans in at an early stage to end the conflict. Saul and his fellows did not, at that point, succeed with their efforts to subvert the rebellion. But Saul ultimately inflicted a greater blow, distorting and converting the Judaism of the Nazoraeans into something it never was, a wider religion for the Roman world.

Rather than two utterly distinct strands there was, I suggest, a degree of ambivalence in the various parts of the movement. Jesus' followers carried arms and were involved in a cat-and-mouse game with the authorities, moving from place to place, a step ahead of the soldiers of Herod Antipas. Jesus' brothers and other disciples had names which suggest militant attitudes and links. Though Jesus did not lead a rebellion, he may have given himself up in exchange for prisoners taken in a riot in which his followers were involved.

The evidence suggests links between the "poor" or Essenes and the early

Nazoraeans, who may either have developed alongside or grown out of an assembly of the poor based in Jerusalem. Like the Nazoraeans, the Essenes also had a militant face. Some at least took part in the battle with the Roman legions sent to take Jerusalem. They also had, at their center in Qumran, a war scroll setting out how they would battle with the "kittim" or Romans. Vespasian certainly saw this group as a threat and took time out from the siege of Jerusalem to destroy the settlement at Qumran and massacre its inhabitants.

There was certainly an overtly militant element that, perhaps even knowing the might of Rome, gave scant attention to the advice of Daniel and took the warrior path advocated in the Songs of Solomon.

Menahem was at the head of one faction of "sicarii" forces, at first conducting hit and run operations against the pro-Roman Sadducee High Priest and his followers and then openly taking part in the rebellion. Josephus also describes another character, "Theudas", in conflict with the Romans, and two others, James and Simon, who were captured and crucified. I have suggested, following the evidence and trying to make sense of the discrepancies, that Theudas was in fact Thaddeus/Judas, the brother of Jesus, and that James, Simon and Menahem were three of his sons. There were not several, but just one messianic movement operating at this time.

What the strained, but still overtly peaceful, wing of the movement sought to do was preserve the integrity of the Jewish religion and thus nationhood, despite Roman occupation. This is why purity of the Temple and its freedom from idolatrous practices and images were issues which really mattered to the Jews. Time and again, it was the encroachment on this, whether through Roman statues, standards or pagan sacrifices, which led to conflict.

James, the brother of Jesus, fiercely and zealously defended religious purity and built up a huge, popular following. But, when he was killed in defending his ideals, a final and fatal rupture occurred between the Sadducee ruling elite and the mass of ordinary Jews, including James' substantial Nazoraean following. The strategy of defending Judaism and waiting in hope was strained beyond its limits. The sicarii stepped up their activities. They gained more and more supporters. Then finally, a critical mass of rage and pent-up frustration was reached, and the populace turned its fury on those who were collaborating with Rome. Although the war was probably lost from the outset, its outcome was not helped by a continuing bloody struggle between zealot nationalists and an establishment still seeking to come to terms.

The death of James lit the fuse for the rebellion and, as Josephus observed, this event may thereby have led to the destruction of Jerusalem.

Paradoxically, this also helped in the generation of a new religion, Christianity. Saul, as the converted Apostle Paul, had been locked in a battle with James, Simon Peter and other leaders of the Nazoraean community over the issue. He had been summoned twice to account for himself before the leaders of the Nazoraeans.

The argument was ostensibly about the rules which should apply to Gentile converts to this movement which operated fully within Judaism, though with one distinguishing feature. This was the belief that one of their number was the Jewish Messiah, who had overcome death and would one day return. What form the looked-for liberation would take on Jesus' return was open to interpretation. This enabled the movement to operate under James within the framework of Roman occupation, though in a state of tension between its twin aspects of spirituality and active resistance.

The Nazoraean leaders were aware of some of what Paul was doing, including advocating that Gentile converts no longer need follow Jewish dietary restrictions or practice circumcision. What Paul had in fact concluded, as his letters show, was that the Torah was defunct and superseded by his new gospel message of faith in Jesus as the risen Messiah, not just of the Jews but of the whole world. James, Simon Peter and the other Nazoraean leaders wielded considerable power. They headed the community in Jerusalem and they were, after all, the followers and kin who had known Jesus. They were, in one of its forms, the direct expression and continuation of the messianic movement.

The Nazoraeans were able to summon Paul, call him to account, make him reaffirm his allegiance to the Torah and undergo a humiliating purification ritual. They intended thereby to send a message to those whom Paul may have wrongly informed and so counteract what he had been doing. As a further measure, they sent their own emissaries to preach the orthodox view to possible converts in Gentile communities.

Paul could not at this point ignore the source of the movement which had the power to cut him off and discredit him. He also needed to retain the links with Judaism, to provide a respectable pedigree and sense of continuity for the new "Christian" religion.

Though Paul also had powerful allies, through his links with the Herodians, the Nazoraeans were a formidable force and might well have prevailed. But they were dispersed and destroyed in the Jewish uprising which had its origins in antecedent struggles over key issues of religious freedom. The death of James may well, as Josephus perceived, have marked the beginning of the end.

Christianity filled the gap which was left by the destruction of the Nazoraeans. It steadily gained ground despite periodic persecutions and was eventually, under the Emperor Constantine, made the official Roman religion.

Christian authors and editors rewrote the texts and redefined what had happened. The messianic movement was effectively hijacked and the Jewish

Messiah cut off from his Jewish roots.

As I have argued, Christianity has imposed ideas of what kind of a man Jesus was that are plainly wrong. He was made into a bizarre, celibate figure without background, without family, without even a proper biological origin, disjointed from his social and historical context and from the movement of which he was a part. A strong anti-Jewish overlay was also introduced both into the description in the gospels of what happened and the things which Jesus is credited with having said.

As far as the sayings are concerned, that is the message that Jesus was preaching, a fair attempt can be made to extricate what is core and probably original. This can be done by analyzing the texts to see what appears in more than one, or several, distinct sources including extracanonical gospels and other writings.

It can be seen that Jesus preached a Kingdom of God that was immanent, in and all around people. It was one that paid no respect to class or status. Indeed, the rich were handicapped by their very wealth in the goal of achieving wisdom. The kingdom was for those like children, lowly and humble, abased and at the bottom of the social hierarchy. The blessed were those who were destitute, downtrodden or outcasts.

Jesus and his followers went to the Temple, were practicing Jews and supported the Torah. But Jesus brought together and gave new emphasis to existing Old Testament values, offering as the greatest commandments the injunction to love God and to love one's neighbor as oneself.

His sayings suggest links with the philosophy of the "poor" or Essenes, and there is submerged evidence in the gospels of involvement with an assembly of the poor in Jerusalem. His advocated code, selecting texts from Deuteronomy and Leviticus, indicates grounding within Pharisaic ideals. There is indeed also evidence in the gospels of congruence and cooperation between Jesus and Pharisees, despite editing to make Jesus appear opposed to the main sects or strands of thinking within Judaism.

If the philosophy offered by Jesus, as transmuted through the gospels, provides an excellent guide for living, then does it really matter that a lot of extraneous and patently false beliefs have been added on in generating a "Christian" religion? It would not perhaps be a matter of great consequence if those taking part could pick and choose, as if from a menu, the best values and the more sensible beliefs.

But it does unfortunately really matter a great deal.

The first reason is that the authority of the Church as an institution depends on individuals subordinating their own critical judgment. So something is maintained as right and believed to be right because the hierarchy of the institution says that it is right, whether or not it is so or can be shown to be so.

This devalues human integrity and intellect. It places higher value on the power of institutions and the preservation of order than on objectivity and the quest for truth. It is neither a healthy intellectual nor a good moral state to be in.

Furthermore, dogma which cannot be defended acts as a barrier to mutual understanding. If something is so patently threadbare that it cannot survive even the most superficial scrutiny, then the only way to preserve the position is to ban discussion and ban all dissent as heresy. Which is the position long adopted by the Catholic Church.

This does not only demean individuals, who are not permitted to think for themselves; it also helps to create religious bigotry. Many central Christian values are common to other religions, particularly Judaism from which these derive. So there is potentially considerable room for a meeting of minds. But when beliefs without factual or logical foundation are added, and must be defended, the barriers arise.

One of the most formidable blocks to mutual understanding lies in the Christian religion's adoption early on of the pagan cult of the sacrificed God. The response to any suggestion that the ideas on which this is based may be irrational, without foundation or derived from something else is rarely to offer to engage in debate. It is all too often, "this is true because we say it is". Or even, "we will burn you, if you continue saying what you do."

Christians have no monopoly of bigotry and such intolerance has occurred, and continues to occur, in other contexts. Killing those who disagree is nonetheless the ultimate expression of censorship.

Ideas do in the end generate a reality of their own. As Eisenman has suggested, "one can say with some justice that it does not matter what really happened, only what people *think* happened." In terms of consequences, including the impact of Christianity on the development of Western culture and values, there is a lot of truth in this. But it does also matter for individual and social integrity what the factual basis is.

This is so, even where say a mistaken belief leads to the adoption of socially desirable values and behavior. There will be occasions when dogma leads to persecution and prejudice, and it is important that individuals are able to question and challenge imbedded social or religious philosophy.

Eisenman points to a further problem, that ideas and stories may appeal to people simply because of their poetic form or beauty. The Passion tale is a compelling narrative which grips the imagination and is, even for anyone first coming to it, already embodied in popular consciousness. This is regardless of any relation it may or may not have to real events that took place in Palestine 2,000 years ago.

In making my own analysis, I have tried to disentangle myself from collectively imbedded ideas and the beauty of the poetic form within the gospel accounts. I have also had to deal with several levels of censorship. The original gospel writers were undoubtedly careful in what they wrote, sometimes leaving out names in order to protect friends and sources still living. Later editors and writers made changes to make Jesus appear anti-Jewish and to distance him from his origins. The Jewish historian Josephus fashioned his story both to please his Roman masters and patrons and to protect himself, and maybe others.

The evidence is there, nonetheless, of a fairly continuous and coherent messianic movement in Israel. It is within this movement that the gospel story is really located in time and context, and where it finally makes sense. The movement led to a rebellion, which was presented both in the gospels and in Josephus as something other than what it actually was.

Though it was a censored rebellion, between the lines and within the lines the reality of what happened spills out. Despite what has subsequently happened to the story, for those with ears attuned to hear, the underlying truth is still there.

FURTHER READING

Beeching P, *Awkward Reverence,* The Continuum Publishing Company, New York, 1974

The Book of the Maccabees, East and West Library, 1949

Crossan J D, *The Birth of Christianity,* T & T Clark, Edinburgh, 1998

Crossan, J D, *The Historical Jesus,* T & T Clark, Edinburgh, 1991

D'Ancona M & Thiede C P, *The Jesus Papyrus,* Weidenfeld & Nicolson, 1996

Eisenman R, *James the Brother of Jesus,* Faber & Faber, London 1997

Feldman L H (trans), *Josephus: Jewish Antiquities,* Heinemann, London, 1965

Joyce D, *The Jesus Scroll,* Angus & Robertson, London, 1973

Maccoby H, *The Myth Maker: Paul and the Invention of Christianity,* Weidenfeld & Nicolson, London, 1986

Noth M, *The History of Israel*, Adam & Charles Black, 1960_

Rubenstein R E, *When Jesus became God,* Harcourt, New York, 1999

Schonfield H J, *The Passover Plot,* Hutchinson, London, 1965

Stirling J (ed), *The Bible, Revised Standard Version,* W M Collins

Vermes G, *The Complete Dead Sea Scrolls in English,* Allen Lane, Penguin Press, 1997

Williamson G A (trans), *Josephus: The Jewish War,* Penguin Books, 1981